EDI Security, Control, and Audit

For a complete listing of the *Artech House Telecommunciations* Library,
turn to the back of this book.

EDI Security, Control, and Audit

Albert J. Marcella, Jr. and Sally Chan

Artech House
Boston • London

Library of Congress Cataloging-in-Publication Data

Marcella, Albert J.
EDI Security, Control, and Audit/Albert J. Marcella, Sally Chan
Includes bibliographical references and index.
ISBN 0-89006-610-8
1. Electronic data interchange 2.Electronic data interchange—Auditing
3. Data transmission systems—Standards. I. Chan, Sally. II. Title
HF5548.33.M37   1993   92-40730
657'.45'0285.—dc20   CIP

British Library Cataloguing in Publication Data

Marcella, Albert J.
EDI Security, Control, and Audit
I. Title. II. Chan, Sally.
384.3
ISBN 0-89006-610-8

© 1993 ARTECH HOUSE, INC.
685 Canton Street
Norwood, MA 02062

International Standard Book Number: 0-89006-610-8
Library of Congress Catalog Card Number: 92-40730

10 9 8 7 6 5 4 3 2 1

To Sean and Stefanie with Love
—S.C.

To Kristina and Andy with Love
—Daddy

May the good Lord be with you down every road you roam.
And may the sun shine and happiness surround you when
    you're far from home.
And may you grow to be proud, dignified and true.
And do unto others as you'd have done to you.
Be courageous and be brave.
And in my heart you'll always stay—
Forever Young, Forever Young.

May good fortune be with you, may your guiding light
    be strong, build a stairway to heaven with a
    prince or a vagabond.
And may you never love in vain.
And in my heart you will remain—
Forever Young, Forever Young.

And when you finally fly away, I'll be hoping that I
    served you well.
For all the wisdom of a life time, no one can ever tell.
But whatever road you choose, I'm right behind you win
    or lose—
Forever Young, Forever Young
            —Rod Stewart

Contents

Foreword

Electronic data interchange, or EDI, is the electronic exchange of business information in a standard format between trading partners. Today, thousands of North American corporations use EDI to exchange purchase orders and invoices with suppliers and customers. The related payments are effected through banks and other financial institutions.

For these corporations, the benefits are clear. The paper trail has disappeared, replaced by more efficient and less costly accounting and processing methods. For auditors, however, the challenges of EDI are just beginning. Due to initial investment costs, standards limitations, and legal constraints, current use of EDI by North American industries represents only a fraction of its potential. But when EDI becomes the norm for thousands of enterprises, as the authors predict it will, the auditing profession must be prepared.

The risks inherent in EDI exceed those in standard computer processing systems. Of particular concern is the risk of linking different systems in the same organization, such as inventory, payments, and accounting systems, as well as with the proprietary systems of trading partners. Included in this book is an interpretation of how the risks of "cross-vulnerabilities," as the authors refer to them, might develop in the coming years. Through this discussion the authors hope to raise management awareness.

The implications of these risks to the auditing profession are significant. Auditors of EDI systems will require more specialized information technology training. They will need to establish whether there are adequate controls over the unique risks of EDI and to test their operation on an online, real-time basis. Finally, they will need to know whether these controls exist at places other than the business being audited.

EDI Audit and Control is an excellent and thorough study of EDI and a valuable tool for understanding the auditing implications thereof. We in the auditing profession are indebted to the authors Sally Chan and Albert Marcella, Jr., for writing this book.

John Merriam
Senior vice president and chief inspector
Royal Bank of Canada, Toronto
April 1993

Preface

EDI will change our lives, just as computers did. It will redefine the ways we work as it pushes us toward a knowledge-based society in which we pursue intellectual challenges while routine, noncreative tasks are assigned to computers.

Gene A. Nelson
"EDI or Die"

Electronic data interchange (EDI), computer-to-computer, or application-to-application, exchange of business information in a standard format, is reshaping business practices and procedures globally. EDI is becoming a technological "bandwagon" of the 1990s, with corporations worldwide connecting buyer and seller and shipper and receiver electronically, in slowly but steadily increasing numbers. Faced with the unattractive prospective of "no EDI, no business," major U.S. multinationals, the world banking community, the European Commission, and many smaller industry players are motivated to climb aboard as well.

As of September, 1992, there are over 31,000 EDI users worldwide (See Chapter 1, Figure 1.1.) The most active users are in transportation, retail, grocery, automobiles, warehousing, pharmaceuticals, and the public sector, with healthcare and financial institutions as the newcomers.

The benefits of EDI include significant cost savings across the board in improved customer response, speed of transaction processing, error reduction, and increased efficiency of operations and administration. However, in their rush to implement EDI, many organizations overlook (or waive) critical controls and safeguards required under normal system migration strategies.

Conducting business electronically, computer-to-computer, introduces new control, security, and legal exposures. These exposures might become the assigned responsibilities of one or more management information systems (MIS) or information technology (IT) departments, data security, internal auditors, legal departments, senior corporate management, and ultimately, end user management.

Because EDI significantly increases reliance on automated communications with customers, suppliers, distributors, and subsidiary units, it is becoming less and less realistic to "audit around the computer." The growing interest of audit professionals is reflected in the number of publications in which internal controls, the amount and form of evidentiary material, and risk assessment procedures are being reexamined.[1] Indeed, the entire audit process itself is changing in ways that are both unstoppable and unavoidable. If EDI is changing the way we conduct business, it must also change the way auditors perform their audits. Yesterday's audit tools are no longer adequate.

As the use of EDI accelerates, end users, auditors, security and MIS personnel, and legal staff will require accurate answers to key questions about EDI and its impact on the business community. Major questions that this book addresses include:

- Exactly what is EDI, and how will it affect the way companies conduct business?
- What are the costs of implementing EDI? What are the cross-vulnerabilities?
- How should organizations go about selecting trading partners?
- How should organizations manage interenterprise partnerships?
- How should third-party service provider agreements be evaluated for liability, auditability, security, and apportionment of risk?
- What control considerations should be incorporated in the design and implementation of a third-party service provider agreement?
- How are appropriate EDI controls established?
- How significant is the records retention issue in EDI?
- What distinguishes financial EDI (FEDI) from electronic funds transfer (EFT) and EDI itself?
- What are the special controls required for FEDI?
- What are the critical audit and security issues in EDI?
- What does conducting an EDI audit entail?

The material in Appendices A through F provides a basis for the development of EDI audit programs and checklists. The individual topics, however, are not inclusive, nor do they provide the final word on internal controls. Rather, these topics are designed to raise awareness of internal control considerations for EDI. In addition, readers are encouraged to be aware that each EDI environment is unique and they must adapt the information provided in this book to their own processing environments.

Both organizations that are considering (or in the process of) implementing EDI or other computer-based technology for business transaction processing and EDI practitioners who are responsible for providing security, internal control, software development and support, risk management and assessment, and legal counsel should find this book helpful. It provides a comprehensive discussion of establishing appropriate internal controls and defining auditability in this emerging technology.

---

1. Refer to Appendix G for a list of publications on EDI audit and control.

Acknowledgments

A book of this nature and undertaking rarely reflects the efforts of one individual. Our efforts in completing this work could not have been successful without the support and assistance of a number of managers, colleagues, and peers. We owe particular thanks to John Merriam, senior vice president and chief inspector, Royal Bank of Canada, for his Foreword; to Frank Allen, manager of advanced technology at the Institute of Internal Auditors, for his Epilogue; to Joseph Rosenbaum, senior counsel for American Express Travel-Related Services Company, Inc., and chair of the Global Networks and Information Technology Committee of the EDI & Information Technology Division of the American Bar Association Section of Science and Technology, for his contribution to the section on legal issues and lawyers in the EDI world; to Leigh Morris, partner, Ernst & Young, Toronto, for his section on the external auditor's view of EDI; and to all who gave personal time to provide support and peer review and permission for material in this book.

Our thanks also go to individuals who provided sources, permissions, and insights into the art of auditing and controlling EDI environments. To these dedicated professionals we are grateful: Jim Holland, vice president, Information Technology Audit and Development, Royal Bank of Canada; Russ Leighton, senior systems analyst with Sterling Chemicals, Inc.; Edward Morrisey, education specialist at the Institute of Internal Auditors; Don Caniglia, director, Data Security for American Automobile Association; Mark Mitchell, president of M. Mitchell & Associates; Joyce Momich, corporate information systems auditor at Westinghouse Electric Corporation; Philip Oddo, manager of internal audit for CIBA-GEIGY Corporation; William Winberg, chief internal auditor at the Illinois Department of Central Management Services; A. Scott Roberson, information systems auditing area audit manager for JC Penney; Benjamin Wright, attorney and counselor, Dallas, Texas; Henry Jablonski, senior project manager, Bank of Montreal; Peter Rumyee, audit manager, Royal Bank of Canada; Donald Van Geete, senior systems auditor, Royal Bank of Canada, for his concepts of cross-vulnerabilities in EDI; Les Bell, EDI project manager, Royal Bank of Canada; Paul Moo, senior manager, EDI Systems and Services, Price Waterhouse; Gilles Vezina, chair, JTC/EDI Finance Working Group; Bob Taylor-Vaisey of Imperial Oil Limited, for his practical insights on EDI records retention; and to the anonymous reviewers provided by the publisher. A special thanks to Kevin Powell, senior EDP auditor with Millers Outpost, whose Masters thesis work on *Security and Control of Electronic Data Interchange Systems* at California State Polytechnic University, Pomona, added a wealth of information to our research and led us to numerous sources on EDI audit, security, and control issues.

And our thanks also go to our spouses, Patricia and Li-Kwong, who provided constant encouragement and support throughout this project.

Chapter 1

The Frontier: An EDI Overview

1.1 EXACTLY WHAT IS EDI?

There is no one authoritative definition of electronic data interchange (EDI) to which all users agree. In layperson's terms, EDI is the *computer-to-computer transfer* of business information in a *standard format* between *trading partners*. In this context EDI can be viewed as a viable alternative to exchanging business information on paper. The *computer-to-computer transfer* can be direct, with two companies using an agreed upon data protocol, or it can be performed by a third-party service vendor. A *trading partner* is any customer, supplier, or business partner with whom documents can be exchanged. Users can communicate business documents, such as purchase orders, price quotes, shipping notices, and even payment orders, electronically to customers and suppliers. Design documents, electronic funds transfers, and database transactions can all come under the EDI umbrella. The format in EDI is governed by a predetermined and institutionally agreed upon set of rules known as *standards*. Standards are the common language spoken by trading partners.

When EDI is fully integrated between trading partners, so that the EDI documents can be directly validated and accepted into the job stream of the receiving partner's processing application, then EDI is also an *application-to-application* transfer. Provided the electronic transfer is based on public or industry format, EDI can be interorganizational and intraorganizational. Free-form fax messages, electronic mail, and video text, which do not use standards, are therefore excluded from this definition of EDI.

1.2 GROWTH OF EDI

EDI is currently used in over 50 industries, including automobile, pharmaceutical, grocery, health care, and manufacturing, with the list continuing to grow. Figure 1.1 provides an overview of the steady growth in EDI utilization over the past six years.

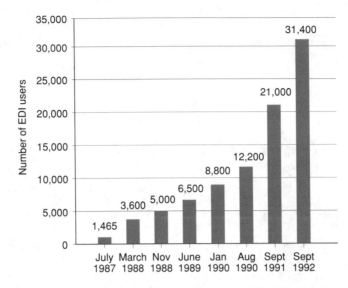

Figure 1.1 Growth of registered EDI users. *Source: EDI, Spread the Word!,* Dallas, Texas. Note: Numbers reflect EDI users worldwide, as listed in *EDI Yellow Pages: The Business Directory.* Reprinted with permission, 1992.

The number of users in the EDI marketplace has grown from under 2,000 in July of 1987 to over 31,000 in 1992. In the period between 1989 and 1992 annual growth of registered EDI users never fell below 70%.

According to a recent report on EDI prospects in Europe published by Ovum Ltd., of the United Kingdom, European sales of EDI products and services will increase from $86 million in 1990 to $396 million in 1994. The same report projects the fastest growth in EDI services, accounting for an estimated 72% of the market in 1994 [1]. In Europe, the United Kingdom and Germany are the most advanced EDI users, with the United Kingdom accounting for 50% of the overall market [2].

Considering that there are more than three million businesses in the United States alone, the penetration of EDI into the business world has not, however, lived up to the lofty expectations of EDI pioneers.

1.3 EDI MARKET ACCEPTANCE

Despite its steady growth, EDI is not without its problems and limitations. EDI users have listed the following five issues as the greatest obstacles to a successful worldwide acceptance by the user community:

1. *Reluctance.* Trading partners are reluctant or refuse to participate in EDI. Either senior management lacks commitment to the idea or the company has difficulty

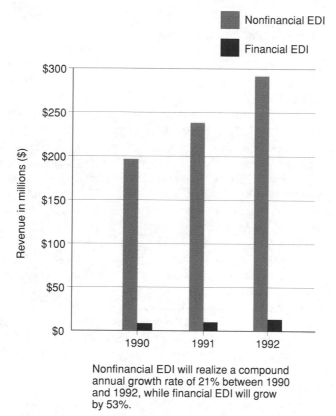

Nonfinancial EDI will realize a compound annual growth rate of 21% between 1990 and 1992, while financial EDI will grow by 53%.

Figure 1.2 EDI growth in North America, reflected in revenue generated between 1990 and 1992. *After: Bank Technology News,* 1992. Information collected by INPUT, a Mountain View, California market research firm.

fitting EDI software developments into an already substantial application backlog.

2. *Quality.* The service quality from current clearinghouse providers is often poor. (Current clearinghouses perform conventional, limited, and specialized services, such as clearing funds and settling accounts. This is in contrast to the envisioned EDI clearinghouse, which would provide various telecommunication and computer-based commercial trading services, to bolster the reliability and enforceability of electronic transaction records, reduce legal uncertainty, and generally facilitate electronic trade. In the United Kingdom, for example, large EDI users have formed pressure groups and insisted on service agreements with their clearinghouse suppliers.)

3. *Multiplicity of standards.* Ideally, there should be a single set of standards covering all EDI message types. That set of standards, referred to as EDIFACT,

is now emerging from the United Nations Electronic Data Interchange for Administration, Commerce, and Transport (UN/EDIFACT) Board. In the interim, there are problems. Current users of generic and industry-specific standards, such as American National Standards Institute (ANSI) X12, used by many industries in North America; the Organization for Data Exchange by Teletransmission in Europe (ODETTE) for the Pan-European motor industry; and Tradacoms, for the United Kingdom retail and related industries are experiencing problems in migrating to EDIFACT standards. Additionally, the development of EDIFACT standards is too slow for many users, and there are gaps in the standards that will also delay the migration process. Users can expect that other standards will be used in parallel with EDIFACT standards for a number of years.

4. *Legal constraints.* Most legal systems are not designed to accommodate EDI. EDI agreements, which stipulate rules for trading between partners or within a community, will help users overcome these problems. The American Bar Association's Electronic Data Interchange and Information Technology Division has readied a model trading partner agreement called the Model Electronic Data Interchange Agreement and Commentary (1990). A similar document, known as the Model Form of Electronic Data Interchange Trading Partner Agreement and Commentary (1990), is available from the EDI Council of Canada. In response to the growth of more complex EDI communities that cross national boundaries throughout Europe, the Commission of European Communities' Trade Electronic Data Interchange Systems program has produced a draft European Model EDI Agreement. In the long term, there is a need to clearly establish the legal status of EDI and harmonize electronic trade documentation.

5. *Security issues.* Most companies believe that current EDI agreements and third-party service providers offer adequate security against fraud and errors in EDI transactions. This is far from true. There is a definite need to upgrade the existing security as the complexity of EDI communities grows. (Security weakness in EDI is discussed in Chapter 4.)

For a manufacturer who supplies large companies (such as auto makers or international retail chains) with component parts or finished goods, the justification for implementing EDI is simple: increasingly, purchasers demand it. Nonetheless, there are several reasons why EDI is experiencing slow acceptance in the marketplace. These include:

- The fact that, currently, few companies are actually capable of carrying out full communication via EDI;
- The costs—both real and imaginary—of implementing and maintaining EDI;
- Loftier than practical expectations of early EDI successes;
- Hesitation among companies waiting for an industry market leader to emerge;
- Resistance by employees to changing technology;
- Standards that are anything but solidified and often confusing or nonexistent in certain industries.

But, despite its slow market acceptance, EDI does offer attractive cost benefits.

1.4 THE COSTS AND BENEFITS OF IMPLEMENTING EDI

Costs and benefits of implementing EDI vary significantly from one user to another. They depend largely upon the level of commitment to EDI and the hardware and software used to support the EDI environment. Jack Shaw, president of EDI Strategies, states that as a rule of thumb, companies might expect to spend 1% of one year's sales over three to five years for a comprehensive EDI implementation. However, a return on investment of 100% per year, he notes, is not out of the question. Thomas P. Colberg, a partner in Price Water-house's EDI Consulting Group, said a typical firm should plan to spend $1 million-plus for EDI and could expect a return of as high as 5% of sales [3].

A study by the Logistics Management Institute (LMI) reported that the U.S. Department of Defense (DOD) could save $1.2 billion over a 10-year period by investing just $79 million in document processing automation, a payback of 15 to 1. LMI computed an average savings per document of $2.40, compared with savings of $10 to $50 per document routinely claimed by the private sector. LMI also figured that every dollar of direct cost savings would be matched by $1.80 from reduced inventories, streamlined operations, reduced interest expenses, and other indirect costs [4].

EDI costs for hardware, software, communications, application enhancements, and replacement can be fixed, as in the case of the cost of the EDI software, for example. Or EDI costs can vary, such as the costs of implementing EDI with trading partners, which are directly related to the number of trading partners. Generally, the costs of establishing an EDI program include the following items [5]:

- *EDI software.* The software used varies widely according to the hardware used (i.e., micro-, mini-, or mainframe computer), the features required (e.g., number of transaction sets processed), and the degree of software customization required.
- *Communications.* Pricing formulas vary by network, but might include one-time setup charges, monthly mailbox rental, storage, and transaction costs. They can be significantly higher if the EDI topology involves a direct connection on dial-up circuits.
- *Training.* Includes training for both internal and trading partner staffs.
- *Integration.* Integration includes creating interfaces to existing applications and translating files from EDI format to internal format and vice versa (i.e., the translation software).
- *Procedures improvements.* Funds should include sufficient resources to underwrite the cost of improving existing systems, such as payables.

A recent industry newsletter quoted James P. Witkins, senior financial officer of Manufacturers Hanover Trust Company, as noting that "Today, 70% of data in a typical firm's mainframe computer was output from another mainframe, compared to 20% five years ago." Eliminating the re-entering of that 70%, which predictably is rekeyed multiple times for many functional systems, is one of the major benefits of implementing EDI.

The benefits of implementing EDI can add dollars directly to the bottom line through significant savings in the following areas: (1) reduced labor processing costs resulting from entering data more efficiently and allowing labor to be utilized more efficiently in problem solving and other activities that require human judgement; (2) better forecasting and decision support for more accurate information; (3) improved customer service, improved internal operations, and faster detection and resolution of operating problems; and (4) increased cash management controls resulting from a reduction in inventory carrying costs, order cycle times, and administrative expenses.

It should be noted, however, that by narrowly focusing on the cost savings, potential users are overlooking the real advantages and benefits of EDI, which can help them

- Improve customer service;
- Improve internal operations and responsiveness to customers;
- Improve accuracy and control of data;
- Increase financial control;
- Reduce labor processing costs resulting from data reentry and clerical error;
- Reduce order cycle time;
- Decrease administrative costs.

1.5 WHO SHOULD USE EDI?

Companies or industries that possess one or more of the characteristics listed below are strong candidates for conversion to EDI [6]. The candidates:

- Handle a large volume of repetitive standard transactions (an important factor in both the transportation and the grocery industries);
- Operate on a very tight margin (a strong influence in the grocery industry's decision to pursue EDI);
- Face strong competition, requiring significant productivity improvements (the major reason the automobile industry has embraced EDI);
- Operate in a time-sensitive environment (the reason retailing is an advocate of EDI);
- Have received requests to convert to EDI from trading partners.

We can add to this list other firms that are suited for EDI. These are financial institutions that have the requisite technology, networks, security expertise, and broad clientele. After all, to close the EDI loop, which begins with request for quotation and ends with final settlement of payments, financial institutions have to be active players.

The use of EDI is steadily growing across all industries. One of the driving forces behind the implementation of EDI is external pressure from customers. For the most part, smaller companies enter the EDI arena out of fear of losing the business of a big customer or supplier to a competitor who agrees to cooperate with the larger organization's request to use EDI. A larger company can dictate that its smaller trading partners must implement EDI if they want to begin or continue to do business [7]. (Chapter 4 further discusses external pressure in terms of interenterprise dependency as a form of cross-vulnerability.)

Figure 1.3 presents an analysis of the reasons users implement EDI.

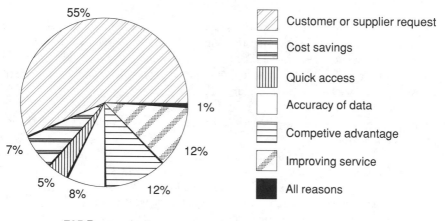

705 Respondents

Figure 1.3 The most important reasons for using EDI. *After:* EDI Research, Ltd., Oak Park, Illinois, 1992 research survey.

1.6 EDI OPERATING ISSUES

EDI directly addresses the operating issue of increasing the volume of processed transactions by connecting trading partners electronically, either directly or through a third party. This electronic connection reduces data entry errors by eliminating repetitive tasks (EDI *will not* prevent input errors from occurring, however) and lowers administrative overhead costs associated with paper-based processing methods. Douglas Aircraft Company, for example, estimates that the manual processing cost of a purchase order is $4 to $6, versus an EDI processing cost of less than $1 for the same document. Others have estimated that the cost per transaction in a manual environment could be as high as $50, with a reduction to $3 to $12 through use of EDI [8].

Studies of efficient data entry and cost savings have shown that even expert-level data entry operators miskey their entries 2% of the time, thus contributing to lower accuracy of processed data. Added to the cost of rekeying data is the increased uncertainty of timely receipt and any interest loss or penalty resulting from mailing and processing delays—which are beyond the control of the sender.

In the traditional paper-based flow of information, manual data entry is performed at each step in the process. In addition, manual reconciliation—comparison of purchase order, receiving notice, and invoice—is also required, thereby contributing to the higher dollar cost of transaction processing and the continued involvement of the end user in the overall process. These two manual processes are eliminated with the substitution of electronic methods such as EDI.

1.7 EDI RISKS

Risk is a powerful word. It tells auditors what to audit and managers what to manage. Therefore, it is important to understand the potential risks and exposures associated with EDI, so that appropriate steps can be taken to minimize them to an economical point. At the initiation of an EDI project, a risk analysis should be performed jointly by users and systems staff. That analysis should focus on these potential risks[1]:

- The EDI application does not meet business objectives or satisfy either user or control requirements.
- Unauthorized users can gain access to EDI applications and initiate unauthorized transactions or destroy data.
- Authorized personnel can initiate unauthorized or erroneous transactions that could result in excessive costs, fraud, embarrassment, or legal exposure.
- Data can be lost, inaccurately transmitted, or altered during transmission.
- Adequate audit trails are not maintained, impairing the organization's ability to evaluate controls or potentially exposing it to legal liability.
- As a result of control weaknesses, the organization is exposed in the trading partner's environment.
- The trading partner agreement does not adequately address liabilities for protection of proprietary data, the required components to constitute a binding agreement, or other necessary clauses.
- Formal contracts with third-party EDI service providers do not adequately address security, system reliability and availability, or responsibilities.

During a risk analysis one should bear in mind that information is an asset, not just a cost of doing business. The asset value (the EDI message) and the potential threats against that asset will provide good insight into the risks. For instance, in financial EDI (FEDI), the value of funds being transferred, not just the cost of transmitting the message, must be considered. The same can be said of the loss of benefit of a business deal and any consequential damages.

The risks listed above confirm that the risks associated with EDI are similar to those found in information systems. If this is the case, are there still new areas of concern? Yes, and these risks, which will be elaborated on in subsequent chapters, include:

- *Cross-vulnerability.* An increased number of partners means a corresponding increase in an organization's dependence on its trading partners. Dependency is

---

1. *Source:* Institute of Internal Auditors Research Foundation, "Module 8: Telecommunications," *System Auditability and Control Report*, April 1991, p. 90.

expanded to include the possible sharing of technology and databases. As EDI business grows and partnerships multiply, the risk of basing mutual reliance on mere trust—without contract or agreement—is risky business.

- *Third-party network risks.* These risks include disclosure of confidential information, errors in transmission or processing, the introduction of invalid or unauthorized transactions by third-party staff, invoicing for services not rendered, service disruption, and lost audit trails.
- *Risks of integration.* When EDI is integrated with a firm's inventory management, production control, issuance of payments, and accounting systems, the domino effect resulting from errors, omissions, and failures increases severalfold. This risk is further aggravated by high speed and volume coupled with low human intervention.
- *Auditability risk.* As mentioned in the Preface, EDI changes the way auditors perform their audits. Electronic records can be forged and altered. Paperless systems are most suited for online, real-time control and audit techniques, to ensure record authenticity and integrity. There is the risk of an auditor failing to master new audit techniques—embedded audit modules, context-sensitive alerts, continuous process monitoring, and knowledge-based risk assessment—that can all be profitably applied to EDI.

1.8 MANAGEMENT CONTROL CONCERNS

As with any innovative application of technology, EDI raises a number of management control concerns that must be addressed:

- *Loss of an audit trail.* No longer is there a formal, paper source document with EDI. While it is an error to associate EDI with a paperless system—EDI transactions can generate plenty of paper—the main element is the source transaction, which is paperless. We frequently are asked the question: "Is there an audit trail produced for all EDI processing activities?" (The subject of an electronic audit trail is fully dealt with in this book.)
- *Business continuity.* As more and more transactions migrate toward an EDI format, organizations will come to rely on and be dependent upon its data processing operations and its trading partners. Computer systems that store EDI transactions must be kept secure; controls designed to maintain the availability of these computer systems must operate as intended. Organizations should have a policy that specifically addresses the domino effect of EDI system outages and failed transactions. Contingency planning can help and therefore is a matter of top priority. (Environmental controls covering contingency planning and related issues are covered in Chapter 7.)
- *Exposure of data to third parties.* As EDI transactions are passed through third-party networks, the data (or at least some of the data) are exposed to potential review and access by the third-party processor. That likelihood forces organizations to consider these questions:

□ Are there adequate controls in place to prevent unauthorized creation of a trading partner?

□ Are there adequate controls in place to prevent data from being transmitted to an unauthorized organization (i.e., the wrong party)?

□ To what extent does the audit department have a right to audit the third-party network vendors?

The answers to these questions are presented in Chapter 3.

- *Potential legal liability.* Internal controls designed to screen or prequalify vendors or suppliers should be in place before the organization engages in business with these entities. (Chapter 5 discusses trading partner agreements and network and software contracts from legal and audit perspectives.)

- *Records retention and retrievability.* Because there are no source documents with EDI, controls must be put in place to ensure that the source data that initiate EDI transactions are retained for an amount of time that corresponds both to business needs and to the stipulations of the firm's legal department. (Chapter 8 is devoted entirely to addressing this topic.)

- *Segregation of duties.* Very often managers are concerned that, because EDI controls are automated and concentrated in the hands of a few individuals, the traditional segregation of duties does not apply. On the contrary, division of labor should still exist. For example, the individuals responsible for maintaining the EDI software should never be allowed to change data. Similarly, dual custody and split knowledge of encryption and authentication keys must be observed.

Although EDI introduces new risks and concerns, there is no cause for alarm. Different risks require different controls. The challenge is to manage the EDI risks that arise in a cost-effective manner.

1.9 GENERAL CONTROLS IN EDI STANDARDS

Understanding the potential risks in EDI is a necessary step in identifying controls required of an EDI environment. It is good news that the two major public standards for EDI, ANSI (North American) and UN/EDIFACT (international), provide basic controls to ensure transaction completeness and, to a limited degree, accuracy of data. These basic controls include:

- Embedded headers and trailers
- Functional identifier code
- Application identifier code
- Segment identifiers
- Acknowledgments
- Batch totals
- File sequence numbers

1.9.1 ANSI

The ANSI X12 EDI transmission and control structure consists of three different-sized electronic envelopes. The structure is designed in such a way that the contents of a smaller envelope become part of a larger envelope. The largest envelope is found at the *interchange level*. This envelope is akin to a package containing one or more smaller envelopes of purchase orders and invoice payments, grouped by functional applications. A *functional group* is one or more similar documents exchanged between trading partners in a single transmission. Inside each functional group are *transaction sets*, which can be treated as electronic image representations of business transactions. Transaction sets are made up of *data elements*, which together are referred to as *segments*. Further details of the ANSI message structure are presented in Chapter 2.

Headers and trailers at the interchange, functional group, and transaction set levels provide basic control structure for EDI and contain parameters critical to the acknowledgment of messages exchanged between trading partners. The ANSI X12 standard codes for headers and trailers as shown in the envelopes are

- ISA   Start interchange
- IEA   End interchange
- GS   Start functional group
- GE   End functional group
- ST   Start segment (transaction set)
- SE   End segment (transaction set)

These codes trigger the beginning or the end of an item. Because of the predictable relationship between a lower level and the next higher level (one being the subset of the other), this relationship can be verified and cross-checked.

1.9.2 UN/EDIFACT

Like ANSI X12, the UN/EDIFACT standard also provides control features in the headers and trailers of its interchange, functional group, and message (known as transaction set in ANSI) envelopes. These controls are

- UNB   Interchange header
- UNZ   Interchange trailer
- UNG   Functional group header
- UNE   Functional group trailer
- UNH   Message header
- UNT   Message trailer

The headers identify and specify the respective interchange, functional group, or message, while the trailers serve as a completeness check of the corresponding envelope, by means of total count and reference numbers.

1.9.3 Acknowledgments

The system of acknowledgments works the same way in both ANSI and UN/EDIFACT. The system informs trading partners that a transaction has taken place. In the event of a dispute between trading partners, the acknowledgment can support the existence of a transaction. Taking the ANSI format as an example, each transaction set (known as a message in UN/EDIFACT) includes an acknowledgment that is only provided by the postal service if the mail is registered. In an EDI transaction set, a *functional acknowledgment* (FA) informs the originating trading partner of the status of the transaction set upon receipt. Basically, an FA is an acknowledgment sent to a trading partner to indicate that the document was received. The acknowledgment also indicates whether or not the document passed EDI syntax standards compliance tests. If it passed the tests, the document enters the EDI interface phase. If it failed compliance testing, the acknowledgment indicates the reason for the failure and either the document is not processed or the processing is subject to further notification [9].

In this way, a buyer knows that a purchase order, for instance, was received by the supplier, and that it was either accepted for processing or rejected and requires correction and retransmission. It is imperative that the functional acknowledgment be correctly interpreted by the sender of the related transaction. (It should be noted that FEDI requires another level of acknowledgment at the application level. This additional requirement is discussed in Chapter 9.)

One of the classic control objectives of businesses is to ensure that transactions are complete. Batch totals and sequence numbers are techniques that ensure completeness but not accuracy. Syntax checking ensures compliance with standards. It is usually performed by EDI translation software, which transforms data into a format that can be understood by an otherwise incompatible system or network at either end of the transmission. Validity checking of trading partners is often accomplished through the use of partner profiles and directories that contain pertinent information about each trading partner.

1.10 EDI AUDIT IMPLICATIONS

The information systems auditor is normally the only dedicated resource who specializes in controls in an automated environment. To offer informed opinions and advice to management on the nature, type, and attributes of the controls that must be designed into an EDI system, this individual must keep abreast of emerging technologies. When it perceives that auditors are adding value to their function with timely recommendations, management might become more cooperative and cease to view auditors as merely a cost of doing business.

In addition to evaluating EDI controls, auditors should pay special attention to potential cost savings, which can result in reduced overhead and improved efficiency in operations. The following are also key audit considerations.

- EDI demands specialized IT training. No longer will auditors examine only paper-based systems and transactions. To accurately assess controls existing in worldwide and domestic telecommunications environments, databases, and data dictionaries—and in FEDI as an initial example—auditors will have to enhance their existing skills base. They will have to become more technically proficient and literate. Emerging technologies will restructure the traditional audit process, approach, methodology, and philosophy.
- Auditors will need to redesign existing audit techniques to establish the controls required to securely manage the EDI system.
- Auditors might have to provide assurances that adequate internal controls exist at locations other than the company being audited (i.e., the billing vendor, shipper, or third-party service provider's premises).
- Auditors will not compromise the objectivity nor independence of the audit function. Organizationally, these individuals do not report to the auditee management and they do not make decisions for the project team. Auditors simply provide an opinion for management's consideration. Auditors can provide valuable service to EDI project teams by getting involved early and focusing on these areas [10]:
  - Finding evidence of proactive planning versus reactive response;
  - Identifying where existing manual controls are substituted by EDI;
  - Assessing the responsibilities for maintaining standards and versions;
  - Reviewing project controls and facilitating cooperative problem solving between trading partners.

A paperless environment is only justified if adequate controls are available. An informed auditor, as a specialist in control, has much to contribute to assuring that such controls are in place.

1.11 SUMMARY

As the decade of the 90s begins to unfold, new international markets are rapidly forming. Industries, as well as governments, are viewing EDI as one of the significant facilitating technologies readily available to support this growth.

Machiavelli, in *The Prince*, said "There is nothing more difficult to carry out nor more doubtful of success nor more dangerous to handle than to initiate a new order of things." The emerging global economies of Europe and the Pacific Rim are changing the order of traditional relationships between companies, trading partners, and those individuals whose responsibility it is to audit these activities. Possibly an even greater risk than initiating a "new order of things" is being unprepared to determine the impact and ramifications of this new order on existing operations.

In this decade, as businesses require (and demand) the ability to requisition goods of varying configurations and have them shipped anywhere in the world as a strategic component of their internal just-in-time (JIT) systems, EDI must command a closer and more detailed review by the audit function. Gone will be the days of paper trails.

An EDI message will be entered into a computer, extracted from a database, transmitted, and processed by the receiving computer, without human interpretation or rekeying. Already EDI vendors are marketing "window-based EDI," "event-driven EDI," and "real-time EDI," allowing users to take a step beyond the standard store-and-retrieve mode of processing [11]. Such changes require that auditors become familiar with the capabilities of EDI, the associated changes in processing procedures and the risks and exposures posed by this data transfer technology. It will not be too long before auditors must assess the impact of EDI on such business functions as marketing, quality and inventory control, production, customer service, distribution, accounting, sales, and IT.

REFERENCES

[1]   Jelovec, Nahid, "EDI Goes International," *3X/400 Information Management*, Vol. 2, No. 1, January 1991, p. 52.

[2]   "European EDI Growth Predicted to Vary Across Industries and Countries," *EDI News,* Vol. 6, No. 19, September 21, 1992, p. 7.

[3]   Colberg, Thomas P., "The Compelling Case For EDI," *The Financial Manager*, Vol. 6, No. 1, January/February 1990, p. 20.

[4]   Anthens, Gary H., "EDI Could Save Defense Dollars," *ComputerWorld*, November 12, 1990, p. 72.

[5]   Colberg, Thomas P., "The Compelling Case For EDI," *The Financial Manager*, Vol. 6, No. 1, January/February 1990, p. 21.

[6]   Emmelhainz, Margaret A., *Electronic Data Interchange—A Total Management Guide*, First Edition, New York, NY: Van Nostrand Reinhold, 1990, p. 4.

[7]   Sucharski, Frank J., "Alamo Corporation: Getting Involved In EDI," *Tech Exec*, March 1990, pp. 35, 37.

[8]   Willenz, Nicole V., *Electronic Data Interchange: A Quiet Revolution*, Chicago, IL: Price Waterhouse, 1988, (Review, 1988, Number 3).

[9]   Leighton, Russ, senior systems analyst, Sterling Chemicals Inc., personal correspondence, September 1991.

[10]   Chan, Sally, "Managing and Auditing EDI Systems Development," *CMA Magazine*, Vol. 65, No. 9, November 1991, p. 12.

[11]   "Demand for Real-Time Communication is Changing the Face of EDI," *EDI News*, July 27, 1992, p. 6.

Chapter 2

EDI Infrastructure and Standards

2.1 THE ESSENTIAL COMPONENTS OF EDI

An analysis of the infrastructure in which EDI operates would be incomplete without an examination of the essential components that make up the EDI environment. Concisely, the essential components are: (1) a set of commonly agreed upon standards (either for domestic or international EDI business communications); (2) appropriate information delivery systems, which might include telecommunications hardware and software and general communication protocols; (3) translation software, which transforms data into a format that can be read by an otherwise incompatible system or network at either end of a transmission. As an extension to translation software, the existing EDI application system must be suitably enhanced to enable it to map the data elements in the EDI transaction set with the application's internal format.

This chapter discusses in detail the components that comprise the EDI environment.

2.1.1 Standards

EDI standards for North America consist of a body of public standards developed and maintained by volunteers from industry and government, largely under the auspices of the ANSI Accredited Standards Committee (ASC) X12 in Alexandria, Virginia.

The Data Interchange Standards Association (DISA) was formed in 1987 to be the secretariat and administrative arm of ASC X12. DISA is a not-for-profit corporation, and its staff manages, among other tasks, standards development and maintenance, publications, communications with ANSI on behalf of ASC X12, and other administrative duties required to support the X12 Committee.

The international standard for EDI is UN/EDIFACT. UN/EDIFACT is a set of internationally agreed upon standards, directories, and guidelines for the electronic interchange of structured data and, in particular, for the interchange of data that relate to trade in goods and services between independent computerized information systems.

2.1.2 Telecommunications Hardware and Software

Telecommunications hardware and software are the components that create the link between trading partners and provide partners with the capability to send and receive EDI transaction sets. This capability is often provided by a third-party network service.

Hardware components, including such peripherals as modem and storage devices, are required to implement EDI and establish the inter- and intracompany links between computerized information systems.

Telecommunications software controls the actual transmission of EDI messages. Features of this software can include automatic dialing, management and maintenance of trading partner phone numbers, and activity logging. The software also interfaces with the system's modem to determine transmission speed and type and to conduct limited error detection during the transmission process. This process works in exactly the same way for incoming EDI messages.

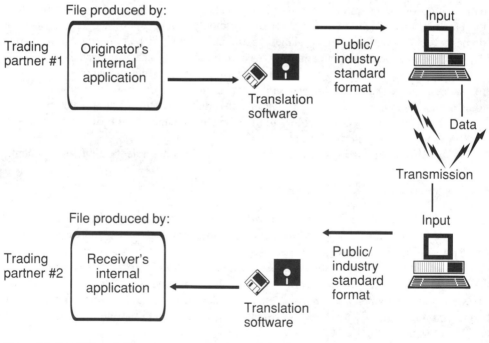

Figure 2.1 How EDI works.

2.1.3 Translation Software

The EDI translation software, which links the application and the communications software, is the conduit that makes the EDI process functional. This software allows for the translation of data from a company's internal format to the industry-specific format—

either the interindustry generic ANSI X12 or the international UN/EDIFACT format. As part of the translation process, the software examines the partner profile for such details as

- Trading partner number/code;
- The standard (ANSI, UN/EDIFACT, or industry-specific) adopted by the partner;
- The codes (seller's catalog number, buyer's part number, etc.) being used;
- The transaction sets being sent;
- The optional data segments and elements that are to be selected;
- The communications protocols (if direct connect) that will be in effect.

EDI translation software has two primary functions. For outgoing data, the software reformats the electronic data into a public or industry standard or into the standard used by the receiving partner. For incoming data, the software reformats the EDI data into the format required by the internal application and performs edit checks.

Because both industry-specific standards and generic ANSI X12-based standards use the same syntax, most table-driven translation software programs can decipher them. This capability is of particular benefit to companies that conduct business transactions with organizations from different industrial cultures.

EDI translation software typically includes these security and control provisions:

- Routines that are designed to report exceptions, including syntax violations, values exceeding preestablished ranges, and the omission of required data.
- Reports of acknowledgment, which are automatic acknowledgments sent to the original sender after receipt.
- Routines that are designed to facilitate sequencing of both sending and receiving EDI transmissions for which (1) sending translations provide error correction, suspense file maintenance, and transmission compression; and (2) receiving translations provide translation verification from public standard format to internal format, as well as provisions for detecting "dropped" data via record control counts.
- Controls that are designed to secure access to the application itself via a logon and password process, restricted table maintenance for translation and vendor validation tables, and (perhaps cryptographically enhanced) authentication capabilities.

EDI software typically consists of a communications link and an application interface. The *communications link* is responsible for sending and receiving teleprocessing commands along the network that connects the trading partners and third-party service providers. The *application interface* controls the sending or receiving of EDI messages, or transactions, to or from the document database. The interface consists of

- *Message database*. This database is the storage area for transactions, which are retained in local application format.
- *Arrangement module*. This software restructures outgoing messages in standard EDI syntax. It also handles batching of EDI messages for transmission.

- *Conversion module.* This module receives and processes incoming EDI messages, restructures them into a locally acceptable format, and stores them in the message database.

Using EDI software and standards, a company can extract information from its database, prepare a purchase order or other type of documentation in company format, and translate the document into a standard format for transmission to a trading partner.

2.2 STANDARDS: EVOLUTION OF A BUSINESS TOOL

Standards in the United States have shifted from company- or industry-specific formats to more general, common formats. The same movement is occurring internationally. Thus, the X12 standard is becoming, in effect, a subset of EDIFACT, with the EDIFACT standard providing all of the X12 data requirements. Moving from the X12 standard to the EDIFACT standard requires some effort, but should not be traumatic [1].

These levels of EDI standards are currently in place[1]:

- *Proprietary.* Standards that one or more trading partners develop to suit their specific situation.
- *Industry.* Standards that an industry group develops for it's specific transaction processing requirements (i.e., TDCC for the transportation industry).
- *National.* Standards that address different industry types within one country (i.e., X12 in the United States and Tradacoms in the United Kingdom).
- *Continental.* Standards that are usually more widely accepted across an entire business community (i.e., X12 in North America and EDIFACT in Europe).
- *International.* Standards that have been developed to facilitate trade among all industrialized nations in a world marketplace. (The most widely accepted international standard accepted to date is EDIFACT.)

2.2.1 The Development of North American Standards

Early electronic data interchanges relied on proprietary formats for information interchange that were agreed upon by two trading partners. However, the disadvantages of programming the widely varying formats required by different partners soon became apparent.

In the 1960s some industry groups began a cooperative effort to develop EDI industry standards for purchasing, transportation, and financial applications. Many of these standards supported only intra-industry trading; others, such as standards for bills of lading

---

1. *Source:* Jelovec, Nahid, "EDI Goes International," *3X/400 Information Management*, Vol. 2, No. 1, January 1991, p. 52.

and freight invoices, were applicable across industries. Eventually, the idea of national standards for use across industries began to receive substantial support.

2.2.1.1 ASC X12 Standards for EDI

Using the pioneering work of the Transportation Data Coordinating Committee (TDCC) and the National Association of Credit Management's Credit Research Foundation, in the late 1970s ASC X12 began to develop its first standards for EDI. In 1983 ANSI published the first five American National Standards for EDI. The 1991 publication (Version 3, Release 2) contained over 100 Draft Standards for Trial Use, including most of the transportation and retail industries' standards. There are over 150 additional standards and guidelines now available or in development.

The primary objective of the X12 subcommittees in developing the ASC X12 series of American National Standards is to minimize the need for users to reprogram their internal computer systems to effect interchange. Standards are designed to facilitate translation of data from internal to external formats and vice versa, so that firms of all sizes and computer environments can use them.

The ASC X12 standards for EDI are based on interdependency. The *foundation standards* define the syntax of X12 EDI, as well as the data elements, data segments, and control structures. These standards are required for the interpretation, understanding, and use of the X12 series of transaction-set standards. The X12 standards, in turn, define the format and data contents of business transactions. The foundation standards are

- *X12.6 Application Control Structure.* X12.6 is the syntax (architecture) document that governs the other EDI standards. It contains the formal definitions of terms related to EDI.
- *X12.5 Interchange Control Structure.* X12.5 contains specifications for the control structure (envelope) for the electronic interchange of one or more transaction sets. This standard provides the interchange envelope of a header segment (ISA) and trailer segment (IEA) for electronic interchange through data transmission and also provides a structure for the acknowledgment of receipt and processing of this envelope.
- *X12.22 Segment Directory and X12.3 Data Element Dictionary.* These standards define, respectively, the segments and data elements that are used to construct transaction sets. They must be used at the same version and release level as the transaction sets.

2.2.1.2 The ANSI X12 Message Structure

The ANSI X12 message structure is made up of four interrelated components: a functional group, a transaction set, a data segment, and a data element.

Functional group. A functional group is a group of similar transaction sets exchanged between trading partners in a single transmission. A functional group, for example, three purchase orders, when transmitted, is bounded by a functional group header (GS) segment and a functional group trailer (GE) segment. Each transaction set is assigned a functional identifier code, which is the first element of the header segment. Only transaction sets that have the same code are considered members of one functional group (Figure 2.2).

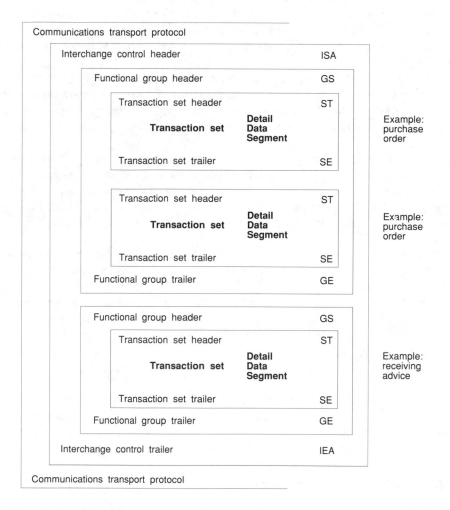

Figure 2.2 EDI transmission and control structure—the ANSI X12 standard EDI electronic envelope. *After: EDI for Managers and Auditors*, Sally Chan, et al., Electronic Data Interchange Council of Canada Library Publication, 1991, p. 10.

Transaction set. Much of the data included in a transaction set is the same as the data found in a conventionally printed document. A transaction set is the information that is exchanged between parties engaged in EDI. It consists of the specific group of segments that comprise a business document, for example, a purchase order or an invoice.

The function of a transaction set type is defined in a purpose and scope statement. Each type is composed of one or more tables that list the segments in a predefined position. Tables display a transaction set header (ST) segment as the first segment, followed by one or more data segments in a specific order and a transaction set trailer (SE) segment.

Many transaction sets are divided into three areas, or tables, that relate to the general format of a printed document. In that configuration, Table 1 is the heading area, and holds information common to the entire transaction, Table 2 is the detail area, which is usually one large loop, and Table 3 is the summary area. Figure 2A.1, in Appendix 2A, provides a diagram of the contents of a transaction set table.

Data segment. A data segment is an intermediate unit of information in a transaction set. A segment—for example, the address of purchaser—consists of logically related data elements in a defined sequence. These data elements are: a predetermined segment identifier (which is actually not a data element); one or more data elements, each preceded by a data element separator; and a segment terminator. Data segment types are defined in the segment dictionary. The definition includes the segment identifier, the segment name, the purpose of the segment, and, in the specified order, the data elements that the segment contains. Figure 2A.2, in Appendix 2A, illustrates the format of the segment dictionary.

Data element. The data element is the smallest named unit of information in the ANSI X12 standard. An example of a data element is a purchase order number. Each data element is identified by a reference number. Data element types are defined in the data element dictionary, which specifies, for each data element, the name of the element, a description, the element type, and the minimum and maximum length [2]. Figure 2A.3, in Appendix 2A, illustrates a data element dictionary entry.

2.2.2 The Development of International Standards

International commerce needs fast, efficient, and accurate information to ensure the smooth flow of goods and services. In addition to being cumbersome, current paper document systems inhibit effective operation, increase the possibility of errors, waste resources, and incur high administrative costs. EDIFACT was developed specifically to solve these universally recognized problems. (ANSI also addresses these problems.) EDIFACT is the standard that the United Nations promotes to member nations.

EDIFACT has established five regional boards as advisors for international standards: Pan-America, Western Europe, Eastern Europe, Japan and Singapore, and Australia and New Zealand. Each regional board has a rapporteur, who initiates and coordinates EDIFACT development work in the geographical area of jurisdiction. A *rapporteur* is someone who is nominated by a government and appointed by the United Nations Economic Commission for Europe Working Party 4 (UN/ECE WP4) on Facilitation of International Trade Procedures. For more than 10 years, WP4 has been developing standards for data elements, codes, messages, and syntax rules for EDI. The EDIFACT standards provide the world market with the necessary ingredients for applying EDI.

In Europe, the Western European EDIFACT Board consists of eight message development groups: trade, customs, construction, insurance, transportation, finance, statistics, and tourism. In North and South America, the Pan-American EDIFACT Board (PAEB) serves as the coordinating body of Pan-American national EDI standards organizations and provides a forum for Pan-American representation and consensus to the EDIFACT rapporteur. EDIFACT standards development, maintenance, and technical assessment in North America is performed by ASC X12 in the U.S. and by the Canadian Government Standards Board (CGSB) and Canadian Standards Association (CSA) Joint Technical Committee on EDI (JTC/EDI) in Canada [3].

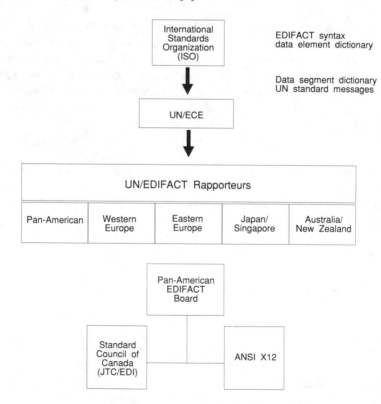

Figure 2.3 International standards development.

One of the most well-known and widely used overseas standards is the Trade Data Interchange (TDI), which is used primarily in the European Economic Community (EEC) for warehousing and distribution. Tradacoms, which was developed in 1982 by the Article

Number Association (ANA), is used throughout the United Kingdom and includes more than 20 documents that cross a wide variety of industries. Other standards include ODETTE, which is used in the European automobile industry, and Data Interchange for Shipping (DISH), which is used in European transportation industries.

EDI is gaining prominence in the global marketplace. The existence of two prevailing standards might lead one to speculate about the future of ANSI and EDIFACT. As it stands, ANSI X12 is mature and, relatively, more stable than EDIFACT, and it recognizes transaction sets covering many industry sectors. EDIFACT standards appear to be in "catch-up" mode, but in recent years EDIFACT has taken a great leap forward. The latest developments suggest that, over the next five years, X12 intends to migrate to or merge with EDIFACT [4].

With the integration of the European Common Market and the creation of free trade agreements, such as the Canadian-United States Free Trade Agreement, the growth of international trade will further underscore the importance of one set of EDI international standards for global commerce.

2.3 THE STANDARDS CONTROVERSY

Standards should imply the reduction of risk and the elimination of uncertainty and entry barriers. However, the standards climate does not seem to be totally congenial. EDI standards are not incontestable and are still subject to reinterpretation.[2]

The following are key perceived risks associated with standards adoption:

- Standards are not absolute and will be superseded. Trading partners can get locked into expensive architectures that have short life spans.
- The central committee that administers a set of standards might be slow to respond to innovations and the needs of local businesses.
- Pragmatic experience reveals that divisive contention exists between corporations and banks over standards; enacted standard networks are perceived as being costly and bureaucratic and as impeding the progress of the business [5].
- Systems that are based on national standards are inflexible. They guarantee little in terms of efficiency and lock partners into obsolete trading relationships that might have high exit costs [6].

Essentially, firms assume a level of risk when they adopt standards; standards are apt to change or evolve and are generally conceived without full regard for the industry or economy in which a given firm operates. A shared exposure or cross-vulnerability between partners has been brought on by the dependency that the standards create. (Chapter 4 discusses cross-vulnerability.)

---

2. We acknowledge the contribution of Donald Van Geete of the Royal Bank of Canada to this section.

REFERENCES

[1]   "McGinnis Expresses Optimism On The Progress of International EDI Efforts," *EDI News*, March 1988, p. 1.

[2]   *An Introduction To Electronic Data Interchange,* Alexandria, Virginia: Interchange Standards Association, Inc., September 1991, pp. 10–13.

[3]   *Introduction to UN/EDIFACT,* Alexandria, Virginia: Data Interchange Standards Association, Inc., April 1991, pp. 10–13.

[4]   Jones, Peter, *Essentials of EDI Law*, Toronto, Canada: EDI Council of Canada Library Publication, 1992, p. 12.

[5]   Peverett, Tracy, "Closing the EDI Loop," *Banking Technology*, May 1992, pp. 29–30.

[6]   Tutt, Nigel, "The EDI Trials," *Banking Technology*, September 1991, p. 22.

Appendix 2A

ANSI ASC X12 Transaction Set Table, Segment Dictionary Format, and Data Element Definition

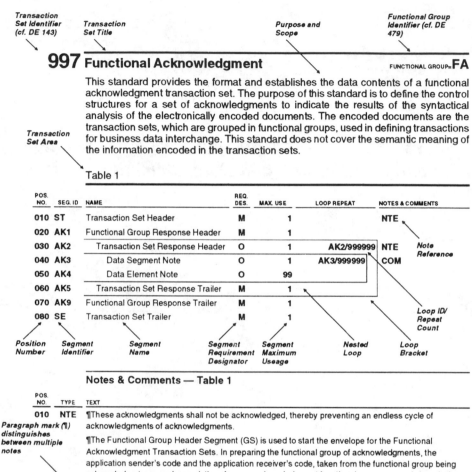

Transaction Set Identifier (cf. DE 143)

Transaction Set Title

Purpose and Scope

Functional Group Identifier (cf. DE 479)

997 Functional Acknowledgment

FUNCTIONAL GROUP=FA

This standard provides the format and establishes the data contents of a functional acknowledgment transaction set. The purpose of this standard is to define the control structures for a set of acknowledgments to indicate the results of the syntactical analysis of the electronically encoded documents. The encoded documents are the transaction sets, which are grouped in functional groups, used in defining transactions for business data interchange. This standard does not cover the semantic meaning of the information encoded in the transaction sets.

Transaction Set Area

Table 1

POS. NO.	SEG. ID	NAME	REQ. DES.	MAX. USE	LOOP REPEAT	NOTES & COMMENTS
010	ST	Transaction Set Header	M	1		NTE
020	AK1	Functional Group Response Header	M	1		
030	AK2	Transaction Set Response Header	O	1	AK2/999999	NTE
040	AK3	Data Segment Note	O	1	AK3/999999	COM
050	AK4	Data Element Note	O	99		
060	AK5	Transaction Set Response Trailer	M	1		
070	AK9	Functional Group Response Trailer	M	1		
080	SE	Transaction Set Trailer	M	1		

Position Number | Segment Identifier | Segment Name | Segment Requirement Designator | Segment Maximum Useage | Nested Loop | Loop Bracket

Note Reference

Loop ID/ Repeat Count

Notes & Comments — Table 1

POS. NO.	TYPE	TEXT
010	NTE	¶These acknowledgments shall not be acknowledged, thereby preventing an endless cycle of acknowledgments of acknowledgments.

Paragraph mark (¶) distinguishes between multiple notes

¶The Functional Group Header Segment (GS) is used to start the envelope for the Functional Acknowledgment Transaction Sets. In preparing the functional group of acknowledgments, the application sender's code and the application receiver's code, taken from the functional group being acknowledged, are exchanged; therefore, on acknowledgment functional group responds to only those functional groups from on application receiver's code to one application sender's code.

¶There is only on Functional Acknowledgment Transaction Set per acknowledged functional group.

020	NTE	AK1 is used to respond to the functional group header and to start the acknowledgement for a functional group. There shall be one AK1 segment for each functional group that is being acknowledged.
030	NTE	AK2 is used to start the acknowledgement of a transaction set within the received functional group. The AK2 segments shall appear in the same order as the transaction sets in the functional group that has been received and is being acknowledged.
040	COM	The data segments of this standard are used to report the results of the syntatical analysis of the functional groups of transaction sets; they report the extent to which the syntax complies with the standards for transaction sets and functional groups. They do not report on the semantic meaning of the transaction sets (for example, on the ability of the receiver to comply with the request of the sender).

Figure 2A.1   ANSI ASC X12 transaction set table definition. *Source:* Data Interchange Standards Association, 1992.

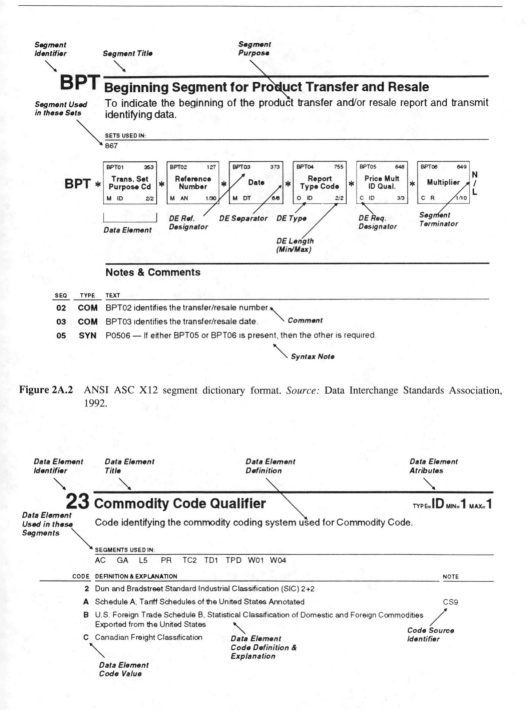

Figure 2A.2 ANSI ASC X12 segment dictionary format. *Source:* Data Interchange Standards Association, 1992.

Figure 2A.3 ANSI ASC X12 data element—definition and explanation. *Source:* Data Interchange Standards Association, 1992.

Chapter 3

Networks and Telecommunications

3.1 THIRD-PARTY NETWORKS

Third-party networks in the EDI community have undergone major changes, emerging as multiservice vendors who offer a wide range of products and services to prospective EDI users. Many of the third-party networks that exist today began as time-sharing networks. They were simply third-party service providers (TPSPs) that offered the basic service of transmitting messages between point A and point B. Competition, technology, and growing demand from sophisticated end users have turned this single-service, linear-focused, time-sharing environment into a land of opportunities for vendors who propose to add value to their baseline products and services.

Generally, most companies begin their serious consideration of switching to a third-party network when their EDI transaction volume reaches between four and six individual trading partners. As EDI usage increases, an end user's needs become more varied and demanding. In response to increased demands for services that traditionally were not part of the TPSP package, TPSPs began to expand the list of service offerings for an additional fee. In this way they created an entirely new species—the value-added network (VAN). Such features as alternative delivery methods, educational seminars, EDI program management, EDI consulting, and even EDI software are now part of the VAN product line.

A third-party network can be used in two distinct ways: (1) as an electronic mailbox or (2) for many of the additional services provided in the TPSP's expanded role of a VAN. Probably the chief benefit of VANs is their flexibility. The operators of VANs are aware of the myriad of local rules, regulations, and infrastructure. VAN service providers are constantly seeking to hook up with new areas so they can offer their customers better access to the global market.

A study conducted by Frost & Sullivan of the market for VAN services in Europe found that demand should grow 120% per year through 1992. According to the study, manufacturers—who represent 2% of VAN traffic—should expect to increase their utilization of EDI by 9% [1].

Table 3.1
VAN Expenditures—Amount Paid in a Typical Month for All VAN Services

Average Monthly Expenditures	All Respondents	EDI Hubs
Under $100	21.2%	5.6%
$100—$500	31.4%	15.8%
$501—$1,000	8.4%	8.3%
$1,001—$2,000	8.4%	11.1%
$2,001—$3,000	3.8%	4.6%
Over $3,000	10.7%	35.2%
Didn't know or refused to respond	16.2%	19.4%
Total respondents	476	108
Average expended	$896	$2,012

Source: The EDI Group, Ltd. (1992)

Simply stated, the VAN is structured into three main components:

1. The *technical component,* which provides message formatting, establishes communications protocol, and determines and maintains line speeds;
2. The *mail component,* which establishes the electronic mailbox in which EDI transactions, or messages, are temporarily held before they are forwarded to their intended destinations;
3. The *link component,* which coordinates the transmission of data through the VAN network or the network of another contracted vendor.

3.2 BENEFITS OF VALUE-ADDED NETWORKS

Given the existence of the telephone and the ability of telecommunications technology to link any number of businesses together, domestically or internationally, why not simply have trading partners communicate by telephone and avoid the headaches associated with third parties (i.e., VANs)? Because, though it is an important business tool, the public phone system cannot, as of this publication date, provide the additional features, services, convenience, and utilities that VANs can provide.

Why, then, doesn't a company manage its own link to its trading partner or partners, via a point-to-point, or direct, connection between computers? This arrangement would provide direct access between the sender's computer and the receiver's computer. But there are obvious drawbacks to this arrangement, particularly when trading partners do not operate in the same computer environment nor use the same data format standard. VANs put order into this EDI world by performing conversions between different trading partner environments, thus enabling many trading partners to work as a single user community.

Thus, the EDI message originator sends data to the VAN in a format, protocol, and transmission speed that is convenient—unencumbered by the format or requirements for data processing used by the trading partner. The same convenience is available at the receiver's end.

Note: VANs are in the EDI business because they offer more peripheral services than direct connect. They also permit subscribers to concentrate on their own business—while the VAN provides connectivity to the rest of the world.

Additional benefits that companies derive from using VAN services include:

- A direct communication link to any trading partner;
- VAN service providers' experience and knowledge of existing EDI standards and evolving EDI technologies;
- The geographical breadth and economies of scale that a VAN provides;
- A VAN's ability to support multiple data format standards;
- The value-added component—customer support, training, software, and consulting services;
- VAN mailbox services, a store-and-forward system of messaging;
- A VAN's ability to support varied protocols and access methods;
- The "7-Eleven" of electronic messaging—VANs are up all night, providing 24-hour message transmission, if required;
- A VAN's ability to provide tracking and control information, with which users audit document and message transmissions between partners;
- A VAN's dial-out services, through which users connect to companies that do not subscribe to the VAN.

It is worth noting that not all VANs are the same. In this volatile market, selecting a VAN should be a carefully considered process. If the benefits listed above (which the VANs claim) indeed exist, managers and auditors should determine whether their organizations are taking full advantage of them.

3.3 INTERCONNECTABILITY: VAN VERSUS POINT-TO-POINT

EDI documents are transmitted electronically through telephone or data lines from one computer to another. This link is supported by a VAN or a point-to-point connection. When trading partners begin to use different third-party networks, in different industries or countries, a common method of transferring messages between numerous VANs is provided by a third-party gateway, or *interconnect*. Interconnects allow companies to communicate with trading partners who use different VANs without having to establish accounts with each separate third-party network.

In a *point-to-point network*, trading partners' computers are linked directly, typically through dial-up circuits. Direct communications are required between all trading partners. Figure 3.1 illustrates a point-to-point network.

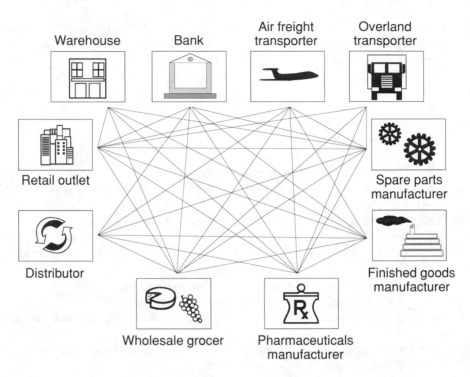

Figure 3.1 Point-to-point EDI network.

A series of three events take place in a point-to-point, or direct-connect, network environment. If, for example, a pharmaceuticals manufacturer communicates with its trading partners via a point-to-point network, the steps would proceed as follows:

1. The manufacturer's computer system is instructed to prepare a number of EDI messages—one for the warehouser, one for the overland transporter, and one for the distributor.
2. The manufacturer's computer initiates a communications link via a common carrier/public telephone network and sends the EDI messages, which are tagged for each of the trading partners. This polling and transmission process continues until all the EDI messages are sent. The trading partners' computer systems must be active and able to receive incoming communications signals (i.e., calls), and, more importantly, all the computer systems involved must be compatible.
3. The reverse process—when the warehouser, overland transporter, or distributor sends an EDI message to the pharmaceuticals manufacturer—is identical to the one described in steps 1 and 2.

The technical auditor who evaluates a direct EDI network must determine the integrity of controls—or the lack of controls—in the network configuration. These controls might or might not exist in the organization's current telecommunications environment—the environment in which the EDI system must operate.

There are key differences between the two alternatives—point-to-point networks and VANs—that organizations must consider. As discussed earlier, a point-to-point system is appropriate for an organization that communicates electronically with only a few trading partners. To create this point-to-point system, the organization must establish a complex and sophisticated communication subsystem and acquire or train the skilled personnel to manage the environment.

On the other hand, VANs do not require organizations to create their own communications subsystems and can provide a more restricted and secure network. And, in addition to these advantages, competition among VAN service providers ensures subscribers lower overall communications costs, better audit control and traffic monitoring, and access to professional EDI support, assistance, and education [2].

Figure 3.2 illustrates an EDI messaging environment that incorporates a third-party (VAN) mailbox service.

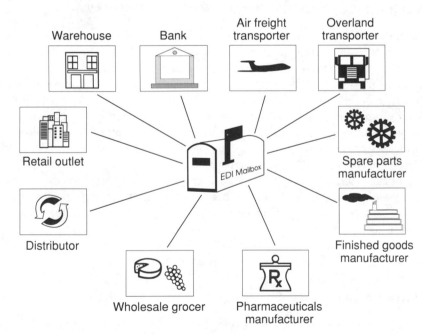

Figure 3.2 EDI messaging via a VAN mailbox service.

3.4 SELECTING A THIRD-PARTY NETWORK

Few boundaries exist between the different EDI VANs. To a degree, by their nature EDI services must be generic. Most third-party network providers can handle public standards, such as X12, Warehouse Information Network Standard (WINS), TDCC, and EDIFACT, and industry standards, such as the Automotive Industry Action Group (AIAG), the Interindustry Communication Standards, and the Chemical Industry Data Exchange (CIDX).

The primary difference between EDI networks is the type of business for which the network was designed. Yet, while this industry-specific characteristic might seem to make choosing an EDI supplier easy, the decision is complicated by the variety of services that trading partners can require of a network. An organization's telecommunications component might receive multiple demands for external EDI connections. Before embarking on an EDI program, decision makers must ensure that the chosen EDI network vendor interfaces with the largest possible number of clients. This consideration is especially important because more companies are beginning to use EDI, and thus, an organization's need to increase trading partner connections continues to grow.

Note: Generally, price is one of the least important factors in deciding on an EDI network. Choosing the right system and an appropriate network is of higher priority.

3.5 INTERNAL CONTROLS IN THIRD-PARTY NETWORKS

With regard to internal controls, a significant benefit that VANs provide is the security derived from an organization not allowing external parties to directly connect to or communicate with its computer—all communications pass through the third party. However, this relationship also has its disadvantages. An organization that both transmits and stores its EDI data messages at an external location risks disclosure to unauthorized parties. Network service providers must be able to assure end users and auditors that the security at the network site and beyond is adequate. Likewise, the organization's confidentiality requirements should be included in the network agreement (i.e., the third-party services contract).

Before deciding on a third-party vendor, an organization's auditor should determine if an audit of the candidate is warranted. Alternatively, the auditor should verify the existence and validity of a third-party audit report. Also, if an independent review of the vendor has not been conducted previously, the auditor might wish to perform a limited data and physical security review, as well as a review of the telecommunications network that supports the VAN, provided the right to audit is included in the VAN contract. (For additional audit-related considerations, refer to Appendix E.)

3.5.1 Access Control

A major concern of many EDI users is that an unauthorized user might gain access to company data. All data that pass through a third-party network are routed via the receiver identification codes in the outer EDI envelopes. These codes indicate the addresses of the sender and the receiver and identify the electronic documents being sent in the transmission. In EDI nomenclature, the outer envelope is called the *interchange envelope*. The interchange envelope contains two data segments: (1) the interchange control header (ISA) segment and (2) the interchange control trailer (IEA) segment. (Refer to Chapter 2, Figure 2.2 for further clarification and example.)

Access to a mailbox normally requires both a specific mailbox identification code and a password. In a third-party network, document flow between mailboxes is controlled through the use of identification and authorization data files, which are maintained by the third-party vendor.

3.5.2 Data Integrity

Some third-party networks offer encryption and authentication of messages, using standards provided by X12. A cryptographic facility must be available to both the sender and the receiver because they share a responsibility for implementing the cryptographic protection. *End-to-end encryption,* for example, protects the confidentiality of data passing between a sender and a receiver, independently of the nodes that the data must traverse. End-to-end encryption can be further refined to address *association encryption*, which protects each transmission sent between sender and receiver.

The method that networks use to physically move data can help prevent data alteration. VANs often use *packet switching* to move data. In this method, messages are broken into packets of characters, moved separately, and then rejoined.

The ANSI ASC X12 subcommittee X12 Finance (X12F) has been charged with the responsibility of developing and maintaining EDI standards and guidelines for EDI documents associated with financial functions. These documents include invoices, payment transactions, bank reports, credit instruments, data content edits, and batch totals. Related issues that require guidelines include security, payment systems, and architecture. X12F is also responsible for developing and maintaining UN/EDIFACT standard messages.

Two technical standards developed by the X12F subcommittee that are particularly important to auditors are: (1) Standard 815, Cryptographic Service Message and (2) Standard X12.58, Security Structures. Standard 815 carries the ANSI reference number X12.42 and uses X12 structures and data formats. Its primary objective is to provide a data format for cryptographic key management, which involves standardizing three functions: key generation, key distribution, and key installation (including automated distribution and exchange of keys).

Standard X12.58, Security Structures, includes ANSI guidelines for encryption, authentication, cipher-block chaining, filters, and relationships between key partners and interchange partners. The specific objective of X12.58 is to define security (authentication or encryption) structures for two levels of EDI message exchange: functional group and transaction set [3]. The security structures provide integrity, confidentiality, and verification of sender to receiver.

To assure the confidentiality and integrity of data being transmitted via EDI—especially when demand for security is high, such as in financial EDI—the auditor should verify that either message authentication or encryption standards are incorporated into the EDI technical system requirements specification. One factor to consider when determining a data integrity scheme is the speed of transmission. In fact, weighing speed of transmission as an important factor can justify the selection of message authentication over a more costly and encumbered encryption methodology. If, however, the nature of the transmission is sensitive and requires utmost confidentiality, the use of encryption methodologies is strongly recommended.

3.5.2.1 Message Authentication Code

Message authentication code (MAC) is a cryptographic checksum value calculated by passing an entire message or the authentication elements of a message through a cipher system. This methodology can provide the additional level of security required for EDI messaging. Auditors should become familiar with message authentication coding and its role in establishing internal control in the EDI environment.

In an EDI transaction, the sender calculates the MAC and appends it to the message prior to transmission. The receiver's software recalculates the MAC upon receipt of the EDI message and compares it to the original MAC. If the MACs agree, the EDI message is processed. If the MACs do not agree, the disagreement indicates that the original message has to some degree been altered. At this point, both the sender and the receiver should be notified of the failure of the MACs to authenticate the initial message. Notification gives both parties the opportunity to investigate the discrepancy and to agree on a resolution.

Message authentication coding is a useful technique for controlling unauthorized attempts to modify, add, or delete EDI messages. Trading partners can create both preventive and detective controls by attaching preestablished and agreed upon identifiers to every EDI message. Messages that do not possess identifiers can be automatically rejected as invalid and unauthorized.

3.5.2.2 Encryption

Encryption is the conversion of plain text into cipher-text data and is performed with a cryptographic algorithm and key. Data are cryptographically disguised in such a way that only the parties who possess the key can view the data in their original form. This cryptographic algorithm (which is a series of characters that represent the product of a mathematical formula) can be of many varieties, but the most widely accepted is the Data Encryption Standard (DES), which is developed and maintained by the National Institute of Standards. Encryption protects the privacy of data passing between a sender and a receiver irrespective of any communications nodes traversed by the message, because only the sender and the receiver are aware of the cryptographic key. However, the message source and destination identifiers must exist in plain-text form so each node on the network knows how to route the message.

X12 cryptographic security can be applied to different levels of an EDI transaction. It can be used at the transaction set level, to encrypt payment orders, for example, or it can be used at the functional group level, to encrypt batches of payment orders and purchases in one EDI envelope. Or encryption can be performed at both levels for the same transmission. However, for security reasons encryption is commonly performed at the transaction set level. Problems encountered at this lower level do not cause the entire functional group to be rejected [4].

3.5.3 Transmission Security

The distribution of products from suppliers to customers typically involves communicating and coordinating various activities among different parties at different locations. Data exchange is as important in distribution as the movement of the goods themselves. Therefore, maintaining the integrity of EDI communications is vital to a company's success and prosperity. Most companies rarely consider the vulnerability of their conversations or messages, believing that the systems are secure. However, according to Michael Bacon, "The truth is that public networks are not secure; information carried over them cannot be confidential, and integrity is not guaranteed [5]." (This issue is further explored in Chapter 4.)

Many of the factors that dictate security and reliability requirements are directly related to the nature of the messages carried through the EDI system. However, there are two basic security requirements that are external to the messages. The first requirement is application software that contains the appropriate error detection and error correction routines. The second requirement is adequate security for local and remote access to the EDI network via a telecommunications medium. The security requirement should incorporate automated call-back procedures, which allow network partners access to the network and automatically log users off the network after a period of inactivity. (Note: The call-forward feature available on many telephone systems, if activated, undermines the control design of the call-back feature.)

As an additional security control, trading partners should be assigned unique passwords, use of which is designed to prevent unauthorized access to another partner's information on the EDI network. Some systems provide the additional protection of checks that establish the level of sensitivity of the data a user can access.

Other key requirements that should be considered as part of transmission security include message authorization, authentication, delivery, and protection. These transmission components are discussed in the following sections.

3.5.3.1 Message Authorization

Message authorization involves the programmed validation (i.e., use of internal controls designed to ensure the legitimacy of a message prior to transmission) and security procedures that ensure the relevancy and authenticity of a transmission.

The authorization process must include the following steps [6]:

- Validate the originating workstation. Is the workstation that transmitted the EDI message a legitimate end-user workstation? Is the workstation an authorized network node? Validation is based on workstation ownership, location, and use and on the appropriateness of the data communication node associated with the workstation (i.e., does the workstation have external data communications capabilities?)
- Verify that the station is authorized to transmit at the specified time.
- Confirm the operator sign-on.
- Validate the message format.
- Verify the operator or workstation's authority to transmit the message type.

- Validate the message numbering sequence.
- Test to ensure that the correct authorization codes are embedded in the message.

Because any errors that the system detects can be part of a pattern indicating an attempt to breach system security, the system must include the capability to detect and log security breaches and provide exception reports to highlight such breaches.

3.5.3.2 Message Authentication

Once an authorized originator has entered a message into the system, the ensuing procedures should address the parameters for message authentication. These specific parameters, which indicate message format and content, must be standardized and strictly adhered to. At a minimum, automated authenticity tests should include [7]:

- Positional edits for correct control characters, address, data fields, and for line and format constraints;
- Validation for routing numbers, addresses, type codes, and user-specific, content-oriented information;
- Authorization checks for coded data, test words, and other security tests (e.g., multiple identical currency fields).

Authentication differs from encryption in that encryption ensures secrecy of data while authentication does not. Authentication does, however, ensure that the data are not altered. Also, authentication can be used as a form of digital signature because it verifies the identity of the sender.

3.5.3.3 Message Delivery

Message delivery controls help ensure that a message was received properly and remained accurate. The controls should validate message routing and provide for authentication. Additionally, the controls should record and track all messages (sent or received) and verify that messages have not been altered or duplicated during the transmission process. This verification might involve retransmitting certain information about the corrupted transaction to the partner who sent the message. This retransmission control would provide an audit trail to verify that the original message was finally received.

Ideally, message delivery controls and routing verification procedures should ensure that [8]:

- The destination is a valid node on the network and is authorized to receive the type of traffic involved.
- A positive connection is made with the station and validated before and after message transmission.

- Verification of receipt of the message is secured from the terminal upon delivery, with terminal identification included in the acknowledgment.
- Unbroken, sequential output numbers are transmitted (or received, depending upon directional flow of transmission) as part of the message.
- A log of all messages transmitted is kept and reviewed for adequacy. This log can be reviewed by end users, data security officers, and internal or external auditors.
- The queuing and routing algorithms (which are performed automatically and are beyond the control of the end user) enable traffic to be processed efficiently and prevent undue delay of messages in transit.

3.5.3.4 Message Protection

In general, there are two ways to provide protection against message interception. The first process, which can be coordinated by the user or the data security function and reviewed by the audit function, is rather expensive and involves the use of monitoring equipment. Use of this equipment can be both burdensome and uneconomical; it requires expensive and complex hardware and techniques to intercept and interpret transmissions. The second method scrambles or rearranges data patterns, making the data unreadable and useless in this form (e.g., encryption). Although this method of message protection is regarded as being one of the most secure, due to the overhead costs (i.e., processing time and expense) required to rearrange the data, it is costly.

There are considerations that can be incorporated into network system design that address the protection of messages. Some considerations of this type that can be applied to EDI are discussed in the sections below [9].

Message encryption. The process of message encryption involves scrambling the contents of a message into a series of numbers and letters. The resulting string of characters is illegible to anyone not possessing the appropriate private key decryption algorithm. Special consideration should be given in the network design process to allowing for the implementation of an encryption scheme. Encryption schemes include DES and the Rivest, Shamir, and Adelman (RSA) scheme. (RSA is explained in Chapter 4.)

Multiplexed transmission lines. Creating multiplexed transmission lines entails combining a number of communications from different lines onto a single line. With this configuration, rather than having to secure multiple lines coming from many locations, the user need only secure one line. Multiplexing techniques use statistical channel derivation schemes to assign capacity on a fixed, predetermined basis.

Multiplexing enhances a system's reliability in several ways. One way a system is enhanced is by being incorporated into an intelligent front-end processor that performs other functions, such as message validation and protocol conversion. Additionally, a multiplexer eliminates the difficulty a user experiences attempting to disentangle myriad messages passing over a single channel.

Synchronous, continuous data streams. Maintaining a continual stream of data within a transmission—which entails employing a repetitive indicator that identifies similar parts in a transmission stream—can be useful when messages become garbled or are lost before reaching final destination.

The highest-speed transmission facilities feasible or available. Incorporating high-speed transmission facilities into a network design ensures that, to read a transmission, would-be intruders must possess equally fast data capture or interpretation devices.

Alternate paths and rotary-line configurations. Providing several means for routing a call, and thus ensuring that an open pathway is always available—even if the primary line is out of service and unable to be repaired—can be accomplished through the use of concentration techniques in combination with multiplexing.

Concentration techniques use schemes in which a number of input channels dynamically share a smaller number of output channels on a demand basis. Thus, concentration techniques smooth the traffic flow across a network. Because the number of input channels surpasses the number of output channels, to determine the optimal path for the message to navigate, the concentrators must be able to handle message queues.

Packet switching. In packet switching a message is broken up into small, fixed-length packets, and the individual packets are routed through the network as channels become available.

Satellite transmission. Satellite transmission requires an expensive and complex reception device that can receive and interpret transmissions and thus discourage unauthorized activities.

3.6 LIABILITY OF THIRD-PARTY NETWORK VENDORS

The liability of third-party network vendors closely resembles that of the U.S. Post Office. When a post office loses a piece of mail, liability, if there is any, normally covers only the cost of the mail service. Such limited liability is meaningless when the message is a payment order. Additional controls must be in place so that the users of FEDI can avert liability under certain circumstances. (This specific issue is examined in Chapter 9.)

Managers, end users, auditors, and the firm's legal counsel should review the liability limits established by a contract with a third-party vendor to determine if the potential exists for the firm to experience loss. In addition, they should assess the extent of any liability or exposure that might occur as a result of the vendor performing or *failing* to perform certain actions—such as failing to establish a network backup recovery facility or failing to control the disclosure of trading partner data to unauthorized personnel.

Liability issues might be handled differently by different countries' interchange agreements. For example, agreements might ascribe liability differently in a situation in which a manufacturer made a payment to a supplier by FEDI and the payment was delayed because the third-party network went down [10]. As another example, if one EDI trading partner is located in France and the other is located in Ontario, Canada, and the VANs across which they communicate are located in England and Ohio, respectively, which party is liable when problems in the EDI transmission cause damages to one or more of the parties [11]? There are no easy answers to questions of liability. For this reason, we highly recommend that legal counsel review all legal agreements made on behalf of the trading partners—between partners, VANs, or any other related entity—prior to execution of the contract.

The electronic messages transmitted between trading partners can constitute evidence in liability cases. However, not all EDI messages are truly of legal status. Some messages are more important than others; some are simply not important at all. Some messages have no legal foundation; others stand on their own as legally binding evidence of electronic transaction processing.

There are two questions organizations can use to determine the importance or value to be placed on EDI messages: (1) Does the message contribute to or establish a contract between the trading partners? (2) Do any government regulations—which can place restrictions on use or require specialized processing—apply to the message?

In many cases the third-party vendor is responsible for any liability arising from the VAN's failure to deliver the electronic message within a specified time frame. However, this is not always true. In the proposed Standard for Interchange Agreement, produced by the Legal Advisory Group of the EDI Association of the United Kingdom, if either party entering into an EDI trading partner agreement instructs the other party to use a third-party network, the party making the request is responsible for any losses incurred by network failure [12].

To reiterate, organizations would do well to enlist the aid of a competent and knowledgeable attorney—someone with prior experience in the legalities of electronic commerce—to review any legal agreements made with trading partners, end users who possess authorization to access the network, and third-party service providers, prior to contract execution.

REFERENCES

[1]   "VANs Hard to Avoid for International EDI," *EDI News*, Vol. 4, No. 17, September 10, 1990, p. 3.

[2]   Diamond, Gerry, and Howe, Edward, *Understanding and Choosing a Value-Added Network*, External Affairs and International Trade, Canada Transportation Services Division, Government of Canada, 1992, p. 15.

[3]   *ASC X12 Status Report: Standards Development and Maintenance Activities*, Alexandria, VA: Data Interchange Standards Association, Inc., February 1992, pp. 61–84.

[4]   Chan, Sally, et al., *EDI for Managers and Auditors*, Toronto, Canada: EDI Council of Canada Library Publication, 1991, p. 44.

[5]   Bacon, Michael, "Assessing Public Network Security," *Telecommunications*, December 1989, p. 19.

[6]   Schwartz, Michael, "Data Authentication," *Data Communication Management, Volume 1*, Boston, MA: Auerbach Publishers, 1987, p. 6.

[7]   Schwartz, Michael, "Data Authentication," *Data Communication Management, Volume 1*, Boston, MA: Auerbach Publishers, 1987, p. 6.

[8]   Isaacson, Gerald, "Security and Reliability: Design and Operational Concepts," *Data Communications Management, Volume 1*, Boston, MA: Auerbach Publishers, 1989, p. 2.

[9]   Schwartz, Michael, "Data Authentication," *Data Communication Management, Volume 1*, Boston, MA: Auerbach Publishers, 1987, p. 6.

[10]   Baum, Michael, and Perritt, Henry, *Electronic Contracting, Publishing, and EDI Law*, New York, NY: John Wiley & Sons, Inc., 1991, Chapter 3.

[11]   Takach, George, "Legal Issues in EDI Implementation—The Canadian Perspective," *EDI for Managers and Auditors*, Toronto, Canada: EDI Council of Canada Library Publication, 1991, p. 106.

[12]   Salamone, Salvatore, "Legal Groups Working On Rules For International EDI," *Network World International Networks* (Section), March 12, 1990, p. 26.

Chapter 4

Cross-Vulnerabilities in EDI Partnerships

4.1 WHAT IS CROSS-VULNERABILITY IN EDI?

The EDI security and control systems that trading partners create and maintain are only as strong as the weakest link in the chain. A potential exposure, or cross-vulnerability, exists when a partner's operation is adversely affected by the mishaps of another partner. For example, two partners awaiting a cash settlement during a VAN outage are at risk.

For the purposes of this text, a *cross-vulnerability* is a major control deficiency in one EDI system that can materially compromise the integrity of other dependent EDI systems. A cross-vulnerability can result from a technical limitation or from imprudent business or management practices. This chapter addresses the issue of cross-vulnerability within the context of current security technologies and then goes on to locate the issue within the context of everyday business and management practices.

4.2 CROSS-VULNERABILITIES INVOLVING SECURITY

Commonalities in security architectures that cross applications, trading partners, and institutions can make these entities equally vulnerable to major system disruption. Cross-vulnerabilities exist between systems that rely on common values for user identification and authentication, such as user IDs and passwords that are stored in shared databases. In the recent North American experience, Mark Koenig's foiled attack on Bank of America's automated banking machine (ABM) network demonstrated that the management of shared security architectures in public networks is worthy of serious review [1].

Both the high visibility of public networks and the potential for harm resulting from unauthorized tampering justify an investigation of other areas in which these networks might be vulnerable. EDI suggests itself as an area worthy of evaluation.

Proactive management of EDI involves looking far down the road to the day when online EDI systems of tightly coupled applications and shared corporate databases are the norm for commercial trading relationships. While such a scenario might not exist in the near future, it is surely the goal of EDI development.

Although the current initiatives taken by Task Group 4 of the X12F subcommittee appear to be addressing many outstanding issues, a review of the security architectures effected by ANSI National Standards Councils on EDI suggests that much work remains to be done.

4.2.1 Point-of-Sale and EDI Security

Financial institutions have always been key players in defining requirements for security and control in electronic payment systems. The X9 series of standards was developed in tandem with the emergence of the banking community's use of electronic devices, which, typically, were ABMs. Since the banking community regards confidentiality and data integrity as key business success factors, there was tremendous incentive to push the issue forward. The main standards, X9.9 for message authentication and X9.17 for wholesale key management, were closely tailored to the banking industry. In Canada, rigorous ANSI-based compliance and certification programs are in place to regulate ABM and, in recent years, point-of-sale (POS) traffic in public networks. ABM networks have been in place for 20 years. Point-of-sale (POS), an emerging business application of the last few years, has learned from the ABM experience and upgraded its security requirements. However, it is interesting to note that the progress that cryptographic security made between ABM and POS has not yet been extended into the EDI area, even though the major exposures in both technologies are similar.

Before the banking industry got involved as financial intermediaries, there was limited security in X12. Most of the initial development and standard-setting effort by the X12 committee was in the area of transaction typing and message structures. The evolution of the 820 payment order/remittance advice service created a need, in the late 1980s, for X9, the message authentication code (MAC), to map to X12, to provide a specification for security within the 820 transaction set. Thus, X12.42, Cryptographic Service Message Transaction Set, and X12.58, Security Structures, were created. As a result, the integrity of the 820 transaction set is reasonably protected, and X12.58 is sufficiently generic to allow any new transaction set to be secured against tampering.

There remains, however, a sharp contrast between what is acceptable in EDI and what is mandatory in POS. POS remains a standard-driven environment of financial institutions, and control is correspondingly stringent. EDI, on the other hand, is characterized by a partner-to-partner relationship that has not kept up with the range of key management and cryptographic practices available.

One major difference between EDI and POS security is the requirement for key change, which involves the periodic recalculation and updating of key values. The objective of key change is to limit the damage that can result from a current key being broken, by frequently replacing it with a new value. In POS there is a closely coupled set of three keys and mandated key change requirements. The three keys are: (1) an encryption key (KPE), (2) a message authentication code key (KMAC), and (3) a message encryption key (KME). The mandated key change requirements might call, for example, for keys to be changed daily or after every 2,000 transactions. These exacting standards require an auto mated key management process to ensure operational feasibility. Financial institutions use online databases of key components and automated hardware security modules so that cryptographic functions can be called by the applications. However, such automation is costly, and, ironically, the average POS transaction is valued at scarcely more than $100!

In EDI, logical access passwords are still the primary security mechanism for nonfinancial messages. Additionally, in Canada, message authentication coding is mandatory for message exchange between financial institutions. By contrast, encryption is not mandated—not even for such detailed fields as dollar balances or account number. While both forms of cryptographic controls are mandatory for POS, they might be no more than de facto requirements for doing EDI with a particular financial institution. EDI key change requirements are settling into a 90-day cycle, while they are a mandatory daily requirement for POS. Organizations seem to take better care of POS transactions than they do higher dollar-value EDI business!

It appears that a certain management lag or, more precisely, a security lag exists in the area of EDI. Managers are not demanding EDI security products, and vendors are not marketing security products as value-added. Within the thin portfolio of EDI security products, ANSI-compliant products have been known to be incompatible due to reasonable but irreconcilable differences in interpretations of standards, particularly at the microcomputer level.

4.2.2 Limitations of Current Security Structures

The concerns discussed in the following sections are rooted in the security of EDI systems themselves. In addition, the ramifications of these concerns suggest that, in the global context of exponentially growing credit fraud, a cautionary review of the state of health of EDI security is warranted.

4.2.2.1 Limitations of Message Authentication Coding

Message authentication coding is frequently used to verify the identity of the sender of a message. However, this practice might not be entirely defensible, primarily, because this type of coding was designed to protect data integrity, not to authenticate message routing. Any use of MAC for verification of a sender's identity is a misapplication of the control mechanism.

It should also be noted that using message authentication coding as a security mechanism hinges on *inferring* that, just because the MAC was verified, a message came from a specific partner who alone shares an organization's keys. The MAC-verified message could just as easily have been inserted fraudulently by an employee within the organization. Alternatively, a third party with unauthorized access might have inserted the message. Possession of the key is everything in cryptography. Furthermore, companies that have not secured their key generation and maintenance procedures cannot place absolute reliance on the integrity of their message authentication coding. Furthermore, for the coding to be reliable, it must be enacted "end-to-end" across the network. In other words, the MAC value must be calculated as soon as the message is created. If the message is routed or stored before the MAC is applied, then the coding process might be useless—the opportunity for unrecorded tampering is left open.

4.2.2.2 Symmetrical Cryptography

Security exposures created by stolen keys are threats to symmetrical cryptographic architectures. By *symmetrical* we mean a kind of cryptography that always encrypts a clear value into the same encrypted value. When the crytography is symmetrical, anyone in possession of the keys and a copy of the key database can reverse all the encrypted values into clear text. The data encryption algorithm (DEA), based on the ANSI data encryption standard (DES), is the most widely used cryptographic algorithm. It is the algorithm used most often in EDI for message authentication coding.

There is reason to suspect that this kind of reversible cryptography is reaching the end of its useful life [2]. This is especially true for the single-key enactment of the algorithm. Because keys are numbers that we combine with other confidential data, the longer the key (i.e., the more characters it contains), the larger the number of values the key can assume and the more difficult it becomes to break. When the 64-bit key DEA architecture was created in the mid-70s, 72 quadrillion options were felt to be adequate for DEA ciphers. In the age of increasingly cheap and fast microprocessors, this assumption might no longer be accurate. Single-length key cryptograms can be *finite-searched* and their clear text contents dumped for fraudulent manipulation. Therefore, all major keys should be extended from 64 to 128 bits, which would make them *double length*. (Note that 8 bits are reserved for parity.) These double-length keys would require considerable effort to break using available technologies [3].

4.2.2.3 Public-Key Cryptography

Message authentication coding constitutes part of what is often referred to as *private-key cryptography*. This implies the privacy of exchange between a very limited number of partners. EDI ushers in the era of public interchange of trading information and of *public-key cryptography*.

Public-key cryptography involves an extra layer of key types and a complex key generation and exchange procedure. If nonfinancial trading partners show reluctance to use DEA-based key management, they cannot be expected to buy quickly into public-key management, with its incremental administrative requirements. Further, the processor overhead of public-key cryptographic computations is a hurdle to adoption, even at current processor speeds. These functions require external mathematical computations for each element within a transaction and, for this reason, are often routed to dedicated processors within the computer—a process that takes time.

The leading public-key algorithm is RSA. Applied to EDI architectures, the algorithm can build *nonrepudiable* electronic signatures that can be appended to the traditional DEA-protected message. In this way, RSA protects the signature in a highly secure manner, establishing contractual certainty. But RSA will probably not replace the simpler and faster DEA process for the bulk of the message. Contractual nonrepudiation under DEA-based message authentication coding is inferential but not absolute. RSA offers the nonreversibility required, but that nonreversibility comes at a cost of additional overhead.

Note, too, that the knapsack algorithm, which, like RSA, is nonreversible, is reported to have been compromised: this suggests that the reliability of RSA would benefit from periodic verification [4]. And, another issue that threatens the long-term reliability of RSA is the reluctance of the Department of National Security to allow sophisticated cryptographic devices to be exported. This constraint will surely delay the rate of adoption of much-needed security by international trading partners [5].

Because users do not demand adequate levels of security, suppliers simply do not make appropriate products available. Security is always difficult to sell to senior management because it adds cost and complexity without adding apparent customer value. The arcane world of 64-bit ciphers does not sell projects or build careers. It appears that management lag has resulted in EDI systems that might not be adequately secured and that expose both partners to the cross-vulnerabilities of fraud and mischief.

4.2.3 Security Solutions

EDI has yet to become the driving force in international commerce that its advocates suggest it will become. Thus, the opportunity exists for the exposures outlined above to receive serious consideration within the context of the future evolution of EDI technology. In addition, EDI users and service providers would do well to note that many of the cross-vulnerabilities outlined above can be regarded as future threats that could proliferate as EDI volumes grow.

The current situation is an excellent and timely opportunity for companies to perform housekeeping of their current security systems, and they should carry out that housekeeping with a view toward ensuring system integrity in future applications. To that end, security should be given consideration in the areas described below. These solutions are best addressed on an enterprisewide basis and will require periodic and routine management review. Implementing them will ensure that a broad and internally consistent security layer is developed and maintained over time and that security evolves along with business practices.

Development methodology. All systems development should proceed according to an effective development methodology, and, as part of that methodology, organizations should ensure that security is appropriately represented in the EDI project life cycle. Most importantly, because these technologies are difficult to retrofit and their implementation requires coordination with operational staff requirements, cryptography and key management should be defined as early as possible in the development cycle. Key generation and injection requirements for interchange keys (e.g., key exchange key [KEK]) should also be defined by both EDI partners as early as possible.

Cryptography. It is important to identify applications that share security. Generally, a cryptographic key should be dedicated to one cryptographic function only. Key sets that are not dedicated to individual communications links should be compensated for by an increased frequency of key change.

Data ownership. A policy of assigning data ownership is indispensable. As a rule, the manager whose business is being supported should be designated the data owner. It is then that manager's responsibility to determine the requirements for security profiles for stored data and to identify the fields that require encryption. Any changes to the security of the system must be communicated to all data owners, and their sign-off recorded. In this manner, not only is segregation of duty achieved, but also business logic is tightly integrated with the cryptographic process. The data owner should also coordinate security with the management counterpart in the partner firm.

Upgrades. To minimize the requirement for future upgrades, all but working keys should be double length. To date, vendors have been slow to upgrade this aspect of their systems. Companies considering an investment in hardware security modules for automated key management should clarify the status with their vendors, particularly with regard to the incremental processing overhead that might be required. Because hardware devices are designed to be tamper-proof, while software is vulnerable to unauthorized copying, hardware-based cryptographic security is preferable to software-based.

Security diagnostics. To facilitate security and network incident investigation, companies should ensure that time-sensitive controls are built into EDI interfaces. A time-sensitive, real-time reporting mechanism can diagnose such occurrences as MAC failures and key synchronization errors. In addition, action steps should be defined—and accountability assigned—to address security breaches. It goes without saying that this security logger should dovetail with the company's contingency plan—to protect against the possibility of mass fraud. Further, an escalation procedure should be in place for confirming and coordinating responses with trading partners in the event of security incidents.

Key archival. Trading partners should agree on a policy for archiving keys and crytograms. The policy should specify the length of time offline records are retained—in anticipation of events that require that whole messages be reconstructed after the fact.

4.3 CROSS-VULNERABILITIES IN OTHER BUSINESS AREAS

The technical exposures generated by shared EDI systems go far beyond the issue of security. Unlike ABM networks, which can occupy both a public and a proprietary domain, EDI exposures and risks imply a shared dependency with at least one partner, and this shared dependency gives rise to additional areas of cross-vulnerability that might require management attention.

Cross-vulnerabilities exist because trading partners are making shared commitments to a technology that is still undergoing change. Still-evolving standards can do little to offset the risk of entry for partners. Financial and other risks could grow incrementally, that growth caused by the vertical integration of partners who were formerly separate but are now linked in the areas of market, cash flows, and business cycle. Other aspects of the link—from competitive cost structures to the legal enforceability of electronic transactions—are exposures that might not be understood fully or managed adequately by users.

Cross-vulnerabilities engendered by various dependencies include difficulties associated with maintaining shared standards, the uncertain legal status of EDI contracts, and conflicts in partners' competitive profiles. These and other business and management exposures are discussed in the sections below.

4.3.1 Difficulties with Shared Standards

Standards should provide a certain reduction of risk and elimination of both uncertainty and entry barriers. But this is not always true of EDI standards; they are still subject to reinterpretation. And, while standards organizations are pursuing the goals of flexibility and certainty, these two desirable features are proving to be incompatible. The area of standards tends, ironically, to be characterized by disagreement and inconsistency. EDI has fallen prey to its own share of contention [6].

As a result of the barriers to standardization, trading partners share the following cross-vulnerabilities:

- A financial commitment made by two profit-seeking partners can be placed at risk by the standards committee redefining standards.
- Vendors build their systems around the same standards, which, in turn, are subject to revision or enhancement.
- Costly conversion cannot be avoided and is required bilaterally.

To summarize, the risks created by the standards controversy are [7]:

- Ever-changing standards cannot guarantee interoperability between systems.
- International standards emphasize a global and normative way of doing business that might not reflect the exigencies of specific industries in specific national contexts.
- Standards represent high entry and exit costs that can undermine a company's competitive advantage.

Despite the difficulties inherent in shared solutions, however, optimism about standards still prevails, based primarily on the fact that the creation of standards is driven by business needs. However, standards will not thrive if users do not support them. Standards organizations have procedures in place that enable effective consultation with users from the industries affected. Participation is voluntary; any organization can join a standards committee.

The logical enactment of standards occurs in translation software and in universal application program interfaces (APIs). EDI users should look for translation software vendors who are attuned to current standards development, capable of supporting the standards approved by the standards organizations, and able to provide cross-translation between X12 and EDIFACT or other industry standards. Whether an organization is a small or a big EDI player, standards development should be on its watch list.

4.3.2 The Uncertain Legal Status of EDI Contracts

The euphoria of implementing EDI might, on occasion, blind organizations to the fact that trading partnerships can turn sour. Be it interdivisional gamesmanship or bad faith among "arm's length parties," certain situations require evaluation of the legality and certainty of trading arrangements.

Concerns are not limited to the reconciliation of disputes. In fact, disputes can be addressed by effective arbitration. Other concerns exist that are related to the exposure created by electronic transactions, evidentiary status, enforceability, and liability, and these concerns might not be provided for in the management procedures of each partner's organization.

There are certain actions organizations can take to avoid or reduce the potential risks and also certain issues they must remain mindful of in forging partnerships. Such prudent actions include enlisting third-party arbitration, signing formal agreements, cost-justifying security measures, and understanding the implications of Article 4A of the Uniform Commercial Code.

Enlist third-party arbitration. Ben Wright offers a cautionary discussion about employing a third party to ensure the basic functioning of the record-keeping system between partners. In the absence of such an arm's length arbitrator, an organization's data integrity is only as reliable as its partner's [8].

Sign formal agreements. Trust has always been an integral part of business relationships. In anticipation of the proliferation of EDI partnerships, businesses are well advised to support relationships with a specific and formal trading partner agreement (TPA). TPAs explicitly define the intent to contract, which might not otherwise be conclusively established. As the number of paper invoices diminishes, the requirement for contracts increases. Even when both parties intend to contract in good faith, because there are no EDI precedents yet, the enforceability of such agreements by law is not certain. Both parties are vulnerable to the higher degree of risk that this uncertainty causes [9].

Cost-justify security measures. There are no standards for care or diligence in EDI, nor is there an established arbitration process for damages, errors, or delays [10]. Both parties in a partnership are likely to remain at risk because of an unavoidable expectation gap involving cost-justification of good security and control. The costs of reconciling expectations and periodically monitoring the shared security layer (i.e., keys and shared corporate databases) are not trivial, and they have to be charged back to the profit and loss statement of the EDI undertaking.

Understand the implications of Article 4A of the Uniform Commercial Code. Although Article 4A covers U.S. wholesale funds transfer, the U.S. courts might also apply this article to funds transfers that involve non-U.S. participants. What this will mean to the EDI community in the 90s is not yet fully defined. However, one consequence is clear: the article establishes liability for performance—which might not be in the best interest of either trading partner [11]. (Chapter 9 presents further discussion of Article 4A.)

In the book *EDI for Managers and Auditors* the authors argue that EDI systems have a greater need for mutual control assurances than other systems [12].

> Whether trading partners like it or not, when EDI becomes integrated with other applications systems, mutual reliance upon other trading partners involves reliance upon their controls as well. This mutual dependency motivates trading partners to seek mutual assurances that controls are adequate and continually functioning as intended.

Control and audit features that are identified and agreed upon by trading partners can be used to establish mutual obligations. Trading partners who agree on mutual obligations are acknowledging that each partner's control environment extends beyond the enterprise [13]. While the TPA itself can be viewed as a form of management control, the terms and conditions therein require that trading partners comply with, among other controls, certain control standards applicable specifically to EDI. It is through control assurance that reliability is established, not through the liability clauses in the TPA. This is not to discount the TPA, which can establish the burden of proof, but to emphasize that a good grasp of the controls up front will save money in legal fees and improve the use of legal services.

Two particularly helpful forms of control assurance, *control self-assessment* (CSA) and the *EDI compliance program*, are described below.

Control self-assessment. CSA is a process that allows management to identify and refine the management control objectives they must fulfill. The process must begin with a clear understanding of the management objectives, the controls that exist to ensure the attainment of those objectives, the nonresidual risks, and the compensating controls. CSA worksheets assess the actual effectiveness of controls against managers' prescriptions for adequate control. They also include action plans for areas of deficient control. Typically, a control coordinator fills out CSA worksheets and then summarizes the information for senior management [14]. (Appendix 4A contains an example of a completed CSA worksheet and worksheet summary.)

EDI project managers should encourage users to identify and evaluate controls up front, during the EDI project life cycle. Managers should also involve their systems auditors, who can provide independent opinions of the CSA worksheets [15].

EDI compliance program. The EDI compliance program involves compliance reporting and compliance auditing—both of which are based on a set of generally accepted standards of control. Compliance reporting involves management issuing a periodic statement verifying that, during the specified time, the organization complied with the set of predetermined control standards. The concept of EDI compliance reporting promotes regular evaluation of controls by management. In addition, exchanged between trading partners, the periodic compliance statements can provide a level of comfort for both parties.

Compliance auditing, on the other hand, involves an auditor assessing the validity of management's statement of compliance with EDI control standards. The auditor's report might be sent to the senior management of the reporting organization and it might also be made available to prospective trading partners [16].

4.3.3 Conflicts in Partners' Competitive Profiles

Not all companies derive economic benefit from their EDI implementations. While information exchange in EDI is a duplex flow, the associated physical flow of goods is frequently one way. Sometimes organizations convert to EDI at the behest of a major downstream trading partner—a partner who is often the ultimate buyer of the goods. This type of conversion is a cost of doing business, rather than an arrangement made for competitive advantage. Current research suggests that, in this type of partnership, the supplier, or upstream partner, experiences no positive impact [17].

Current research also reports a substantial need for organization and workflow redesign. Far from yielding competitive advantage, EDI might turn out to be a process that makes management stand on its head to satisfy major partners' expectations about maintaining competitive edge [18].

Seen from this perspective, EDI creates a new kind of synergistic business risk for companies. Internally, there is a tight coupling of application integration and strategic consolidation at the corporate-database level, and management and accounting information systems are integrated. In the most extreme form, there is a tight coupling of production schedules—as an organization's back-end relationship with its own suppliers begins to be influenced, if not determined, by a partner's marketing budget.

EDI exposes partners to new competitive risks they might not possess the management skills to control. Exposures that come with partnership can involve

- *New products and services.* A freight transportation company, for example, couples its services closely with that of its retailer partner and assumes primary responsibility for assessing the freshness and shelf life of the retailer's products.
- *New competitive intervention.* An organization can use its EDI management information system (MIS) to identify the most profitable clients in the marketplace. However, if it then focuses its efforts on that group only, the company might find itself servicing only problem accounts and accounts most sensitive to price.
- *New trade practices.* These might involve, in particular, timing and liability at the payment or settlement level.

Given these new risks—which can often involve added cost—the much anticipated savings provided by EDI (through reduced paper exchange, the elimination of postage stamps, etc.) is very possibly offset by the increased costs of doing business in an EDI environment. New EDI-related costs include: transaction cost (which is lower on an individual, variable-unit basis but possibly many times higher in terms of investment and fixed assets); higher legal costs (i.e., the cost of legal assurance that the TPA is valid); the implicit financial cost of shifts in capitalization; and the cost of experiencing obsolescence without the required risk premium.

4.3.4 More EDI-Related Exposures

In addition to the cross-vulnerabilities described above, there are other exposures trading partners might share when they integrate their systems. For example, there are exposures related to the shared usage of VANs. Until a standard emerges for VAN services, management should not assume that risks are covered.

Partners might also experience repercussions stemming from the use of financial institutions as intermediaries. While many organizations consider financial institutions to be the drivers of security and payment, in some parts of the world, the banking community is considered to be inflexible and cost-inefficient. In those areas, there is a movement toward using independently financed, industry-specific VANs for payment transfers. Where the common ground lies is not currently clear. Interestingly, financial institutions and their intermediary relationships with trading partners are, at this point, beyond the purview of ANSI and UN/EDIFACT [19].

A third source of shared exposure could involve management reevaluating its use of auditors. While the highly codified public audit process might be appropriate for assessing the fairness of a set of consolidated financial statements, it might not be appropriate for determining the adequacy of the security and control system between partners. The skill set required by public auditors needs enhancement. Audit risk increases as public auditors—often trained in traditional, historic-cost-based shops—try to grapple with unfamiliar topics in EDI [20].

Partners might try to meet their new audit process requirements—and offset incremental expense—by employing a specialized audit firm. This solution could be provided for in the TPA. But, regardless of how partners decide to resolve this issue, developing the appropriate skill set in public accounting firms can only be expected to increase fees and extend lead times. The level of assurance that will be required from an EDI-conformed audit process to satisfy shareholders has still to be defined. (This aspect is explored further in Chapter 10.)

Organizations should identify all the possible cross-vulnerabilities during the planning stage of an EDI project. These issues need to be addressed and their effects quantified up front, in a manner that reflects the environment and risk and reward profiles of each partner. This consideration will ensure an effective and informed executive buy-in to the process—an essential driver if EDI is to become a viable business strategy.

4.4 SUMMARY AND RECOMMENDATIONS

EDI has created shared business and system risks about which partners might not be thoroughly knowledgeable, and the related cross-vulnerabilities need to be addressed as management issues. In other words, it must be clear to the partners that issues involving cross-vulnerabilities cannot be resolved in the same manner and at the same time as technical issues.

In addition to employing the sound control and audit practices recommended in this book, to bring the risk of cross-vulnerabilities into line with management's expectations, organizations should also follow the prescriptions discussed below.

Demand security components as standards rather than features of EDI products. Organizations across industries should send a message to EDI product and service vendors that more is required in standard products than is currently available. To achieve consistency and cost-effectiveness in their products, vendors can include security measures as value-added components of off-the-shelf products, rather than as features that are only available in custom products at custom prices. Larger information system shops can be more assertive in communicating the need for security components to their preferred suppliers. And smaller shops should be aware that the requirement for security does not come cheaply: they should manage their profit expectations to provide for security or understand that they are assuming a higher degree of risk than in non-EDI partnerships.

Broadly speaking, the vendor relationship can yield two types of incremental security software features:

1. *Preventive controls.* In the long term, increased emphasis on nonreversible encrypting devices, such as RSA and automated key management hardware, is appropriate, given the dollar traffic of EDI applications. In the short term, this is expected to be a costly innovation.
2. *Detective controls.* The success of automated fraud detection in the credit business suggests that there is tremendous potential for knowledge, or expert, systems in EDI applications. Expert systems are an interesting possibility for smaller companies because they are relatively inexpensive. PC databases are in the same price range as off-the-shelf PC software. EDI users could employ these systems to analyze anomalous traffic by source and to build message history files for offline processing and review.

Anticipate incremental risk. Adherence to standards is a necessary aspect of business— even while short-term risks are inevitable. And, in the case of EDI, as the applications that partners share become more integrated, the associated risks are bound to increase. Therefore, at the same time that organizations using EDI must follow the sound business custom of adopting and practicing strict adherence to standards, these organizations must also incorporate within their standards the flexibility that will allow their control systems to evolve in response to incremental risk.

Profit from shared dependency. Partners can benefit from being keenly aware of shared dependency at the outset of their relationship. For example, management on both sides of the table should welcome the opportunity, provided early on, to let the superior control system of a stronger partner leverage the control and security systems of lesser partners. Consultative, proactive relationships should be encouraged, with the stronger partner likely adding more value to the process. The consultations should be recorded and their cost estimated. Even if the costs are not charged back to the lesser partner, they should still be blended into the overall true economic cost of the business relationship, and these records should remain available to support future decisions.

In summary, implementing EDI and other paperless systems is only justified if and when the new perceived risks are carefully managed. This management is translated into new control techniques for EDI, which are the subjects of Chapters 6 and 7.

ACKNOWLEDGMENT

The authors acknowledge the substantial contribution of Donald van Geete to the concept of cross-vulnerability and the security and control issues presented in this chapter.

REFERENCES

[1] "ATM Scam: Anatomy of a Failed Computer Fraud," *EDPACS*, Vol. XIX, No. 3, September 1991.

[2] Garon, Gilles, and Outerbridge, Richard, "DES Watch: An Examination of the Sufficiency of the Data Encryption Standard for Financial Institution Security in the '90s," *Cryptologia*, November 1990, p. 3.

[3] Daly, James, "High-Tech Movie Highlights Realistic Security Concerns," *Computerworld*, September 14, 1992.

[4] Hellman, Martin E., "The Mathematics of Public-Key Cryptography," *Trends in Computing*, August 1979.

[5] Anthes, Gary H., "Export Barriers on Encryption Eased," *Computerworld*, July 27, 1992.

[6] Emmett, Arielle, "Breaking Barriers to EDI," *Datamation*, April 1, 1991.

[7] Norris, Richard, "Corporate Strategies and Tools for Making EDI Standards Work," *EDI Forum,* Vol. 3, 1990, pp. 96, 99.
     Carley Joseph G., Jr., "The EDI Standards Debate," *EDI Forum*, Vol. 2, 1989, p. 126.
     Dalton, Gary, "The Relationship between EDI and E-Mail," *EDI Forum*, Vol. 4, 1991, p. 28.
     Tutt, Nigel, "The EDI Trials," *Banking Technology*, September 1991, p. 22.

[8] Wright, Benjamin, "EDI Legal Issues: Important but Not Alarming," *EDI Forum*, Special Edition, 1990, p. 126.

[9] Baum, Michael S., "EDI and the Law," *EDI Forum,* Vol. 2, 1989, pp. 80–82.

[10] Baum Michael S., "EDI and the Law," *EDI Forum,* Vol. 2, 1989, pp. 80–82.

[11] Ballen, Robert, and Diana, Natalie, "Walking a High Wire," *Banking Technology,* July and August 1991, p. 38.

[12] Chan, Sally, et al., *EDI for Managers and Auditors,* Toronto, Canada: EDI Council of Canada Library Publication, 1991, p. 123.

[13] Jones, Peter, *Essentials of EDI Law,* Toronto, Canada: EDI Council of Canada Library Publication, 1992, p. 41.

[14] Leech, Tim, "Control Self-Assessment: The Dawning of a New Era in Control Governance," unpublished paper, Leech & Associates, 1990.

[15]   Chan, Sally, "Managing and Auditing EDI Systems Development," *CMA Magazine,* Vol. 65, No. 9, November 1991.

[16]   Chan, Sally, "Managing and Auditing EDI Systems Development," *CMA Magazine,* Vol,. 65, No. 9, November 1991.

[17]   Taylor, David L., "From EDI to Inter-Enterprise Systems: A Scenario for the 1990s," *EDI Forum,* Vol. 4, 1991, p. 22.

[18]   Benjamin, Robert, et al., "The Realities of Electronic Data Interchange: How much Competitive Advantage?" *EDI Forum,* Vol. 4, 1991, pp. l04–10.

[19]   Peverett, Tracy, "Closing the EDI Loop," *Banking Technology,* May 1992, pp. 29–30.

[20]   Powers, William, "EDI Control and Audit Issues," *EDI Forum,* Vol. 4, 1991, p. 124.

Appendix 4A

Control Self-Assessment Worksheet and Summary

System: PC-EDI purchasing pilot

Date:
Prepared by:

Management Control Objectives	Existing and Proposed Controls		Compensating Controls	Control Adequate	Exposure	Severity of Exposure	Probability	Action Plan	Target Date
Control Technique	Y/N/NA	Explanation	Explanation	Y/N	Explanation	H/M/L	H/M/L	Explanation	DD/MM/YY
Controls should be in place to ensure purchase order accuracy									
• Syntactic checks	Y	ANSI X12-850 Checks by translation software	—	Y	—	—	—	—	—
• Special edits	N	No reasonableness check for unusual quantity	Visual verification prior to release	Y	—	—	—	Review this item when system is upgraded to mainframe	Dec. 19XX
• Criteria for positive acknowledgment	Y	ANSI X12-997 at functional group level only	—	Y	—	—	—	—	—
• Criteria for negative acknowledgment	Y	ANSI X12-997 at functional group level only	—	Y	—	—	—	—	—

H = High
M = Medium
L = Low

Figure 4A.1   Control self-assessment worksheet.

Business or System:

Department: Information Technology

Unit: Business Systems Development

Date: December 19XX

CSA rating: Good

Current CSA Components	Improvements During Prior Year	Residual Risks	Recommendation	Target Date
Organizational controls: Department standards Organization plan Corporate culture	All issues raised in the 19XX audit report were addressed. Audit rating improved from fair to good.	—	—	—
Systems development and change control: Development methodology Project management Authorization of changes	No significant improvement over prior year. Low level of systems development control, especially in the area of testing.	Quality of systems delivered cannot be ensured.	Develop long-term strategy and have senior management address it on an organizational level.	December 19XX

Figure 4A.2   Control self-assessment worksheet summary.

Chapter 5

Managing Interenterprise Partnerships

5.1 CHARACTERISTICS OF INTERENTERPRISE PARTNERSHIPS

A 1990 report by the Gartner Group that evaluated EDI software and service vendors described EDI as a tool for developing interenterprise systems that could introduce fundamental changes, not just in the way a company operates, but also in the very definition of the company itself [1]. Interenterprise systems require that managers work closely with trading partners' systems and with user counterparts to form a development platform for joint systems and project management.

Interenterprise systems are also known as cooperative systems, which implies that the companies cannot act alone [2]. The concept of working together has a significant impact on the management style of corporate managers. Recognizing that an EDI system is only as good as its weakest link, managers must now reach beyond their own organizational boundaries to look for win/win solutions, or solutions that will benefit all partners.

Objectives of interenterprise system or partnership management should include:

- Aim for win/win solutions;
- Favor mutual reliance on good controls over reliance on trust;
- View each partner as able to bring value to the relationship;
- Encourage sharing of experience and collaboration to foster improvement;
- Develop cooperative systems;
- Facilitate intercompany communication and synergy.

5.2 SELECTING TRADING PARTNERS

In the EDI business cycle, trading partners are sometimes called members of a value chain. Emphasizing the idea that values are added by each partner along the chain reinforces the concept that EDI is indeed a cooperative system in which the reigning philosophy is to aim for solutions that work for every partner in the chain. Obviously, this mindset is at odds with the distrust that has existed historically between customers and suppliers.

An organization should base its selection of a trading partner on how much value the prospective partner can add to the organization or, in other words, on how critical the prospective partner is to the organization's success. Then the organization should look for a partner who represents high transaction volume with low dollar value per transaction. Also, the viable candidate should be running or have the capability to run under an EDI environment and should be a company with whom the organization anticipates it can form a good relationship. Finally, the organization should compare its performance measures (which can include profit, costs, financial stability, market share, and quality of service) with the prospective partner's performance and with the performance of the organization's competitors. These comparisons will provide a benchmark for monitoring improvement.

Once an electronic trading partner relationship is established, the partners must determine some key requirements, such as the transaction sets they will exchange; optional data segments and elements they will allow; the product, company, and shipping point identification codes they will use; and communication protocols they will follow. In addition, partners must consider such things as mutual training needs, transmission security, retention, and contingency planning (in the event that the EDI link is rendered inoperable).

5.3 THE TRADING PARTNER AGREEMENT

Before exchanging data, trading partners must reach an agreement on several technical matters, including transmission standards, communication protocols, and data coding syntax. They might also have to deal with legal terms. Typically, in the traditional paper processing environment, the legal terms by which each trading partner agrees to be held bound are neatly printed on the reverse side of invoices and purchase orders. In contrast, EDI and its associated lack of paper documents precludes the preprinting of terms and conditions on original source documents. EDI trading partners' legal terms should be agreed upon beforehand and included in the TPA. (Some companies do, however, agree to forego TPAs.)

The existing legal framework for commercial transactions is defined for a paper environment, which creates legal insecurity for EDI users. The problem can be mitigated through contract, but the insecurity will become more acute as EDI expands and organizations move from trading with partners they know to trading with new and unknown partners. Normally, to anticipate this eventuality, the TPA should include criteria for prescreening and selecting trading partners. A well-drafted TPA might provide certainty for trading partners and reduce the chance of future disputes. Finally, the TPA should specify how partners intend to apportion risk and, therefore, any liabilities that might arise.

To date, within the U.S. court system, no cases have considered whether an EDI transaction is enforceable as a contract, although a substantial argument can be made for enforcement. The Statutes of Fraud might bar enforcement of an EDI transmission due to the lack of the written and signed evidence that commonly accompanies a nonelectronic contract. A well-crafted TPA can help overcome this problem. Partners can agree that if an EDI message is recorded in some lasting fashion (e.g., to disk, to tape, to CD) it is deemed "written." They can also agree that incorporating an appropriate authorization code (e.g., the password or ID of the individual initiating the EDI message) into an EDI message warrants the EDI transmission "signed."

This approach of providing safeguards in the TPA has not received extensive testing in the courts, nor is it guaranteed to succeed in the event of litigation. Establishing agreed upon procedures in this manner, however, might reduce the likelihood of a dispute or of a contract that is challenged being annulled under the Statutes of Fraud [3].

Despite the fact that there are numerous proposals in EDI legal and security literature having to do with the reliability of electronic records and signatures, there is still no generally accepted method that EDI trading partners can adopt to ensure record integrity and legal enforceability. What constitutes reliable record-keeping will largely have to be determined by each user. This approach is inefficient. Difficulties can arise if one trading partner is the dominating force and dictates terms to the weaker partner. Similarly, differing philosophies on control, security, and risk-taking can impede EDI implementation. Records that are written to disks, tapes, or CDs can be erased easily, either accidentally or deliberately. Write protect medium, such as write once, read many (WORM) disks, optical disks, or computer output microfilm (COM), are more sophisticated devices, but they require additional controls to prevent them from being copied and subsequently altered and replaced by a new unit. Without such controls, the medium itself is ineffective as a control device. Serial numbers on storage units can qualify as an effective control, provided the hardware inventory is well maintained and audited on a surprise basis.

Simple passwords and user IDs are very weak control techniques that might not qualify as substitutes for a signature on paper. (It should noted, though, that traditional signatures can be forged and disguised easily.) Theoretically, a signature is unique to an individual. A signature placed at the conclusion of a document also serves as an affirmation of the document contents. On the other hand, an access code or password is independent from a message and so cannot affirm the contents [4]. It is a commonly known fact that masquerading is especially easy when no policy exists for password expiration dates, minimum length requirements, rules about nontrivial passwords, and individual ownership of passwords. And, even when these restrictions are applied, they are easily bypassed with a little ingenuity and collaboration. To guard against tampering, at a minimum, password files should be encrypted and the security of electronic signatures should be administered by an employee who has no self-interest in forging the signatures required in EDI transactions. For high-value and sensitive transactions, passwords should not be transmitted in clear text to the trading partner. Additionally, more advanced techniques, such as using digital signatures or adding challenge and response stipulations to dial access, should be considered as part of the cost/benefit analysis. Trading partners who take an extra ounce of prevention should be at an advantage when disputes arise.

To compensate for the fact that EDI transactions are paperless, EDI users might wish to negotiate written TPAs to preauthorize the EDI transaction and set terms and conditions. Typical terms in a TPA include:

- Payment terms. Faster payments are possible through FEDI.
- Liability. Who is responsible for a transmission error and to what extent?

- Need for acknowledgment. EDI provides for instantaneous acknowledgment.
- Signature requirements. What do the partners deem to be an acceptable signature? Will an authorization code do? Is an additional security procedure needed, such as sending the trading partner's identification code along with the signature?
- Message ownership stipulations. When is an electronic message legally delivered— when it arrives in the receiver's mailbox or when the receiver checks the mailbox for EDI transmissions? Should partners be required to check their electronic mailboxes for messages by a certain time each day?
- Receiver's acknowledgment. Should a party always be responsible for functionally acknowledging receipt of messages?
- Errors.What happens if a partner fails to detect an error? To what extent is each partner liable? What happens if fraud results from inadequate security?
- Traffic. What percentage of transactions do the parties expect to send via EDI?
- Communication charge. Who pays the data transmission charges? What types of documents will be sent via EDI?

In short, the issues listed above can be summarized in three fundamental questions. And these are questions that all EDI project team members, not just auditors, must answer. The fundamental questions are: (1) Who is responsible for controls? (2) How will we manage the control agreement with our trading partner? (3) If the controls fail, who is liable? Along the same lines, every EDI participant should ask: What controls are necessary and appropriate? Who is responsible for implementing, monitoring, and reporting on the controls, and to whom do they report? How is responsiblity for the risk of failure allocated?

These issues of responsibility and control are addressed in subsequent chapters. In addition, managers and auditors in EDI environments who want to learn more about the legal implications can refer to Appendix G for recommended readings in this area.

5.4 OTHER EDI AGREEMENTS

The auditor's examination of the EDI legal environment should not be limited to reviewing the TPA. There are several other types of agreements, such as third-party network agreements and EDI software agreements that, if applicable, the auditor should review.

Essentially, vendors maintain their own standard contract forms, which purchasers must endorse prior to delivery. Purchasers understand that the contract is usually written for the benefit of the vendor; it maximizes the vendor's rights and minimizes exposure to liabilities. The auditor should ensure that the purchaser's legal counsel reviews contracts for goods or services prior to their execution.

Managers and auditors should ensure that these control points, or principles, are addressed or evident in contracts entered into with third-party service or goods providers:

- The wording of the contract is clear and concise and satisfactory;
- The contract contains necessary, required, and agreed-upon wording and describes goods to be delivered or services to be performed;

- All technical terms are clearly and completely defined;
- The contract clearly details all limitations or operating parameters placed on the vendor's ability to warrant the contracted goods or services and to accept liability for failure of the product or service or failure to deliver.

5.4.1 Third-Party Network Agreements

There are two general approaches to examining third-party network systems. The auditor might (1) perform the audit directly or (2) use the reports of other auditors who have reviewed the system. These reports are usually referred to as third-party audits or reviews.

There are certain controls and provisions that a third-party network agreement should contain to ensure a secure and accountable EDI operating environment. The agreement should ensure that

- Customer data is held separately and confidentially; in other words, the third-party network cannot commingle customer data.
- There are restrictions that prohibit the third-party network from monitoring the volume, direction, type, or details of customer data traffic.
- The customer maintains a right to audit the operations of the third party. If direct access to the third-party system is not allowed, meaning that audits cannot be conducted by the customer's personnel or appointed representatives, the agreement should provide for an appropriate third-party review that is available to the customer upon reasonable request.

5.4.2 Application Software Agreements

In reviewing application software (including translation software) for EDI, the auditor is generally reviewing software developed by a third party. In other words, the software is not typically developed internally. In addition, the third-party software is not sold directly to the customer. Rather, the vendor licenses the use of the software to the customer, usually for a specific purpose, at a specific location, and for a specific computer.

The licensing of software creates a concern that management and auditors should be aware of. By using a software license, the vendor usually restricts access to the software's source code, thus controlling access to upgrades and modifications. Limiting access to the source code also prevents the customer from either internally updating the source code or seeking an external individual or firm to perform updates. Additionally, should the customer and the vendor disagree and suspend their business relationship, the customer is without access to the EDI software and, potentially, unable to continue the EDI operations involved. The auditor should ensure that the following points (which are not inclusive) are in the software agreement. The agreement should contain wording to the effect that

- The vendor agrees to place in escrow a current copy of the software source code (replaced or updated as appropriate). Thus, if there is a falling out between the parties or the vendor ceases operations, the customer has a legal avenue to obtain a current copy and retain hopes of continuing operations.

- Maintenance fees cannot increase above a specific percentage over a defined period.
- Should the vendor decide to cease operations, the vendor must notify the customer within 90 days prior to termination of operations.
- The vendor agrees (with some restrictions and limitations) to repair or replace defective software on a timely basis and to provide updates as they become available.

The agreement clauses noted above are not inclusive; they are provided as initial considerations. Again, prior to the execution of any agreement, the auditor (with customer consent) should request that the agreement be reviewed by the firm's legal counsel.

5.5 LEGAL ISSUES, LAWYERS, AND AUDITORS

For years the legal and audit professions have been frowned upon as impediments in EDI development. In March 1989 the Gartner Group reported: "Some people argue that involving lawyers and auditors in the EDI planning process is the 'kiss of death' for the project [5]." As recently as March 1991 Deloitte & Touche published yet another alarming fact. Their survey of Canadian business revealed that 95% of CFOs said audit and legal issues were their biggest obstacles to obtaining the benefits of EDI [6]!

The comforting news is that comments such as these will soon become a thing of the past. The legal and audit professions have made considerable progress, not just in clarifying their roles, but also in being perceived as adding value to the EDI development and implementation process.

> When a legal issue like EDI does come to court, judges will be able to look to a rich body of law dealing with signatures, contracts, computer records, and the like to assist them in determining how the law should apply to EDI...Judges and other legal decision makers usually do not act irrationally when they come in contact with new technologies.[1]

As with any discussion of legal issues, this analysis will be considered too long by some and not long or detailed enough by others.[2] It is the objective of this discussion to alert readers to the basic legal issues related to EDI transactions; point out to practitioners areas in which legal, audit, security, risk, and financial issues overlap; and, in general, pre-

---

1. Phone interview with Benjamin Wright, attorney and author of *The Law of Electronic Commerce (EDI, Fax, and E-Mail: Technology, Proof, and Liability)*, Boston, MA: Little, Brown and Company, 1991.

2. The remainder of Section 5.5 and Sections 5.5.1 through 5.5.5 were written by Joseph Rosenbaum, senior counsel for American Express Travel-Related Services Company and chair of the Global Networks and Information Technology Committee of the EDI & Information Technology Division of the American Bar Association, Section of Science and Technology.

sent a better understanding of why EDI creates some novel and interesting legal problems—and will continue to do so for some time.

Some legal commentators consider the much hailed advent of EDI and so-called "paperless trading" as much ado about nothing. After all, for hundreds if not thousands of years orders, offers, acceptances, negotiable instruments, and other paper documents were transmitted in a variety of ways, and commerce and business flourished. Why worry about legal issues related to EDI when for all these years—in fact, up until perhaps twenty years ago—successful business transactions relied on relatively few lines of writing on paper? Indeed, even if one assumes that there are legal issues related to performing paper-based transactions, why make a fuss when the world decides to automate and perform electronically, optically, or digitally the same transactions previously performed manually?

Unfortunately, the analysis is not quite that simple. Not only have computers and telecommunications networks automated an existing manual process, they have also created a completely different commercial environment from one based on paper. The speed, complexity, and volume of EDI transactions—which can be initiated, confirmed, and consummated in an instant—have gone well beyond what even the most visionary business leaders imagined a scant few years ago. As an example, a few years ago the computers at a major banking institution in New York failed on a Friday morning. As a result, the primary U.S. government securities dealers were unable to reconcile their trades until the following Sunday afternoon. Imagine the chain of possible consequences that could result—such as failure to deliver funds—from a major financial institution experiencing a system crash.

In addition to being concerned about the risks associated with a computerized environment and the speed with which risks can develop into problems that wreak havoc, in an EDI environment, business trading partners must also contend with the fact that the legal and judicial system has not kept pace with the rapid advent of the technology. The fact is that it has taken all of those hundreds and thousands of years that commerce has relied on pieces of paper inscribed and transcribed with magical words for major jurisdictions to wrestle and come to grips with the tough issues defining business conduct with some degree of certainty. The notions of offer and acceptance, proper evidence, intent to be bound, meeting of the minds, payment terms, and the like have been opined upon, adjudicated, and defined over the years, so that business people can understand, with reasonable certainty, the ground rules for commercial trading.

In a paperless world, what constitutes evidence and how it is proven authentic is not always clear. For example, are magnetic directions, electronic impulses, and digital signals considered to be the same as directives in written form? The brief discussion that follows is an overview of the basic legal issues that arise as a result of using EDI as a vehicle for commercial trading.

5.5.1 Fundamental Questions

Virtually every issue related to the legal framework of EDI transactions hinges on the simple fact that the medium through which these transactions take place is fundamentally different from those in which information exchange depends on paper or other tangible symbols or items. Devices that depend solely on electromagnetics or optics are faster and more easily duplicated and transmitted than paper.

Essentially, there are two legal questions that creep into any analysis of contractual and legal implication raised by commercial EDI transactions: (1) How does one know that there has been a deal agreed upon? (2) How can the deal and the parties be identified and demonstrated with sufficient certainty to be legally enforceable? In simplistic terms, when does sign-off take place and how can the fact that sign-off has occurred be proven when required? The legal and audit concerns seem almost married in the EDI world.

In the United States the primary legislative pronouncement of the commercial law that governs sales in virtually all jurisdictions is the Uniform Commercial Code (UCC). UCC Section 2-201(2)—more popularly known as the Statutes of Fraud—specifies that a contract for the sale of goods in excess of $500 is not enforceable unless there is a writing that is signed by the party against whom the contract is to be enforced. The UCC's definition of what constitutes a writing is framed by a requirement that there be an intentional reduction to tangible form.

If one looks internationally, the Transport Convention for the Unification of Certain Rules Relating to International Carriage by Air (Warsaw, 1929) requires a writing to produce very specific legal effects and implications. Similarly, the 1958 Convention on the Recognition and Enforcement of Foreign Arbitral Awards requires that agreements to arbitrate certain disputes or agreements fixing the jurisdiction over contracts be in writing.

Legal scholars can debate whether the definition of a writing should be changed to include electromagnetic and optical media, or whether the whole notion of a writing should be eliminated in favor of a more comprehensive legal construct, i.e., any authentic, reproducible, and verifiable (auditable) evidence of an intention to be bound. The bottom line, however, is that current law has not come to grips with this issue.

The second major issue related to the integrity of EDI transactions—how to prove that a deal has been struck—is no less troublesome under current legal doctrines. Must each party retain a record of every original transmission received or sent? If so, how, in what form, and for how long? In fact, one could also ask what really constitutes an "original" in an electronic or optical environment? In an age in which electronic devices can intercept, retransmit, amplify, switch, duplicate, and broadcast messages instantaneously, how does one know that a message sent ostensibly by one party is really from that party? In a medium in which the goal is to minimize human intervention in the contract formation, approval, and payment process—to permit greater speed and increasingly complex domestic and multinational transactions—how can practitioners ensure that computers have not created an unintentional or inaccurate but nonetheless binding obligation?

Clearly, parties must implement authentication and verification procedures that are secure and auditable and, therefore, of legal import. These requirements are most commonly framed in legal terms as *evidentiary questions*. When is an offer made, accepted, or revoked? Are the terms offered identical to those accepted or have there been modifications (counter-offers) and, if so, by which party? How can a party be sure there is due authority to consummate a transaction—should the mere receipt of a message from the computer or telecommunications switch of one party bind that party? Or should there be additional authentication to verify, with some degree of reliablilty and auditability, who the party initiating a message is? At some point, commercial trading partners might be held liable, either under contract or in tort (i.e., negligence) for failing to install or to use auditable, verifiable security and systems measures that prevent loss or damage. This is especially true in situations in which it is considered reasonably prudent to impose security measures because of the potential for damage or loss. There have been notable cases in which the absence of safeguards that might have prevented personal or property damage have resulted in liability suits.

Auditors too, are interested in determining that transactions are accurate, complete, secured, and auditable, and that the system has the appropriate controls.

5.5.2 Creating an Enforceable Contract

Most binding commercial relationships begin with some form of offer and acceptance. In an EDI environment, much of this process is automated—sometimes outside the control of the contracting parties. Thus, it is increasingly possible that a message is sent and a contract is formed that does not reflect the intent of the contracting parties. In addition, given the lightning speed of communication in EDI, it is increasingly probable that messages contain incorrect or imprecise information. That problem can remain undetected by both the sender and the receiver until the inaccurate contract has already been consummated.

To form a contract properly, common sense (and the law) recommends that parties ensure that the buyer's acceptance matches the seller's offer. Parties must be sure that an offer was not revoked or modified prior to acceptance. They also need to verify that the buyer and seller are who they claim to be and have the authority to create binding obligations. These are hurdles for which, in a paper-based society, the law has provided jurisprudence both to guide us and to be overcome. And, while the continuing volume of litigation suggests that not all the questions have been settled, nevertheless, considering the tremendous amount of commercial trading that takes place around the globe, the current system does seem to work.

No such jurisprudence exists for the electronic formation of contracts. (To date, there has not been a single case involving EDI.) Nor has anyone tested in the courts the question of authority or authentication in paperless trading. Indeed, in an electronic world—where messages might be formatted in data centers far from the remote terminal or device originating the transaction, where telecommunications switches and message traffic routing might function across a variety of jurisdictions, and where offers and acceptances might represent the consolidated buying and selling power of multiple participants around the globe—in such a world, how can we even fix the time and the place of contract formation? The problem is difficult enough on paper, electronically, it might well be impossible.

5.5.3 A Matter of Evidence

From both an audit and a legal perspective, evidence (i.e., facts) is probably one of the most important elements in determining the outcome of any dispute. While the law can be viewed as a framework—the set of rules or the playing field upon which relationships between commercial enterprises are formed—the individual fact patterns and transactions are the elements against which laws must be applied.

Over the years a set of standards for evidentiary determinations has evolved. These rules state, for example, that an original is better evidence than a copy, and they describe what the best evidence is for a large majority of situations. As a general rule, hearsay (i.e., evidence gleaned from secondary sources) is not admissible in court. But, because a business entity cannot give testimony in its own behalf and, thus, sometimes the individuals involved cannot testify to their first-hand knowledge, a Business Records Exception to the rules of hearsay evidence has evolved.

In the United States, under Rule 803(6) of the Federal Rules of Evidence (Records of Regularly Conducted Activity), a communication is admissible as evidence if it was

> . . . kept in the course of a regularly conducted business activity, and if it was the regular practice of that business activity to make the memorandum, record, or data compilation, all as shown by the testimony of the custodian or other qualified witnesses.

If EDI transaction records are maintained in a secured, reproducible, and verifiable manner, it is likely that they can be defended under the exception to the hearsay rule and, thus, be admissible as evidence. However, at this point in the life cycle of legal theory, there remains the challenge of determining who, how many, and what types of individuals can be considered "custodian or other qualified witnesses" for the purpose of giving testimony in court.

For evidence to be credible, clearly the party seeking to introduce it must be able to validate that it has not been altered or tampered with in any way. This qualification is particularly difficult to meet when evidence is in electronic form. In fact, there are some who question whether records kept in electronic form are even "readable" and whether the process of translating electronic records from binary, ASCII, or another file format to a language readable by humans doesn't constitute an alteration that renders the records inadmissible. Further, the potential conflict posed by this seemingly esoteric questioning pales in comparison to the issue of whether an intangible series of signals or magnetic or optical coding can even be considered a "record"—when courts have traditionally focused solely on documents and written materials as evidence.

Hand in hand with the evidentiary questions go the issues of storage and retention of EDI transactional information. While many questions can be resolved using analogies to paper and filing systems, others do not lend themselves so easily to resolution. For example, are the original electronic messages the ones that are kept? If translation or reformatting occurs when messages are received, should the translated versions also be kept? Given the fact that software programs are routinely updated and modified, must copies of the particular versions of translator or reformatting programs be retained as supporting evidence of process integrity? Must senders retain copies of all the messages they send?

As noted previously, the issue that tends to receive the most attention is information security and integrity. How can parties ensure that the information received, sent, retained, and stored accurately reflects the actual events as they occurred. In other words, how can organizations ensure an accurate, verifiable audit trail that will qualify as legal evidence? Unlike in a paper world, in an electronic world it is easier to keep digitized or optically stored copies of everything (i.e., to err on the side of over-storing information), but it is harder to ensure the security and integrity of the data by keeping it "locked up."

It is worth noting another fact that remains a serious legal consideration but is often overlooked in EDI discussions—particularly discussions concerning evidence. Usually, each party considers the storage, retention, and retrieval of information an opportunity to ensure that *its* legal position will prevail in court or in a factual dispute with a second party. It is also true, however, that the well-organized storage, retention, and retrieval capacity of often voluminous (and sometimes unnecessary) amounts of information can be a tremendous burden and potential disadvantage in litigation—especially during the discovery process. If everyone was completely honest, never miscommunicated or misled another, and honored commitments in a timely manner, would parties need to store, retain, and retrieve the volume of information that buyers and sellers keep? For that matter, would we need so many courts, lawyers, and auditors? Sadly, parties can not rely on such scrupulousness, and the right balance of what information should be retained and for how long requires input from lawyers, auditors, and risk managers, as well as from senior business management who relies on the information to make sound decisions. (Record retention is further discussed in Chapter 8.)

Two final issues that require mention are documents evidencing ownership and security. In the world of EDI, ultimately, paper will be unnecessary in all phases of transaction. Such elements as title and security interests will still require documenting, but the traditional concept of written documentation—recorded deeds and mortgages, for example—will no longer be applicable. We are still quite a ways from replacing the written and tangible documents that evidence ownership, the passage of title, and secured transactions with purely electromagnetic devices and media. But that time is coming, and lawyers and auditors must deal with related issues that arise.

5.5.4 Managing Liability and Risk

One role of auditors and lawyers is as advisers. They can assist decision makers in recognizing issues and understanding risks and provide a reasonable map through all aspects of EDI. In all likelihood, the allocation of transactional and relational risk that evolved over years of paper-based trading requires adjustment for the EDI environment.

As an example of questions related to risk management, in this world in which computers permit instantaneous communication, should a party be obligated to acknowledge, in a secure and verified manner, that it has received a message (e.g., return receipt)—even if no response of legal import (e.g., acceptance) is yet required? At a time in which business can be transacted in nanoseconds, should the standard for reasonable or prudent business practice be updated? Left to the courts, the standards for liability in the EDI environment will, of course, evolve—just as our current paper-based jurisprudence did.

Practitioners must also wrestle with determining the role and legal responsibilities third parties will have in the EDI process. EDI clearinghouses and EDI systems and network providers will spring up. Telecommunications companies and common carriers will see an opportunity for additional business and, perhaps, additional intermediation revenue. It is unlikely over the long term that all of the potential buyers and sellers around the world will have direct and bilateral EDI TPAs with each other. Consequently, the roles, responsibilities, and liabilities of these intermediaries must be well defined and understood in the marketplace. This role definition will, in turn, ensure that EDI is a universally viable medium for commercial trading.

5.5.5 Conventions, Guidelines, and Agreements

Probably the greatest contribution lawyers, auditors, financial advisors, and government can make to EDI usage is to promote standards that allow commercial trading partners, intermediaries, and related parties to have a common basis for transacting business. Adhering to these standards would afford the parties, by mutual consent, the certainty of a judicial or statutory framework.

The EDI and Information Technology Division of the American Bar Association has promulgated a model electronic payments agreement and associated commentary for transactions relating to domestic credit transfers. Similarly, the Commission of the European Communities' Trade Electronic Data Interchange Systems program has also produced a draft European model EDI agreement. The EDI Council of Canada has produced the Model Form of Electronic Data Interchange Trading Partner Agreement and Commentary. Unlike contracts or agreements for particular goods or services, these models attempt to harmonize and standardize the EDI transaction process. As a contractual framework, these documents provide a starting point for trading partners to formulate clear and understandable rules for using EDI.

A set of Uniform Rules of Conduct for Interchange of Trade Data by Teletransmission (UNCID) has been published by the International Chamber of Commerce. These rules represent a codification of trade practices that parties can follow, refer to, or simply use as the beginning of discussions about their relationship. It is increasingly likely that similar sets of rules, guidelines, conventions—and perhaps even treaties between governments—will be created in the future.

5.6 SUMMARY

If the preceding discussion has created more questions than answers, your auditor's sixth sense has begun working. The legal issues surrounding EDI are only just emerging, and many are being tested, in most cases, for the first time. Our understanding of these legal issues is far from comprehensive. Auditors are advised to keep abreast of changes, maintain contact with firms' legal counsel, and above all, question all the answers!

ACKNOWLEDGMENT

The authors acknowledge the assistance of Joseph Rosenbaum, who is senior counsel for American Express Travel-Related Services Company and chair of the Global Networks and Information Technology Committee of the EDI & Information Technology Division of the American Bar Association, the Science and Technology Section. Mr. Rosenbaum contributed substantially to describing the concepts put forth by lawyers, as well as the legal and auditing issues presented in this chapter.

REFERENCES

[1]   Gartner Group, "EDI Software and Services Vendor Evaluation Strategic Analysis Report," July 1990, p. 1.

[2]   Norris, D.M., and Waples, E., "Control of Electronic Data Interchange," *Journal of Systems Management*, March 1989, p. 35.

[3]   Wright, Benjamin, "Auditors Should Be Aware of EDI's Legal Issues," *The EDP Auditors Journal*, Vol. 1, 1990, p. 55.

[4]   Jones, Peter, *Essentials of EDI Law*, Toronto, Canada: EDI Council of Canada Library Publication, 1992, p. 120.

[5]   Gartner Group, *A Decision Maker's Guide to EDI*, March 27, 1989, p. 12.

[6]   Deloitte & Touche, *Computing for Executives*, Canada, March 1991, Vol. 6, No. 3, p. 5.

Chapter 6

EDI Application Control Issues

6.1 INTERNAL CONTROLS IN INFORMATION SYSTEMS

Earlier chapters of this book examined the general background, costs, benefits, infrastructure, standards, and risks under which EDI operates; Chapter 6 introduces the controls that establish EDI reliability.

For the user, auditor, project manager, information security officer, or any other participant concerned about control of EDI, it is worth noting that EDI controls are not very different from controls employed in any computer environment. There are four basic internal control categories, and these categories should be present in any information system: application controls, security controls, environment controls, and project controls. Chapter 4 discusses security controls. Chapter 7 discusses environmental and project controls. This chapter focuses on application controls.

Auditors should participate in the early stage of EDI development and evaluate EDI controls with the rest of the project team. In addition to providing an independent opinion on required controls, the auditor should verify, prior to implementation, that the proposed controls actually function as promised.

6.1.1 Application Controls

Application controls guide the inputting, processing, and outputting of transactions and the use of interfaces through which files pass from one internal system to another.

6.1.1.1 Input Controls

Input controls are exercised over data entry, data validation, and error handling. The prime examples of input controls are:

Authorization controls. These controls, which ensure that transactions are properly authorized, range from simple user IDs and passwords, to joint custody and split knowledge of

---

access keys, to segregation of entry and release functions, to sophisticated techniques, such as digital signatures and *challenge and response* added to dial access. The level of authorization should be commensurate with the type and value of transactions and the potential risks inherent in the operating environment. For example, authorizing payment orders or purchase orders for defense equipment should be accorded more stringent authorization control than a remittance advice or request for quotes.

Validation controls. These controls prevent or detect errors or omissions in the recording, preparing, and entering of data for processing. In an automated environment, much of the manual preparation and verification of source documents is replaced by interchange-, functional group-, and transaction-level editing. (See Table 6.1.) Details of application-level editing, which is normally not performed by the EDI translation software, should be specified and agreed upon bilaterally by trading partners. Where timeliness is important, validation controls should be on line and in real time. Online real-time controls require prompt attention to the critical problems and errors that the system identifies. For example, a set of predetermined criteria for transaction acceptance should be built into the validation routine to provide timely resolution of context-sensitive alerts and supervisory interrupts.

6.1.1.2 Processing Controls

Controls must be built into application programs to ensure that the right data are processed. Accuracy in processing requires that the correct records and files be read and updated. The logic of computer processing integrity can be tested via independent programs run from a separate job stream. Errors in processing can be automatically written to an error suspense file for subsequent correction. EDI has not changed such processes.

6.1.1.3 Output Controls

Generally, output controls pertain to processing balance, reconciliation (e.g., of financial data and record counts), output distribution, records retention, and output error handling. Control techniques include control totals, scheduled deletion of unused files and reports, and compliance with the organization's record retention policies.

In accounting systems, *reconciliation controls* require that total credits must equal total debits before a transaction can be accepted for further processing. In the EDI environment, reconciliation control includes a *completeness check* that ensures that all transactions are processed, with no duplicates or omissions. Control totals and unique sequence numbers in trailer records are techniques that ensure completeness. These techniques are further discussed in Section 6.2, Controls for Transaction Accuracy and Completeness.

6.1.1.4 EDI System Interface

When EDI is fully integrated into and streamlined with an organization's internal applications, the interface files produced by EDI are automatically fed to the applications for

Table 6.1
Common Control Information in ANSI X12 and UN/EDIFACT

ANSI X12	Control Information	UN/EDIFACT	Control Information
ISA interchange control header	Authorization information Security information Interchange/communications (sender and receiver) Date and time stamp Standard and version information Interchange control number Acknowledgment request Test indicator	UNB interchange header	Syntax identifier Interchange sender and receiver information Date and time of preparation Interchange control reference Recipient reference password Application reference Processing priority code Acknowledgment request Communications agreement ID Test indicator
GS functional group header	Functional group ID code Application sender and receiver codes Date and time stamp Functional group control number Responsible agency code Version, release, and industry codes	UNG functional group header	Functional group identification Application sender and recipient identification Date and time of preparation Functional group reference number Controlling agency Message version Application password
SI transaction set header	Transaction set ID code Transaction set control number	UNH message header	Message reference number Message identifier Common access reference Status of the transfer
SE transaction set trailer	Total number of segments Transaction set control number	UNT message trailer	Total number of segments in message Message reference number
GE functional group trailer	Total number of transaction sets Functional group control number	UNE functional group trailer	Total number of messages Functional group reference number
IEA interchange control trailer	Functional group total Interchange control number	UNZ interchange trailer	Interchange control count Interchange reference number

processing. Standard interface controls, such as application identification, file-to-file control totals, and batch record count, can be applied. Any special editing that a source (sending) application or a target (receiving) application requires should be specified and adequately tested.

6.1.2 Security Controls

Security controls ensure that computer facilities, software, data, and programs are protected against any unauthorized access, disclosure, or modification, which, in turn, can cause loss or destruction of current or future processing capabilities. Security controls are also called *safeguarding controls* in the accounting environment. (Information security is addressed in Chapter 4.)

6.1.3 Environmental Controls

Environmental controls cover such areas as computer operations, continuity of processing, and the distribution of software changes and releases, program libraries, operating systems, and database management systems.

6.1.4 Project Controls

Project controls are exercised to ensure that (1) the system meets requirements and quality standards agreed upon by the users and the developer; (2) projects are completed on time and within budget; (3) appropriate development methodology is followed; (4) appropriate control, security, and auditability features are designed into the system; and (5) acceptance testing, training, and documentation are adequate.

6.1.5 EDI Standard-Driven Controls

A comparison of the common control information incorporated into the design of ANSI and EDIFACT messages reveals that similar controls are found in both EDI standards (see Table 6.1). In fact, the trailer information for both standards at the interchange, functional group, and transaction set/message levels is virtually the same. The information contains the total count for each envelope and a control number that references the corresponding envelope ID code in each header. These two control elements ensure completeness of information at each level.

Most of the header control information is the same for the two standards; however, EDIFACT does have additional controls at the interchange level (application reference and priority of processing), the functional group level (application password), and the message level (common access reference and status of transfer). These additional control fields are explained below.

At the interchange level, EDIFACT header control information includes:

- *Application reference.* The interchange agreement must state whether this data element will be used. It should also state what information must be carried. Optionally, if the interchange contains only one type of message, this reference code can be used for message identification.

- *Processing priority code.* This code is used if it is specified in the interchange agreement. If it is used, the interchange agreement must state the possible codes and their meanings.

At the functional group level, EDIFACT header control information includes:

- *Application password.* This password offers additional flexibility. It can be carried to the recipient's division, department, or sectional system, if required.

At the message level, EDIFACT header control information includes:

- *Common access reference.* This data element allows the creation of a key that associates all subsequent data transfers with the same business case or file. Within its 35-character set, the interchange agreement can specify component elements. This is a very important feature of the audit trail for auditors who have to recreate the full history of a cluster of transactions relating to one business operation.
- *Status of the transfer.* This information is composed of two data elements; the first indicates the sequence of transfers and the second specifies whether the transfer is the first or final transfer of the same type of message relating to the same topic.

The fact that ANSI and EDIFACT control information is basically the same, with EDIFACT control fields supplemented by the information described above, ensures that, if the industry does migrate from ANSI to EDIFACT, no significant ANSI information will be lost.

6.1.6 Other EDI-Specific Controls

The controls described above are available in both ANSI X12 and EDIFACT standards. Once this control structure is in place, other controls must be exercised to ensure proper implementation. These are (1) trading partner validation, (2) syntax checking, (3) application-level editing, and (4) a system of acknowledgments.

6.1.6.1 Trading Partner Validation

An adequate check on a trading partner must go beyond merely matching the trading partner number with the directory listing to confirm the partner's existence. Ultimately, the extent of validation should be determined bilaterally, based on business need.

To provide effective validation, a partner profile must be accurate and up-to-date. Authority to make changes to a profile should be restricted to a few personnel. In addition to the mandatory information needed for a transfer, other pertinent control information can include: valid transaction types, limits on purchase quantities per order and in aggregate, types of products purchased, *buy only* or *sell only* stipulations, the standard version used, and any information that would be useful for monitoring the partnership, such as the financial stability of a trading partner.

6.1.6.2 Syntax Checking

Syntax checking is based on the standard release, or version, used. Syntax checking information is included in the interchange and functional group headers, as well as in the trading partner profile. The check is usually performed by the translation software, which, at best, ensures syntactic correctness; the presence of acceptable values, types, and codes; and compliance with the standard version. Whereas application-level editing focuses on substance over form, the syntactic checking exercise places form over substance. Special editing is outside the scope of translation software.

6.1.6.3 Application-Level Editing

Parties should identify the control and audit features they consider desirable for EDI-based trading. They should also advise each other of any special editing required they might have involving data dictionary items during application-level editing. To bring data items in line with the special requirements of a recipient's computer system, sometimes additional translation is necessary after syntactic checks. In critical applications, such as, for example, Canadian FEDI, which uses a positive application acknowledgment to signal transfer of funds, the editing criteria at the transaction set level must be bilaterally agreed upon and included in the TPA.

Application-level editing requires that validation of data segments be based on bilaterally-determined editing criteria. Examples of validation checks include checks for reasonableness, range, null values, predetermined codes, and cancellations. To reduce the chance that problems are compounded at later stages of processing, trading partners should promptly notify each other of negative results in application-level editing. As a safeguard, procedures for error logging and incident reporting should be outlined in the TPA.

6.1.6.4 System of Acknowledgments

Both ANSI X12 and EDIFACT have a system of acknowledgments at the interchange, functional group, and transaction set/message levels. A positive acknowledgment indicates that the control information at each level has been matched. Transaction completeness and uniqueness and serial continuity are acknowledged at the interchange and functional group levels. Application-level editing ensures transaction accuracy.

6.2 CONTROLS FOR TRANSACTION ACCURACY AND COMPLETENESS

Accuracy and completeness, the essence of transaction integrity, should be the primary control objective of every EDI user. The controls that ensure accuracy and completeness should be designed up front and built into the system before implementation. The controls fall into three catagories: (1) inbound transaction controls, (2) outbound transaction controls, and (3) transmission controls.

The following controls can be applied to both inbound and outbound transactions:

- Compliance with standards used by the translation software;
- Bilaterally agreed upon special edits and controls;
- Application interface edits;
- Maintenance of up-to-date trading partner profiles and adequate partner validation;
- Prompt action on trading partner requests;
- Timely follow-up and resolution of error and exception reports;
- Regular review of warehoused transactions at third-party sites;
- Cross-checking of the number of messages sent or received between trading partners at agreed upon intervals.

Partners should consider using VAN control reports. Most VANs provide reports that track EDI transmissions and create audit trails. VAN control reports include [1]:

- *Unretrieved documents report.* Provides an up-to-date listing of all documents sent to but not yet received by trading partners.
- *Monthly statistics report.* Summarizes all documents sent and received during the previous month.
- *Receiver status report.* Lists the current status of all documents received.
  Sender status report. Lists the current status of all documents sent.

6.2.1 Inbound Transaction Control Considerations

Control information from the sender should include these elements: (1) transaction set count totals and batch control totals, built into the functional group header; (2) sequential control numbers, built into the interchange header; and (3) segment count totals, built into the transaction set trailers.

Logging of transactions is more important for inbound transactions than for outbound transactions. For every inbound transaction, a record is created at the sender's end. The record log is used primarily for investigation and audit purposes and is useful in the event of disputes. Partners should agree on the retention period for such a log.

Controls must be in place that ensure that data are received properly, regardless of transmission errors caused by such interruptions as line noise or equipment failure. Partners should also consider implementing a control that generates and sends a functional acknowledgment (FA) to the sending partner when a transmission is received.

6.2.2 Outbound Transaction Control Considerations

EDI software features should be used, in conjunction with user-developed control techniques, to ensure that outbound transactions are received and acknowledged properly by trading partners. VAN unretrieved documents reports can be used to identify transactions sent to trading partners but not yet received.

To ensure that EDI transactions are ready for application processing, organizations can employ these control techniques:

- Document procedures to ensure that a request for information that is generated as a result of a nonreceipt is acted upon on a timely basis.
- Apply standing corporate security and access measures to protect intermediate files from unauthorized alteration between the time of generation and transmission.
- Use *event-driven* EDI to automatically match transactions at different stages of processing, e.g., match a purchase order with a payment order or a bill of lading with an invoice.

6.2.3 Transmission Control Considerations

As previously mentioned, the controls applied to EDI for computer input, processing, and output are similar to the controls commonly used in information systems. This is not to say, however, that all EDI control requirements are met with information system controls. For example, EDI introduces intercorporate message transmission as a new area of concern. This is because EDI messages entering or leaving an organization are worth more than the cost of transmission. Disputes and potential liability can be caused by loss, disruption, delays, or unauthorized disclosure occurring while a message is enroute to a partner. (Transaction and transmission security are discussed in detail in Chapters 3 and 4.) The following list summarizes the key transmission controls partners should exercise:

- Ensure data is routed to the intended receivers by employing user IDs, passwords, trading partner profile validations, dual IDs, or a combination or by routinely reviewing critical transactions.
- Implement appropriate controls over communications, such as sign-ons, passwords, call backs, and port protection.
- Use redundancy or parity checks to verify data completeness and integrity.
- Apply appropriate levels of EDI message acknowledgment to ensure message completeness. For critical transactions, consider using message authentication to ensure that messages are not altered and re-sent.
- Use serial numbers and unique transaction sequence numbers to ensure that messages are transmitted once only.
- Use controls that verify that transmissions occur at scheduled times (unless a nonscheduled time is approved by management).
- Incorporate transmission error detection and correction functions in communications software.
- Provide a facility that can trace data transmissions to their sources.

- Maintain a log of all data transmissions. The log should contain the batch ID, transaction set control numbers, date and time stamp, sender and receiver IDs, and transmission status.

6.3 CONTROL AGREEMENTS BETWEEN PARTNERS

While almost all the header and trailer data elements are mandatory for transfer purposes, the exact values that will be stored in the fields are bilaterally agreed upon by partners. In arriving at agreement, partners should observe three control checkpoints: (1) determine the values and control procedures related to subsequent changes; (2) involve lawyers and auditors in evaluating the significance of control information (for example, should control definitions be included in the TPA); and (3) perform adequate systems and user testing of controls to ensure that they actually work as designed.

REFERENCES

[1]   Karson, Jerry, "Keeping EDI Under Control," *Tech Exec*, March 1990, p. 33.

Chapter 7

EDI Management and Environmental Control

7.1 ENVIRONMENTAL CONTROLS: AN OVERVIEW

Environmental controls cover a broader range of EDI transaction components than the controls that govern input, processing, and output activities of particular applications. Environmental controls ensure data integrity by controlling the development, maintenance, and operation of computer systems, as well as data and program security. For interenterprise systems such as EDI, ensuring that there are adequate environmental controls might entail evaluating various VANs and seeking assurances from multiple trading partners that their EDI control environments are adequate.

This chapter discusses controls that support these aspects of the EDI environment:

- Operations and management
- Computer operations
- Data and program security
- Contingency planning and disaster recovery
- Project management
- Selection of vendor-supplied translation software

7.2 OPERATIONS AND MANAGEMENT

Operation and management control considerations vary according to industry, organizational structure, existing facilities, and other resources. One key area management should review for environmental controls is the TPA. This agreement, which defines the trading relationship and processing requirements of trading partners, should contain (1) valid transaction sets, (2) definitions for the electronic signatures of sending and receiving parties, (3) the EDI standards agreed upon by the trading partners, (4) authorized verification procedures, (5) rules for determining responsibility for lost or stolen data, and (6) timing considerations for transmission sequences. (These issues are covered in greater detail in Chapter 5.)

85

Because trading partner relationships are generally close ones, poor planning in the handling of system availability and reliability issues can alienate customers and suppliers, cause operational disruptions, and prove costly to both the sender and the receiver [1]. Corporate contingency planning and communications policies should be revised to incorporate EDI requirements.

Before launching EDI, management should assess the marketing, financial, and organizational dimensions of the EDI business plan. Organizations that implement EDI as a result of external pressure should not lose sight of other improvements EDI can bring, such as the opportunity to redesign work flow or to discover other applications that might be candidates for inclusion in EDI. As noted in the opening chapters of this book, ad hoc implementations do not yield the kinds of benefits that EDI promises. A long-term commitment to EDI requires executive support and management buy-in as well as representation and participation in industry groups and industry standards.

7.3 COMPUTER OPERATIONS

Because EDI involves the operation of a separate computer system—and sometimes separate hardware—there are additional requirements for computer operations controls. These requirements include developing restart and recovery procedures for EDI processing and backup procedures for programs and, more importantly, for transaction and master files. Additionally, a disaster recovery plan must be prioritized and its procedures updated to include the complete EDI processing cycle.

Consideration of EDI security should begin with an analysis of the potential risks unique to the EDI system in its role as an information asset. In other words, the EDI system should not be treated as just one of the suite of systems in the computer operations area. (EDI security is covered in detail in Chapter 8.) In summary, the following areas must be risk-assessed:

- Security of the internal EDI processing system, including access to data, program files, and transaction initiation facilities;
- Security of the network used to transmit data via VANs or directly to partners;
- Data encryption or passwords built into the interchange, functional group, or transaction set level—especially if transaction data are confidential.

7.4 DATA AND PROGRAM SECURITY

Providing an adequate security blanket around EDI might require physically securing hardware, data, and programs and restricting logical access to system data and programs. Whether communication is direct or through a VAN, at a minimum, access controls should require that users provide a user ID and password to gain admittance to the computer system. Adequate security controls are critical in an EDI environment, particularly when multiple parties are communicating across common links, mailbox facilities, or both.

To safeguard records retention, organizations should exercise the controls listed below. (Refer to Chapter 8 for details.)

- For recovery purposes, retain all EDI transaction records.
- For tax, audit, and management purposes, review the retention cycles for EDI transaction files and data.
- Examine record management procedures. Ensure that electronic documents are maintained properly and securely for an appropriate length of time.
- As part of the file retention policy, determine the form of storage required for transaction files and data.
- Duplicate critical data files and send them to an off-site storage facility.
- Track all data files and segregate the responsibility for the physical custody of files from the users responsible for data entry.

7.5 CONTINGENCY PLANNING AND DISASTER RECOVERY

Increasingly, organizations are relying on computers to perform daily routine business functions, and, consequently, the need for a comprehensive contingency or recovery plan is becoming critical.[1] Unfortunately, the escalating complexity of systems, coupled with the growing practice of distributing computer resources across user communities, has made it difficult for most organizations to develop and maintain a functional contingency plan. Consider for a moment the possible impact a long-term EDI outage could have on a firm's business. The more critical EDI is to day-to-day operations, the more important an operational contingency or recovery plan is to the EDI system.

Every firm is capable of developing a customized definition of exactly what constitutes a disaster and what impact that disaster would have on continued operations. For example, one organization might consider loss of the functional acknowledgment receipts information file merely a nuisance, while another organization would consider it a serious problem. Managers should analyze the unique EDI operating environment to determine not only the applications that are critical to continuing business operation, but also how long the organization can withstand a prolonged absence of the EDI gateway link or VAN services. In their analysis, implementors should also bear in mind that local disasters, such as fires and accidents, can result in outages lasting more than a day. Even human error can result in outages of over 24 hours. Organizations must determine how long the business, and, in particular, the EDI processing environment, can withstand an outage.

Contingency plans and recovery plans should *not* depend on the availability of one particular individual or group of individuals. Instead, a plan should describe key activities and critical decisions in sufficient detail so that any staff member can perform recovery tasks. A contingency plan should be comprehensive and should document preestablished

---

1.   The authors wish to acknowledge the generous contribution of Russ Leighton, senior systems analyst with Sterling Chemicals, to this discussion of contingency planning and disaster recovery for EDI.

criteria for making decisions in a crisis. It should document required recovery actions and retention and storage policies. As an organization accumulates information about disaster and recovery experiences, the plan becomes a valuable aid to decision making.

Auditors should seek complete understanding of all phases of the EDI link. Familiarity with potential failure points along the link is paramount. Knowledge of those points will inform the auditor's assessment of the contingency plan. The auditor should know, for example, if the contingency plan addresses the issue of switching to a separate power grid in a power failure. In fact, the auditor must verify that any existing contingency plan has been updated to address EDI transmissions and transaction processing. The plan should also provide instructions for moving EDI processing between VANs, in the event that the firm's primary VAN is compromised or unable to maintain an acceptable level of service. Procedures for the timely replacement of such items as cable interface cards, modems, and fax boards should also be included in the plan.

A recovery plan should be based on the worst case scenario (i.e., the loss of telecommunications capabilities for an extended period), but the plan should also define recovery procedures for basic interruptions that, if not addressed efficiently, might result in a full-scale disaster. For example, management should ensure that backup communications links for the primary EDI gateway link are separated from the normal communications path. Also, because telephone networks have been known to fail (e.g., the Bell fire in Hindsdale, Illinois in May 1988 and the AT&T Signaling System 7 software failure in New York in June 1991), backup phone lines should be routed through separate phone systems.

Some VANs maintain their own disaster recovery plans, but firms are wise to consider negotiating a contract with an alternate VAN, so trading partners can continue doing business if the primary VAN fails. Using an alternate VAN during an emergency might require modification of the trading partner relationship. Most VANs can accommodate firms recovering from a disaster by performing a global switch for all the firm's trading partners. A few VANS, however, require that the individual trading partners' VANs perform the switches for the partners. As part of the control process, managers must verify whether the firm's VAN or the trading partners' VANs will perform this function for the partners. The legal department should determine if this information belongs in the TPA.

As with any critical process, firms should thoroughly document the recovery plan and distribute it (with concern for security and disclosure of confidential information) within the company and to trading partners and their VANs. Firms should also test their plans periodically. Finally, it is worth noting that involving all parties in creating a recovery plan and performing recovery procedures greatly increases the probability of success. (See Appendix F for a detailed list of audit questions related to contingency planning and disaster recovery controls for EDI.)

7.6 PROJECT MANAGEMENT

Chapter 5 discusses the concept of interenterprise partnership and suggests that, as an approach to conducting business, interenterprise partnership requires a particular mindset and style of management. The project manager must view EDI implementation as an opportunity to enhance intercompany effectiveness, rather than merely as an obligation to develop new software to replace existing paper documents. EDI projects must be part of the overall strategic plan of the company. Ad hoc and piecemeal implementations do not yield the benefits EDI is capable of.

The following sections describe the key controls that project managers should consider in EDI implementation.[2]

7.6.1 Learn About EDI

Firms should take time to learn about what other companies are doing with EDI. Lessons learned from pilot implementations and other trading partners can help firms avoid the pitfalls others experienced. Educational efforts should include finding out about the software, network, and communication decisions and the adjustments to business practices that similar companies made. One of the best opportunities for learning about EDI comes from participating in user groups, conferences, and standards-setting bodies for the industry. As with any emerging technology, EDI's problems must be tackled with knowledge.

7.6.2 Gain Executive Commitment and Management Buy-In

Studies have shown that sound business strategy and executive commitment is of prime importance to EDI success [2]. To interest employees in EDI, project managers should make EDI marketing, training, and education an integral part of the project plan. They should involve and enlist the support of all departments that will be impacted by the implementation, including accounts payable, merchandise processing, accounts receivable, shipping and receiving, and marketing. Each department should participate in analysis, design, testing, and implementation phases to ensure the accuracy and completeness of the results.

Since quality systems are distinguished by their ability to fulfill customer expectations, project managers should treat all ultimate EDI users as customers. For the EDI system to be of high quality, commitment from management in development and user areas must be a given. Interenterprise systems require that developers, users within the firm, and trading partners work synergistically.

7.6.3 Establish Quality Project Plan

A quality project plan ensures that processes are defined up front, that users (the customers) understand what they will get, and that developers (the suppliers of software and services) understand what they are expected to deliver within a defined cost structure. Addressing quality without addressing cost and time is one-dimensional management and

---

2. The discussions in Sections 7.6.1 through 7.6.11 build upon information in the Uniform Code Council Voluntary Interindustry Communication Standards publication *Retail Industry Conventions and Implementation Guidelines for Electronic Data Interchange, Version 2040* (April 1990, Section 2, p. 5). The views expressed, however, were developed independently by the authors and should not be construed in any fashion as being the views of the Uniform Code Council.

does not produce the desired results [3]. Quality should be designed into EDI before, not after, implementation. As in all systems development projects, expectation gaps between the customer and supplier will exist. Those gaps should be managed throughout the development process as an aspect of quality control.

The EDI project plan should be a two-way agreement between the user and the developer. In other words, for the agreement to be successful, both parties must profit. In this regard, establishing an EDI project plan is similar to negotiating terms and conditions in the TPA. The objective of the EDI project plan is to arrive at a win/win situation that truly reflects the spirit of interenterprise relationships and cooperative systems.

The EDI project plan should contain a responsibility matrix of the project team that includes the EDI coordinator and both internal business and technical contacts and their trading partner counterparts. The coordinator should come from the user community, rather than from the IT group, because it is the coordinator's responsibility to see that trading partners are properly selected and brought into the organization, whereas the IT group's key responsibility is to provide EDI services. The EDI project team should include lawyers and auditors, even if they have to be educated along with the organization.

7.6.4 Review Business Processes and Internal Systems

All business departments should take a hard look at their processes to determine if they can be improved through the use of EDI. Implementing EDI in an inefficient or archaic process will only provide a speedier exchange of bad or incomplete data [4]. A review might reveal that the existing process requires reengineering. After reengineering, EDI can be implemented to further streamline the new process.

Firms should perform a thorough system analysis, which should include recording the current process for creating business documents, mapping current document flow, and analyzing any rules or procedures that affect the life cycles of documents. Superficially, these steps appear to be the same in any system analysis, but, in fact, EDI requires that analysts go beyond normal document review to critically examine electronic document creation and retention cycles.

Understanding a new project requires learning about the appropriate definitions, concepts, and recommendations. Firms should consult available reference materials before they attempt to rewrite business procedures. The following list of reference materials, although not complete, should be made available to project teams: 1) applicable ANSI X12 or UN/EDIFACT publications, 2) industry-specific standard subsets of the X12 or EDIFACT protocol, 3) size and color code tables from the National Records Management Association (NRMA) or an industry-related association, and 4) network supplier manuals.

7.6.5 Conduct Surveys

Conducting a survey of trading partners identifies personnel who will be participating in the network, outlines their responsibilities regarding the system, and provides contact procedures. (Refer to Chapter 5 for a discussion of the considerations firms should bring to trading partner selection.)

After completing trading partner surveys, firms should evaluate the communication procedures and hardware equipment each trading partner will use. This evaluation helps establish contacts within the industry and identifies transmission requirements. It also identifies communications protocols and mainframe, PC, and emulator types.

7.6.6 Review Standards and Documents to be Exchanged

The prospective mapping of each business document should be reviewed against the ANSI X12 or UN/EDIFACT standard. This review should determine whether internal documents contain all mandatory data elements. Optional data elements can also be identified and their applicability discussed with trading partners. Deviating from the standards established by a partner's industry will require creation of cross reference lists or tables. The constant maintenance required to keep these cross references current might pose problems in the future.

The data elements that determine accuracy and completeness should be tested to ensure that they do function as designed. (As an example, Chapter 9 examines the data elements that perform control functions in FEDI.)

7.6.7 Choose Translation Software

There are four major types of translation software in the EDI software market: (1) home-grown, (2) vendor-developed and mainframe-based, (3) vendor-developed and PC-based, and (4) network-based.

Four factors that can identify the software that best suits an organization are (1) the existing system's hardware platform, (2) systems' resource availability, (3) the organization's ability to maintain multiple versions of software and standards in use and manage the change control process, (4) the flexibility of the implementation schedules. Most generic selection criteria for vendor packages can be applied to EDI; specific criteria are described as one of the last topics of this chapter.

In the last few years, organizations appear to have favored vendor-supplied products and services over software developed in house. This preference is likely the result of the maturation and acceptance of ANSI and UN/EDIFACT standards.

7.6.8 Choose a Network Provider

Organizations should pursue and discussions with prospective trading partners should support finding the most cost-effective means of transmitting EDI documents. The decision on that means should come early in the development process because it will influence future decisions.

As an alternative to a commercial network, trading partners can establish direct, or point-to-point, links. This route requires that trading partners accept the burden of maintaining the connection, coordinating the polling schedule, producing audit reports, and—if costs are to be shared—generating invoices. (Chapter 3 discusses network selection.)

When possible, partners should obtain a copy of the external auditor's report on the control environment of the software or service supplier's organization. Or, better still, they should negotiate a *right to audit clause* in the legal contract. If audit reports are not available or the suppliers have not been audited, the trading partners should decide whether a network controls review is warranted.

7.6.9 Design, Develop, and Test the System

For the most part, the tasks associated with designing, developing, and testing an EDI system are the same as those required in non-EDI system projects. But it is particularly important in EDI system projects that participants establish open communication between trading partners and share experiences—be they successes or failures. Sharing information is especially critical in the testing of the EDI components, i.e., the translation software and network connection. The relationships required in EDI system projects exemplify the operation of cooperative systems development.

7.6.10 Cut Over to and Implement the EDI System

There are several considerations involved in deciding when the "cut-over" to EDI implementation should take place. Processing cut-off dates must follow completion of all contract negotiations and the final signing of partnership agreements, and they must coincide with the accounting cycle, staff availability, and partner and departmental readiness. A sign-off document listing the participants in the project, including senior management, should be signed by all before implementation begins.

7.6.11 Perform Postimplementation Review

During the early days of implementation, partners should monitor all transmissions closely and log all problems, so they can determine the initial success or failure of the development project. Staff should perform data collection during the first few months of operation so partners can assess the cost and benefits of the project. Partners should periodically compare performance issues, system availability, and user satisfaction to ensure continual improvement. This evaluation process will confirm or invalidate the assumptions made before and during the project.

7.7 VENDOR-SUPPLIED TRANSLATION SOFTWARE

In recent years, a growing number of EDI software vendors have begun to offer a wide range of products and services. The maturation of ANSI and UN/EDIFACT standards will likely encourage many users to purchase vendor-supplied software instead of developing in-house EDI applications. Purchasers will come, in particular, from companies in which in-house development and maintenance of translation software and multiple versions of standards cannot be cost-justified.

Managers and auditors must consider many questions in their examination of EDI software packages. These questions fall into three general categories and are listed below. A fourth list groups miscellaneous considerations.

1. Questions related to the standards a software package supports:

   - How many standards and versions of standards does the package support?
   - What is the average lag time between standard adoption and subsequent software upgrade?
   - How long does the vendor continue to support an old standard or version?
   - Does the software allow trading partners to use different releases of the same standard?
   - Can information be translated from standard formats to internal formats and vice versa?

2. Questions related to cost:

   - How are purchase and maintenance fee payments structured?
   - How much do upgrades cost? Hotline support? Training?

3. Questions related to software capabilities and control features:

   - How many transaction sets, or message types, are supported?
   - Does the software perform qualifier and user code conversion?
   - Which translation protocols are available?
   - What mapping capabilities are supported, e.g., online, flat-file, user-defined interface or menu-driven?
   - Can the software be upgraded from microcomputer or minicomputer use to mainframe?
   - Does the software provide backup and error-handling routines?
   - Does the software track both the number and type of inbound and outbound transactions?
   - What acknowledgment capabilities does the software have?
   - Does the software provide audit and control reports?

4. Miscellaneous questions:

   - How has the software been tested?
   - Is the documentation of acceptable quality?
   - Can the software interface easily with internal application systems?
   - What kind of training is provided?

- Is there a user group?
- Will the vendor participate in establishing an escrow for the source code?
- Are risks reasonably apportioned between the vendor and the purchaser?
- Is there an external auditor's report or opinion on the service organization's control procedures?
- Does a potential purchaser have the right to conduct an independent controls review?

REFERENCES

[1]   Powers, William J., and Carver, Thomas, "EDI: Control and Audit Issues," *The EDP Auditor Journal,* Vol. 1, No. 1, January 1990, p. 25.

[2]   Brooks, J.K., "The Strategic Use of EDI: Competitive Edge or Competitive Ledge," *The 1990 EDI Source Book,* p. 77.

[3]   Shaw, Jack, "EDI for Quality," *EDI News,* September 7, 1992, p. 4.

[4]   Meier, Jeffrey J., "EDI: A Practical Approach," *CMA Magazine,* Vol. 66, No. 7, September 1992, p. 30.

Chapter 8

EDI and Records Retention

The records retention, or record keeping, issues that relate to EDI are similar to those in conventional paper-based systems. The primary concern still pivots on the reliability of an electronic record and whether an electronic record's existence and authenticity can be validated. Another concern has to do with the environment in which electronic records reside and whether controls are exercised to ensure that the integrity of records—and EDI records among them—is not compromised. A third concern is that a records retention schedule for all documents is developed to support the business application in the EDI environment.

This chapter applies record keeping requirements for computer records to EDI applications and highlights some of the areas of EDI that warrant special consideration.

8.1 THE RISKS OF POOR RECORDS RETENTION

Exposure resulting from ineffective records retention policies and procedures can involve a lot more than just storage cost [1]. When files that are critical to operations are lost, the result is not always as simple as a temporary shut-down in the organization; the loss might also affect the operation of a trading partner who was waiting to receive the file. In fact, the entire EDI business cycle could be disrupted.

If, because of poor record keeping, they cannot produce the information needed to satisfy the legal requirements of various regulatory agencies, firms can incur substantial fines and penalties. A company's directors and officers might even be held personally liable for missing information. Inadequate records retention also threatens an organization's auditability. An independent review can be thwarted if there is insufficient documentation for an auditor to form an objective opinion.

All information systems share the risk that inadequate data protection can result in the loss, disclosure, or unauthorized manipulation of critical information. A particularly significant risk of exposure lies in delegating the custodianship of records to a third party at a separate location. Some organizations that use EDI store transaction information at a third-party site, either temporarily or as a backup option, and, thus, risk exposure. Note that this storage practice is not the same as having shared records distributed among trading partner organizations, and the risks and controls are not the same.

As a critical component of records retention, firms must develop, publish, and communicate a cost-effective retention schedule that is in line with the level of risk the organization is willing to accept. There are two costs: the cost of not taking any risks and the cost of taking too many risks. Businesses must grapple with balancing risks and controls.

According to Dianna Booher, writing in *Quality Progress*, Americans create 30 billion original documents annually. In addition, 80% of these documents are somehow, erroneously, retained. For every dollar we spend to print forms, we spend $20–$80 to process, copy, distribute, store, and destroy them [2]. Viewed from this perspective, the consequences of ineffective record keeping can be far-reaching.

8.2 THE OBJECTIVES OF GOOD RECORDS RETENTION

Records are kept for a number of purposes, one of which should not be "just in case we need them." Records should be kept long enough to satisfy business (operational, administrative, financial, and historical), statutory, and regulatory requirements. Records for which no legal requirements exist should be destroyed after a reasonable period, based on an organization's specific business needs. Some experts recommend three years as an adequate standard retention period [3].

Knowing the legal requirements for record keeping is not always an easy task. Statute law does not always define or describe what records should be kept. The best way to deal with this lack of information is to rely on existing interpretative works, such as Donald Skupsky's seminal work, *Recordkeeping Requirements* (1989, Information Requirements Clearinghouse), and, in Canada, Anson-Cartwright's *Records Retention: Law and Practice* (1991, Thompson Professional Publishing, Canada).

It is important to develop a record keeping strategy for applying EDI, and that strategy should include preparing and publishing records retention standards and practices. An approved corporate records policy can reflect an understanding of and compliance with corporate responsibilities for record keeping. At the same time, the policy, with its attendant standards and guidelines, can assist the corporate initiative to reduce the volume of paper still used "in the normal course of business."

8.3 THE BASIC PRINCIPLES OF RECORDS RETENTION

In the EDI environment, as in any business process, participants must determine in the normal course of business

- The records to be created;
- The records to be kept and stored;
- The procedure or rationale for proving that all records are both acceptable (i.e., compliance reporting) and admissible (i.e., jurisprudential);

- Where originals and copies should reside;
- Originals that reside outside of an organization, the provisions for storing, accessing, and retrieving documents for both internal and external audits;
- Provisions for backup in the event of loss of the corporate copy.

The basic principles of record keeping are as applicable to paper documents as to electronic records.[1] These principles are:

1. A business document must contain all the components that together constitute legally acceptable evidence of a completed action.
2. The documented proof of completed business transactions must be created, processed, and retained to comply with corporate policy and business practice and with external statutory and regulatory needs.
3. The retention of documents must follow standards outlined in an approved institutional records retention schedule.
4. For firms that engage in EDI activities, there should be bilateral agreement between trading partners regarding record retention for each message type or data element. Agreement should extend to third-party network providers or service bureaus for applicable transactions or transaction groups.

Principle 1 suggests that records must be accurate, complete, and authentic. Principles 2 and 3 call for organizationwide policies to address records retention issues. They imply the need for a sound records management program to implement such practices.

The emergence of EDI justifies consideration of a fourth principle to deal with intercompany retention issues. Principle 4 requires all parties to adopt consistent records retention practices, which, in turn, promotes good business practices.

8.4 PAPER VERSUS ELECTRONIC COPIES

Discussion about the medium in which corporate records should be maintained is confounded by the fact that most corporate records are available in both electronic and hardcopy form. To some extent, this duplication is unnecessary, and it raises the questions: which records *must* be maintained in hard-copy form and which records can be maintained *in either form*, depending on the business needs of the document's owner?

The corporate retention schedule identifies the records for which a company wants originals kept. Currently, there are many initiatives to reduce the records required by a company. An opportunity for the future lies in combining and downsizing forms and records without compromising a company's legal and audit obligations. Some statute law does define the format in which records can be stored; nonetheless, the opportunity lies in

---

1. These three basic principles of record keeping are succinctly outlined by Bob Taylor-Vaisey in "EDI and Records-Keeping: A Strawman for Discussion," an unpublished paper (1992).

creating fewer and better records, not in spending excessive time determining the best medium in which to store records for judicial or other examination.

Need for a hard-copy document is driven by a company needing to produce evidence that proves that it intended to do something and either did it or entered into an arrangement with a second party to have it done. If an electronic copy can be produced on demand and can be certified as the true copy (by audit evidence, compliance program, or control procedure), then the real issue is not whether the evidence is in hard-copy or electronic form, but whether it can be proven that the evidence, in whatever form, is authentic.

The validity of this thinking is also supported by the new U.S. Internal Revenue Service (IRS) rule 91-59, which became effective for taxable years beginning after December 31, 1991. This IRS procedure states that taxpayers who maintain records in an automated data processing (ADP) system can use EDI, rather than conventional paper documents, for commercial transactions. As a result, taxpayers who meet this classification restriction are not required to make or keep paper documents. Auditors should be aware of this ruling and of the fact that EDI records of transactions can be just as trustworthy as paper documents, so long as the EDI records are subject to adequate controls [4].

The IRS rule does, however, impose these requirements: the tax document must be retained for as long as tax laws require; records created on older ADP systems must be retrievable by the replacement system; and documentation of the system, including system changes and security controls, must be maintained. And it goes without saying that companies must provide the resources for examiners to review electronic records.

It is interesting to note that the "machine-sensible recordkeeping requirements" described in Section 5 of IRS procedure 91-59 are no different from the environmental controls auditors seek as assurance that records are maintained in a secure environment.

Revenue Canada does allow taxpayers to use electronic media to file tax returns. But progress in standardizing electronic retention of tax-related commercial transactions has been slow. The agency permits companies to keep microfilm copies of original entries and source documents (see information circular 78-10R2 for guidelines), but it does not yet permit such materials to be kept in electronic form only. Revenue Canada's records retention requirements need further investigation, especially since new requirements have been introduced (beginning in 1991) for the Canadian Goods and Services Tax (GST). In fact, the agency is currently soliciting input from the public on electronic record keeping.[2]

8.5 THE ADMISSIBILITY OF ELECTRONIC RECORDS

To demonstrate to a court that a computer-originated document is admissible evidence, taxpayers (or their representatives) must fulfill four requirements. They must prove

1. That the document in question is of a type that was regularly processed and stored on the computer;

---

2.   Donald Pounsett, chairman, Technology & Computer Law Group, Fraser & Beatty, Toronto. Personal correspondence. September 1992.

2. That, at the time the transaction was finalized and a record of it was created, the computer on which the work was performed was used regularly for processing and storing information;

3. That the computer was working properly all the time or, if it was not working properly, that any breakdowns could not have affected the accuracy of the document;

4. That the system was reliable enough to ensure accurate and complete recall of finalized documents and, in particular, that there was no possibility that the document could have been tampered with after finalization. (There is always the possibility that documents have been tampered with and, therefore, it is important to prove that they have not.)

There are differences between the first and second requirements and the third and fourth requirements. The first two requirements depend on proof of the reliability of the system's documenting of transactions and on the contemporaneity of the document itself. The last two requirements demand that the company produce a record of all computer breakdowns that occurred between the date the document was finalized and the date it was printed out for presentation in court. It might be helpful if the record contains an explanation of the cause, duration, and effect of each breakdown and detail any remedial action. This kind of tracking requires a system for recording breakdowns. And whether requirement 3 is indeed satisfied depends, of course, on the nature of the breakdowns. If a large scale breakdown occurred, during which finalized documents were corrupted or deleted, obviously, the requirement will not be satisfied. Requirement 4, in particular, resembles a control objective taken directly from an auditor's manual. (Chapter 7, which discusses environmental controls, identifies all such controls needed to ensure records reliability.)

8.6 KEY CONSIDERATIONS FOR AN EDI RECORDS MANAGEMENT PROGRAM

The best method an organization can use to ensure proper record keeping is a records management program. The Association of Record Managers and Administrators (ARMA) defines records management as "the systematic control of all records from creation or receipt through processing, distribution, maintenance, and retrieval to ultimate disposition [5]."

The creation, receipt, and processing of EDI messages has been the focus of EDI research and publication in recent years, but there is still a dearth of information or understanding about the rest of the life cycle of EDI-based documents. Many systems professionals have yet to see that the long-term fate of electronic information is just as important as the task of bringing a system from development to production [6].

A sound records management program should clarify the scope of records keeping, which can include examining legal and business requirements in these areas[3]:

---

3. On page 20 of *Recordkeeping Requirements*, Donald Skupsky provides a record-keeping checklist. (See References.)

- General business activities
- Record locations
- Regulatory agencies
- Industry
- Products and services

Of particular interest is the issue of the location of the record keeper. With EDI, partners sometimes have the option of storing records with a third party, such as the VAN provider or a service bureau. Some critics, though, offer the objection that third-party record keepers might have a vested interest in manipulating a client's data and are, therefore, not impartial. The risk of information being disclosed without a firm's knowledge is serious, but it can be reduced through the use of such processes as encryption. Encryption, though, is an expensive and cumbersome technology to use with archives and, in particular, with long term archives.

This chapter does not provide full details of an EDI records management program. Most of the existing principles of records management can be applied to EDI. EDI practitioners in the United States should consult the ARMA and the standards of the National Archives and Record Administration (NARA) for guidelines. (See Appendix G.)

The Canadian Information and Image Management Society (CIIMS) has submitted a draft standard entitled "Microfilm and Electronic Images as Documentary Evidence" to the Canadian Standards Board for approval. The standard is expected to be released by the Standard Council of Canada in 1993.[4]

The following sections present the major EDI records retention issues. The descriptions are designed to generate awareness and further discussion.

8.6.1 Storage Media

The rules for storage media are no different for EDI than for any other system that automates business transactions. And the *type* of storage media used for EDI is not as important as the *security* of the media—how well it is protected for both current and future use. In developing a program, the records management staff should solicit input from business users, information system (IS) development staff, and legal, audit, and tax advisors. The information will help records managers define procedures for archiving and purging EDI records and choose appropriate storage media for both business application documents and the data that support the EDI environment.

The fact that records are retained on magnetic media poses a significant threat to auditability. What medium or media present the least risk to records retention? Benjamin Wright states, "Records could be written to non-rewritable medium, such as a write once, read many (WORM) optical disk, computer output microfilm, or even paper. Controls such as serial numbers on storage units could prevent a forger from lifting information

---

4.   The draft standard was submitted to the Standards Board in June 1992. For more information, contact the CIIMS. (See Appendix G.)

from one unit (such as a WORM disk), changing it, and writing it to a substitute unit [7]." A word of caution here: "write-protect" media, such as WORM disks, optical disks, and computer output microfilm (COM), might be sophisticated devices, but they require additional controls to prevent them from being copied and subsequently altered or replaced. Use of these devices can produce a false sense of security, and a dangerous one at that. What good are the serial numbers on the storage units if the hardware inventory is not well tracked and audited on a surprise basis?

After a document has been analyzed and confirmed as recorded evidence of an intention (or the execution of an intention) and any data required to validate the completeness and accuracy of the document has been captured, processed, and validated, the document should be stored on either paper, COM, or read only optical disk. A fourth option is magnetic tape, which requires the same controls as the first three—the issue with using magnetic tape is whether the choice is practical and justified by a business case.

One final issue has to do with the long-term retention capabilities (i.e., five years or more) of electronic media. Given the rapid obsolescence of technology, some of today's media might be outdated in the next three to five years. Data recorded today might not be retrievable in ten years, not because of data degradation but because of obsolete equipment and media. An organization should remain aware of changes in media and recording devices that could impact their long-term retention requirements and make provisions for transferring data in a secure manner.

8.6.2 Auditability of Records

There are proven cost savings associated with avoiding paper manipulation and data reentry. Clearly, organizations should reduce if not eliminate excessive paper manipulation; EDI can help them achieve that goal. Two conclusions can be drawn from current business practices: (1) a paper trail might still be essential in organizations that maintain only this type of record, and (2) the opportunity exists to replace paper trails with a better audit trail—one that uses acceptable and admissible storage and retrieval media. This new audit trail is alluded to in *EDI for Managers and Auditors.*

> Audit trails or management trails should contain sufficient details to prove the existence and evidence of an obligation. This refers to the classical items, such as date/time stamp, access information, operator ID, terminal ID, attached to a transaction which is machine-readable and can be produced on demand [8].

The world that uses EDI maintains the essential integrity of an audit trail, but the requirements for tracking individual documents change. Because much of the information is repetitive, it becomes essential for organizations to track, time, date, and authorize in an authenticated way the items that comprise each part of a sequence of related EDI transactions. Organizations must be able to ensure, for example, that the component parts of a purchase order can be identified. The key is to audit the sequence of relationships in business events, keeping in mind that sometimes the events transcend corporate boundaries.

8.6.3 Records to Consider Keeping

We suggest that four groups of records be considered.

Planning records. These documents prove that EDI was an accepted strategic direction, agreed to within the terms of an internal agreement.

Contractual records. These records document the rights and obligations of all parties who will ultimately require records to be kept. Examples are network agreements, TPAs, and the exhibits to vendor/customer agreements that define records retention schedules.

System records. These records track transactions from the point of capture (assuming that initiating transaction documents are kept according to correct records retention requirements) and include any changes made to the system that creates the records (e.g., program changes). Maintaining and controlling these records means being able to prove, at any given point, that they were produced by the system in question. System records include:

- Changes made to transactions before transfer to the EDI environment
- Transaction logs
- Test logs
- System logs
- Maintenance logs
- Editing rules
- Program library records
- Table files
- History files
- Security incident reports
- MAC or other authentication and verification failures
- File retention records

Transactional records. These records track

- The sequence of electronic messages, including those between a second and third party;
- Transaction logs, which indicate messages that have been sent or received;
- Evidence of the reconciliation of transactions;
- Audit logs;
- All authorizations;
- Each completed business transaction, which includes a date and time stamp and correct authorization;
- Output documents;
- Records of messages and controls.

The records and types of records listed above are offered as a checklist or starting point for organizations faced with the task of determining what records they should retain.

8.7 RETENTION REQUIREMENTS FOR EDI

Organizations must address clearly the issue of records retention for EDI. It is important to note a basic principle: the period during which a transaction is completed has no relevancy to retention of the documentation of that transaction.

Retention does not depend exclusively on the relevant laws; in fact, it depends more on the particular business activity being executed and the extent to which provincial or state and federal regulatory agencies require that organizations be able to produce for examination documentation of the business activity. The general notion that records are only retained for auditors *from audit to audit* is arguable. In most situations, audit retention requirements are not so different from business requirements. What is good enough for the business reflects fairly closely what the auditors require. Any special audit requirements can be accommodated in audit databases, which can be managed by the audit department, and, therefore, remain outside the control of the auditees. In the systems environment, how frequently audits are performed depends largely on the inherent risks associated with the application or environment. Basing retention requirements solely on standard audit intervals does not make good business sense because an illogical correlation is created—the lower the risk, the longer the retention period.

It is difficult to distinguish between the current way of doing business, which is document-based, and the EDI process, which also depends on commonly agreed-upon templates (or document layouts). Thus, the records identified in document-based corporate retention schedules and that fit document-based business event life cycles are also considered the standard records for *transaction-based* business. Among these record types are such documents as: access violation reports, audit logs, and control reports. In other words, EDI technology might have reengineered the way we process our business, but it has not changed the documentation requirements of those processes—with one exception.

The one change that EDI brings to business document processing involves document retention sequencing. In the document-based environment, individual items in a related series of documents can have different retention period requirements. This is not unusual; requisitions, for example, predate and require a shorter retention period than purchase orders. Conversely, in the EDI environment, organizations will be able to link requisition information straight through to order finalization. In other words, a single document will contain all the data for the entire process. Consequently, that document will warrant a longer retention period than individual components might. Hence, organizations gain on the one hand and lose slightly on the other: EDI eliminates the need for multiple documents, and thus reduces paper costs, but it requires that some information be kept for longer periods. The real benefit of EDI is that the negative impact of the former greatly outweighs imposition created by the latter.

ACKNOWLEDGMENT

The authors acknowledge the generous contribution of Bob Taylor-Vaisey, of Imperial Oil, Limited, to various issues discussed in this chapter. The authors also thank Donald F. Pounsett, chairman, Technology & Computer Law Group, Fraser & Beatty, Toronto, Vigi Gurushanta, president of the Canadian Information and Image Management Society (CIIMS), and Margaret Wright, KPMG, computer audit partner, Peat Marwick, Sydney, Australia, for their views and comments.

REFERENCES

[1]   Lecker, David L., "Records Retention—A Critical Internal Control," *EDP Auditor Journal*, Vol. 1, 1991, p. 61.

[2]   Booher Dianna, "Quality or Quantity Communications," *Quality Progress*, Vol. 21, No. 6, June 1988.

[3]   Skupsky, Donald S., *Recordkeeping Requirements*, Information Requirements Clearinghouse, 1989, p. 52.

[4]   Wright, Benjamin, "The Taxman Has Spoken: IRS Rule 91-59," A special edition of *EDI FORUM, EDI Legal and Audit Issues*, 1992.

[5]   Skupsky, Donald S., *Recordkeeping Requirements*, Information Requirements Clearinghouse, 1989, p. 36.

[6]   Betts, Mitch, "Ignore Archive Issues at your Peril," *Computerworld*, March 2, 1992, p. 74.

[7]   Wright, Benjamin, *The Law of Electronic Commerce (EDI, Fax, and E-Mail: Technology, Proof, and Liability)*, Boston, MA: Little, Brown and Company, 1991, p. 87.

[8]   Chan, Sally, et al., *EDI for Managers and Auditors*, Toronto, Canada: EDI Council of Canada Library Publication, p. 55.

Chapter 9

The Control Dimensions of Financial EDI

9.1 WHAT IS FINANCIAL EDI?

A discussion of financial EDI (FEDI) must begin with a definition of electronic funds transfer (EFT). In general terms, *EFT* is monetary transfer between banks, or financial institutions (FIs), via computer or other electronic means.[1] Such transfers result in debits and credits of the payor's and payee's accounts, respectively. This definition of EFT is well understood. It is important to note, however, that simply equating FEDI with EFT obscures the wealth of information an EDI payment message contains. (FEDI is also referred to as EFT/EDI.) Table 9.1 compares the two transfer types.

Table 9.1
A Comparison of EFT and FEDI

EFT	*FEDI*
Payment transaction	Payment transaction
Value transfer only	Value and remittance transfers
Funds driven	Information driven
Retail or corporate customers	Corporate customers
Interbank proprietary formats, for example, S.W.I.F.T., CHIPS, FEDWIRE, ACH	Public format: ANSI ASC X12 or UN/EDIFACT
CPA-005 (Canada only)	CPA-023 (Canada only)

---

1.   Banks and FIs are regulated by different governing agencies, however, for the sake of simplicity, this book uses the two terms interchangeably.

While there are a number of similarities between EFT and FEDI, one key feature sufficiently distinguishes these forms of electronic payment. FEDI transactions can carry the desired level of remittance information with payment; thus, these transactions create more options for corporate payments information processing. Consequently, FEDI prompts auditors to look beyond the controls built into EFT.

Both EFT and FEDI carry basic payment information, which includes the payment amount, the value date, the payor and payee's account numbers and respective FIs, the method of payment, and transaction reference information. For the EFT message, this information forms the bulk of the payment record, but for FEDI, these items constitute only one component of the message information. FEDI message information can also include remittance, credit, or debit advice, and information to facilitate balance reporting, accounts reconciliation, and cash management. If EDI-capable FIs and their clients are sophisticated in the use of the technology, they can rightsize many of the traditional treasury, accounts receivable, and accounts payable functions. And in the future, when EDI has matured, these functions will be fully automated and their effectiveness greatly increased as a result of the likely integration of credit granting, determination of payment terms, delivery schedules, funds transfer, and, ultimately, financial transaction reporting.

9.2 ANSI X12 VERSUS UN/EDIFACT PAYMENT FORMATS

Two public EDI standard formats handle payment messages. An analysis of the current version of the ANSI X12 and UN/EDIFACT payment message formats reveals similar objectives behind the construction of payment-related information.[2] The only visible difference between these two formats is that the ANSI format gathers aggregate information into one transaction set while the EDIFACT format segments the information into several messages. Either approach can capture the same types of payment information.

At the same time that the ANSI standard is more stable and mature, recent activities of the EDIFACT Joint Rapporteur Team suggest that EDIFACT is catching up. (Table 9.2 contrasts ANSI X12 and UN/EDIFACT payment formats.) In September 1992, the team met in Oslo to discuss the use of multifunctional finance messages. The participants agreed upon the concept and the Pan-American EDIFACT Board is preparing a proposal. The meeting also addressed the need to better tailor the remittance information section to the needs of various industries. Most of the existing remittance information was designed by the food and transportation industries. Today, such industry groups as health services, construction services, and financial services have different needs [1].

If the ANSI 820 transaction set carries payment order information only (in the opening data segment for payment order or remittance advice [BPR]) and the EDIFACT

---

2.   This discussion uses version 3020 of ANSI X12, published in December 1991. For more information, see Richard Bort's article "The ANSI X12 820 Transaction Set," *EDI Forum*, No. 2, 1991. The UN/EDIFACT financial messages are found in the Pan-American EDIFACT Board UN/EDIFACT 1991 Trial Directory, April 1992. These directories are currently available: the 1991 Status 2 (91.2) Directory, which supports 19 messages; the 1991 Status 1 (91.1) Directory, which supports 34 messages; the 1990 Status 2 Directory; and the 1990 Status 1 Directory.

Table 9.2
ANSI ASC X12 versus UN/EDIFACT Payment Formats

ANSI X12 Version 3020		*EDIFACT Status 91.2*
820 (Payment order/remittance advice)	PAYORD	Payment order only
	PAYEXT	Payment order and remittance advice
	DEBADV	Debit advice
	CREADV	Credit advice
	CREEXT	Credit and remittance information
	REMADV	Remittance advice only

PAYORD message is used, arguably, it is correct to say that FEDI is just another form of EFT. Both the BPR data segment and PAYORD carry the basic funds transfer information that is carried by other wire transfer mechanisms.

When, as in the scenario described above, FEDI is a variation of EFT, the two share similar risks and exposures. Essentially, these risks involve

- The acceptance and subsequent processing of unauthorized, inaccurate, or incomplete transactions;
- Unauthorized access to information;
- Compromised confidentiality;
- Fraud and money laundering;
- Internal collusion;
- Missed settlement windows;
- Failure to acknowledge or confirm transactions on a timely basis;
- Failure to detect when transfer limits (daily/aggregate) are exceeded or excess is not authorized;
- Incorrect debiting or crediting of accounts or amounts;
- Misdirected or lost payment messages;
- Failure to respond to investigations promptly;
- Inadequate backup, recovery, and contingency planning provisions.

If they apply general EDI environmental controls and existing EFT controls, users should not have specific concerns regarding a limited use of FEDI. However, it is important to note that, in both EFT and FEDI, definite criteria must be met before funds can change hands. In EFT, successful authentication is mandatory. In the ANSI world, Canadian FIs have officially announced that a positive application level acknowledgment is the key requirement.[3] EDIFACT provides authentication for PAYORD, PAYEXT, DEBADV, CREADV, and CREEXT message types but not for REMADV messages (Table 9.3). The

---

3. See CPA Standard 023—*Standards and Guidelines Applicable to EDI Transactions* (November 18, 1992), Canadian Payments Association, 50 O'Connor Street, Suite 1212, Ottawa, Ontario, K1P 6L2.

success or failure of authentication is stored in the AUT segment of these messages. It should be noted that the REMADV message is not necessarily a finance message; it is exchanged between two corporate entities and does not carry any payment instruction. REMADV messages might have gained the label *finance message* because, in North America, both JTC/EDI finance and X12 finance groups own the message. In Europe, the trade group owns the message.

Table 9.3 lists the control fields used in EDIFACT payment messages.

Table 9.3
Control Fields in EDIFACT Payment Messages

Message Type	Control Field					
	UNH	BGM	DTM	REF	AUT	UNT
PAYORD	X	X	X	X	X	X
PAYEXT	X	X	X	X	X	X
DEBADV	X	X	X	X	X	X
CREADV	X	X	X	X	X	X
CREEXT	X	X	X	X	X	X
REMADV	X	X	X	X		X

ANSI 820 transactions and EDIFACT payment messages contain similar control fields. Table 9.4 compares the key auditability features that exist in both forms to ensure completeness and integrity.

Table 9.4
A Comparison of ANSI and EDIFACT Control Fields

ANSI 820		EDIFACT Equivalent	
ST	Transaction set header	UNH	Message header
BPR	Beginning segment	BGM	Beginning of message
DTM	Date/time/period	DTM	Date/time/period
REF	Reference number	REF	Reference
SE	Transaction set trailer	UNT	Message trailer
		AUT	Authentication result

As previously mentioned, the feature that distinguishes FEDI from EFT is the additional information that FEDI messages can carry. Because it can affect many of the traditional accounts receivable, accounts payable, and cash management functions of an organization, the ability of FEDI messages to carry various types of payment-related information deserves critical attention.

9.3 FINANCIAL EDI IN INSURANCE

An ANSI payment transaction set created for the insurance industry that is similar to ANSI payment transaction set 820, created for the financial industry, was published in December 1991. Health insurers use ANSI transaction set 835, *Health Care Claim Payment/Advice* (Version 3, Release 2) to make payments or to send remittance advice or explanation of benefits (EOB) remittance advice to health care providers. Insurers can send transactions either directly or through financial intermediaries. The Finance Subcommittee develops standards for transaction set 820. The Insurance Subcommittee develops standards for transaction set 835. Many of the controls designed for 820 are applicable to 835 as well.

9.4 THE FINANCIAL EDI INFORMATION COMPONENT

The information component of FEDI, generally referred to as the *remittance component*, can be viewed as an electronic check stub that possesses multiple levels of detail. Potentially, this component carries all the information necessary to reconcile invoices and payment receipts at the payor end. It can also affect the accounts receivable and collection function within the payee organization.

Before the advent of EDI, trading partners' accounts receivable and payable departments commonly practiced the basic financial controls listed in Table 9.5.[4]

Additional controls are built into an ANSI X12 820 payment transaction set. While all the general security and controls governing any ANSI X12 message are applicable to FEDI (see Chapters 4, 6, and 7), the format requires additional controls. For example, a control is needed to define what constitutes the finality of payment between the FIs on behalf of their respective payor and payee. Among Canadian FIs, a positive application advice (ANSI X12 824) is the key consideration; thus, their evaluation of FEDI controls revolves around criteria for a positive 824.

Controls in EDIFACT payment messages include transaction headers and trailers, date/time periods, reference numbers, and, most importantly, the AUT segment, which contains details of authentication. In ANSI, security structure (X12.58) is not embedded in the payment message. Instead cryptographic security can be applied at the transaction set

---

4.   The basic financial controls for cash receipts and disbursements can be found in any textbook on internal auditing. The key controls listed here are adapted from *Auditing: An Integrated Approach* by Alvin A. Arens, Canada: Prentice Hall, 1984, pp. 388-389, 636-637.

Table 9.5

Basic Financial Controls in Accounts Receivable and Accounts Payable

Accounts Receivable Controls	*Accounts Payable*
Segregation of duties between cash handling and record keeping	Segregation of duties between accounts payable and custody of signed checks
Policy governing approval of cash discounts and write-offs of bad debts	Monthly bank reconciliation by an employee independent of recording of cash disbursement or custody of assets
Immediate endorsement of incoming checks	Checks prenumbered and accounted for
Use of remittance advice or prelisting of cash	Control procedures for authorization of payment and timely recording of transactions
Periodic reconciliation of accounts	Internal verification of calculations and large or unusual amounts
Regular monthly statements to customers	
Internal verification of the recording of cash based on existing control procedures	

level, functional group level, or both. In Canada, transaction set level security is mandatory for inter-FI messages. Functional group level security can be added on a bilateral basis. The advantage of using transaction set level security is that problems encountered at this level do not cause the entire functional group to be rejected.

To indicate that a functional group is to be secured, ANSI uses an S1S segment (security start) after the GS segment (functional group start) and an SIE segment (security end) before the GE segment (functional group end). A similar pair of segments (S2S and S2E) provides security at the transaction set level. These segments are placed after the ST segment (transaction set start) and before the SE segment (transaction set end).

Considering the future plan to merge ANSI and EDIFACT, this comparison provides comfort by showing that no basic ANSI controls will be lost in the merger.

The key controls in FEDI are

- The Model Electronic Payments Agreement (American Bar Association);
- The Canadian Payments Association Standards and Guidelines Applicable to EDI Transactions;
- Audit trail requirements built directly into application edits;
- Validation of the trading partner and FI profile;
- Validation of the existence and authenticity of accounts;
- Authorization and authentication requirements for payment transactions;
- Strict adherence to the settlement window;
- Compliance with the settlement or credit limit as agreed upon by the FI and payor;
- Mutually agreed upon application edits, to be accomplished without these errors[5]:
  - □ Unusual or large amounts

---

5. The error codes attached to most of these error conditions are documented in ANSI 820 and 824 standards publications, such as the publication cited in Footnote 3.

- □ Duplicate or missing data
- □ Out of range data
- □ Invalid date
- □ Data that doesn't match
- □ Invalid combinations
- □ Other errors defined in the bilateral agreement[6]
- Availability of control reports, including:
  - □ Reconciliation report
  - □ Security violation report
  - □ Message cancellation report
  - □ Missing account report

As these FEDI controls indicate, when FEDI payment replaces paper checks, many accounts receivable and accounts payable controls become irrelevant. Instead of duties being segregated, different operators can perform the data entry and release function. Corporate policies on cash discounts and authorization of payments become part of the application edit or table search routine. No checks are endorsed and there is no physical custody of signed checks. In addition, controls built into EDI messages automatically handle transaction completeness and uniqueness.

Some organizations still believe the notion that, if they use FEDI, payors will miss out on the *check float*—the free use of funds between the date a check was mailed and the date the account was debited. This situation is more relevant in the United States than in Canada, where the speed of clearing (one day across Canada) has largely eliminated any float advantage. While it is true that EFT or FEDI eliminates most of the float enjoyed by the payor, in favor of timeliness of settlement, there are terms the payor can negotiate to compensate for the loss of float advantage. For example, the American Bar Association's recent draft agreement, the Model Electronic Payments Agreement and Commentary, contains provisions that allow trading partners to change payment due dates to achieve *float neutrality*.[7]

The number of existing accounts receivable and accounts payable reports that can be eliminated depends, in part, on the amount of remittance information included in the FEDI message. From the perspective of accounts receivable staff, the usefulness of the aging report or collections reports or even the periodic reconciliation of accounts is questionable. Bad debts will be rare, except in situations in which payment is cancelled in the FEDI system prior to value date, and trading partners will have to resolve those occurrences outside the FEDI system.

---

6. Additional validation is encouraged. For example, the trading partner profile might specify *buy only* or *sell only* for only certain product codes. Other validations include placing limits on quantity and dollar amount.

7. See Section 4, Timing of Payments, in the *Model Electronic Payments Agreement and Commentary— For Domestic Credit Transfers*, American Bar Association, August 1992. This draft document was presented and discussed at the 1992 annual meeting of the association. Note, however, that the agreement has not yet been approved or endorsed by the numerous authorities within the association.

The ANSI 820 transaction set *detail area* and the EDIFACT PAYEXT message are capable of accommodating all the remittance information the payee needs to apply to outstanding invoices and to dispose of any adjustments claimed by the payor. The new version of the 820, published in December 1991, can accommodate multiple paying entities, receiving entities, or both [2].

If a trading partner sends remittance information with payment to an FI, payors can outsource some or all of their accounts receivable or accounts payable functions. In North America, some FIs are calling themselves *value-added banks* (VABs) or *information banks*. Instead of simply playing the role of financial intermediary, these FIs can also process purchase orders and invoices and generate the MIS reports their clients specify. Payors and payees should ensure, though, that in outsourcing functions they are not also relinquishing controls. They should seek assurances from their VABs that the controls that existed for outsourced functions are matched by acceptable controls on the VAB's end. This includes matching the requirements of IRS rule 91-59. The focus must be on managing intercompany bookkeeping and the associated risks. (These management tasks are discussed in detail in Section 9.10, which describes controls from payor, payee, and FI perspectives.)

9.5 THE CANADIAN FINANCIAL EDI AUDIT TRAIL

An example of the new control in Canadian FEDI is the audit trail that logs the movement of 820 and 824 transaction sets.[8] Figure 9.1 depicts this transaction movement. A clearing member of the Canadian Payments Association (CPA) is a direct participant in the Canadian payments system. The originating payor's FI might or might not be a direct participant, but must assign a trace number to the transaction set. As the 820 or 824 travels from one financial trading partner to the next, each must append a CPA-assigned code to the trace number to form a continuous payment audit trail. This comprehensive logging and referencing system gives both the partners and the auditor evidence of the existence of an authentic transaction. Similarly, the U.S. Uniform Commercial Code, Article 4A places the onus on banks, FIs, and corporations to provide evidence of the audit trail in electronic environments. If something goes wrong with a transmission, the courts assign liability according to the audit trail [3]. The party that breaks the audit trail is thus placed in an unfavorable position.

This logging process is a positive feature of the Canadian FEDI audit trail. One issue must, however, be clearly understood. The addition of a trace number by the FI does indeed alter the message and, therefore, the modified 820 must be treated as an entirely new message. Users must recognize that the 820 comes in (from the payor or FI) is not the same as the message that goes out (to another FI or the payee). The two messages possess, among other items, their own reference numbers and dates of creation. For the purposes of

---

8. *Electronic Contracting, Publishing and EDI Law* provides an excellent illustration of a nonfinancial EDI audit trail. (See Chapter 3 Reference 10.)

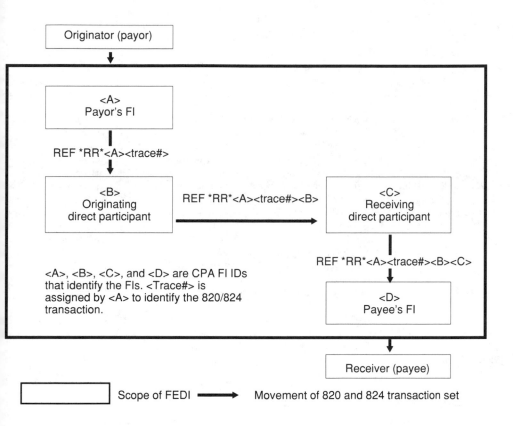

Figure 9.1 The Canadian FEDI audit trail. *Source:* CPA Standard 023–*Standards and Guidelines Applicable to EDI Transactions*, November 18, 1992.

archiving, each message must be considered and tracked. Table 9.6 details the critical archiving steps that payors, payees, and FIs should seriously consider.[9]

Used in conjunction with the Canadian FEDI audit trail, translation and communications software possess referencing capabilities that can provide ostensibly sufficient proof of where transactions began and where they ended.[10] In addition to this proof, auditors can request that audit trail and control information be stored separately in a database restricted

9. The authors acknowledge the insights of Gilles Vezina, chair of the JTC/EDI Finance Group, for the suggested archiving points for FEDI.

10. The reference numbers consist of the EDI transaction set sequence number and functional group number, which are supplied by the translation software, and the interchange number and communication session number, which are supplied by the communications software. Control and business requirements dictate the level of referencing or logging.

Table 9.6
Critical Archiving Points to Consider in Canadian FEDI

Payor	*Payor's Financial Institution*	*Payee's Financial Institution*	*Payee*
1. Prepare 820	1. Receive transaction	1. Receive interchange	1. Receive interchange
2. Add security segments S2S and S2E	2. Verify syntax	2. Verify syntax	2. Verify syntax
3. Add GS and GE segments	3. Issue 997	3. Issue 997	3. Issue 997
4. Add ISA and IEA segments	4. Authenticate 820	4. Authenticate 820	4. Authenticate 820 (if payor and payee use different FIs)
5. *Archive*	5. *Archive*	5. *Archive*	5. *Archive*
6. Transmit	6. Strip security segments S2S and S2E	6. Strip security segments S2S and S2E	6. Strip security segments S2S and S2E
	7. Perform application edits	7. Perform application edits	7. Perform application edits
	8. Issue 824	8. Issue 824	8. Issue 824 to FI, as required
	9. Process by application	9. Process by application	9. Process data in accounts receivable system or FEDI system
	10. Create new 820	10. Create new 820	
	11. Add trace number	11. Add trace number	
	12. Add security segments S2S and S2E	12. Add security segments S2S and S2E	
	13. Add GS and GE segments	13. Add GS and GE segments	
	14. Add ISA and IEA segments	14. Add ISA and IEA segments	
	15. *Archive*	15. *Archive*	
	16. Transmit	16. Transmit	

for audit use.[11] A dedicated database allows auditors to perform trend and statistical analysis, which, in turn, provides information about the behavior of controls. If trading partners also create databases, periodic comparison of key control information can enhance the authenticity of transactions.

Trading partners should agree on EDI environmental control; to facilitate the enhancement of controls for mutual benefit. Auditors should begin to participate early in the EDI development cycle, to allow time for their views to receive project team buy-in.

9.6 UNIFORM COMMERCIAL CODE ARTICLE 4A: FUNDS TRANSFER

The U.S. Uniform Commercial Code (UCC) is a comprehensive set of rules that defines the rights and obligations of parties to wholesale wire transfers. Prior to the creation of Ar-

---

11. The concept of an audit database is alluded to in two recent publications, *EDI for Managers and Auditors*, pp. 65–66 (see Reference 5) and *Electronic Contracting, Publishing, and EDI Law*, pp. 176–177 (see Chapter 3, Reference 10).

ticle 4A, such rights and obligations were largely determined by the laws of individual states. Article 4A relates primarily to the relationships between banks and funds transfer systems and between payors and payees and their respective banks. The Article governs only U.S. wholesale funds transfer; however, U.S. courts might apply the Article to U.S. funds transfers involving non-U.S. participants.

It is important to note that Article 4A does not govern relationships between trading partners. Moreover, the particular information transfer issues that characterize FEDI are not covered. Many FEDI issues, such as remittance information processing, will have to be resolved in trading partner contracts. Such outstanding issues, in fact, underscore the need for an FEDI-specific agreement, such as the Model Electronic Payments Agreement and Commentary.

9.7 THE MODEL ELECTRONIC PAYMENTS AGREEMENT AND COMMENTARY

The Model Electronic Payments Agreement and Commentary document bridges the gap between existing model electronic trade agreements and UCC Article 4A. The agreement was drafted on the assumption that Article 4A would be applicable. It provides a framework for the implementation of FEDI between trading partners and both integrates and resolves the EFT and FEDI issues for all partners [4].

These individual sections of the agreement discuss the control dimensions of FEDI: Section 6, Receipt, Acknowledgment, and Verification; Section 7, Security Procedures; and Section 8, Confidentiality. Partners can define the confidential information that must be verified and retained and the security procedures that must be followed in an appendix to the agreement. (Chapters 4 through 7 of this book discuss the implications of these stipulations to the Model Agreement.)

9.8 CANADIAN INTERFINANCIAL INSTITUTION EDI CONTROL AND AUDIT STANDARDS

Canadian FIs have developed an interfinancial institute (inter-FI) compliance reporting and auditing program based on a set of control and audit standards recommended by the Inter-FI EDI Audit Task Force [5]. The task force also developed a set of guidelines, called *Corporate to FI EDI Control Guidelines,* to communicate the control responsibilities of all EDI participants.

9.9 UNIFORM CONDUCT FOR THE INTERCHANGE OF DATA BY TELETRANSMISSION

EDIFACT recommends that EDI trading partners follow the International Chamber of Commerce provisions contained in the Uniform Conduct for the Interchange of Data

(UNCID) rules.[12] In reality, these rules are guidelines for parties intending to implement EDI; they become binding obligations only when parties specifically adopt them in a contract. The following list contains the key EDI issues that UNCID rules identify [6]. (The items include the chapter of this text in which they are discussed.)

- Identification of the standard to be used (Chapter 2);
- Security of data (Chapter 4);
- Authenticity of messages (Chapters 3 and 4);
- Integrity of messages (Chapters 3 and 4);
- Acknowledgments of transmissions by the receiving party (Chapter 6);
- Storage of data (Chapter 8);
- Use of third-party networks for EDI transmissions, transmission risks (Chapter 3).

Both the American and Canadian model TPAs contain clauses of the type found in the UNCID rules, but the scope of the agreements are expanded to include and detail other clauses.

Evaluation of the security and controls for FEDI should begin with a clear understanding of all of the documents described in the preceding sections. This knowledge base is a prerequisite to tackling the specific payment issues in each trading partner's organization. Figure 9.2 provides a diagrammatic representation of the FEDI environment.

9.10 FINANCIAL EDI CONTROLS

The following sections discuss FEDI controls from the perspective of payors, payees, and FIs. Table 9.7 summarizes the controls each of these groups must be concerned with.

9.10.1 The Payor's Perspective

The payor and the originating FI should agree on the extent to which transaction sets, or messages, are edited. Some common edits check for unusual or unreasonable data items, daily limits, or transaction limits. The entry and release function (system segregation of duties) is no different from the controls currently existing in EFT. What is different is that many FEDI systems treat a positive application acknowledgment as an order to pay and that payment is considered final.

A typical FEDI system can process advance payment notices. Therefore, sufficient time must be allowed to meet payment dates, taking into account any differences in holiday, business, and nonbusiness schedules. If organizations use default limits, they should ensure that those limits are approved by the appropriate user. Overrides of default limits and individual payment dates should be accounted for. In addition, audit trails must exist for such exception transactions.

---

12. *Essentials of EDI Law* includes a reprint of the UNCID rules in their entirety. (See Reference 6.)

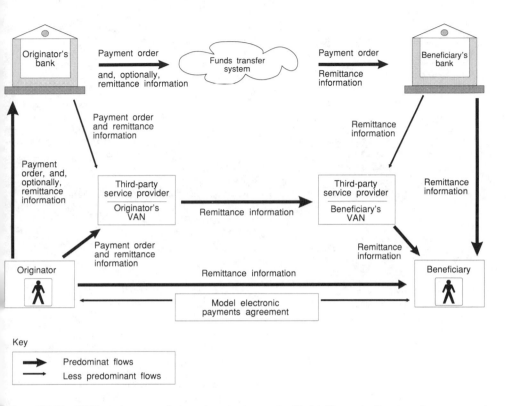

Figure 9.2 The FEDI environment. *Source: Introduction to the Model Electronic Payments Agreement and Commentary,* 1992. Reprinted with the permission of the American Bar Association.

FEDI is time-sensitive. Provisions for alternate and emergency delivery, if required, should be part of contingency planning. (This aspect of contingency planning is covered in Chapter 7.)

9.10.2 The Payee's Perspective

A typical FEDI system requires mandatory application acknowledgment between the payor and the originating FI and between the originating and the receiving FIs. If the payor and the payee use the same FI, one application acknowledgment is sufficient for funds to change hands. No application acknowledgment is required between the payee and its FI, the rationale being that, at this point, payment has already been effected. What remains to be communicated is the remittance information; therefore, a functional acknowledgment usually suffices.

Logging of inbound transactions is more important than logging of outbound transactions. When an outbound transaction is sent, a record is automatically created at the sender's end that is readily available as proof of payment. Inbound transactions are logged

Table 9.7
FEDI Controls for Payors, Payees, and Financial Institutions

FEDI Controls	FEDI Participants		
	Payors/Purchasers	*Financial Institutions*	*Payees/Suppliers*
Management controls	Effective electronic payment agreements	UCC Article 4A (U.S.)	Effective electronic payment agreements
	External and internal audit reviews	Inter-FI control and audit standards compliance (Canadian FIs only)	External and internal audit reviews
	Control self-assessment	External and internal audit reviews	Control self-assessment
		Control self-assessment	
		Definition of liability (application level acknowledgment)	
Application controls	(Outbound messages)	Funtional acknowledgment	(Inbound messages)
	Functional acknowledgment	Proper authorization of payment instructions	Functional acknowledgment
	Proper authorization of payment instructions	Extended edits	Transaction validation
	Significance of application acknowledgment from the FI	Validation of FI files	Transaction logging
	Entry and release of large-value or unusual transactions (i.e., event-driven EDI)	Authentication and encryption	Accuracy and completeness of consolidated payment information
	Message generation (timeliness, uniqueness, sequence, authorization, authentication, and application and operating system security)	Use of smartcards	Timeliness of settlements
		Security incident logging and reporting	Reconciliation of purchase orders and payment receipts
	Controls over warehoused payments	Automated and manual key management	
	Management controls over payment cancellations and credit returns	Settlement reports	
	Status reports	Reconciliation reports	
	Reconciliation of outbound messages		
	Control totals		
	Automated or manual key management		
	Matching of invoice and payment amounts		

primarily for investigation and audit purposes. These logs can prove useful in disputes, and retention periods should be established for them.

A typical FEDI system can also consolidate payment information from several sources, such as ANSI X12 820 or ACH (Automated Clearinghouse) files or output to ANSI X12, printed formats, or other specified formats, including CCD, CTP, and CTX.[13] The payee must verify, through adequate testing, the accuracy and completeness of payment information processed by the FEDI system.

Ultimately, payees must ensure that security measures are in place for all the advising methods and destinations they use. Missing account reports, which list the accounts from which outstanding payments are due the payee from its FI, and advance payment notices are useful control reports that payees should request.

9.10.3 The Financial Institution's Perspective

In addition to maintaining a directory of standard trading partner validations, FIs also maintain their own directory of FIs that allow additional transaction checking. It is in the nature of banking for security to be stringent. In Canada, FIs that conduct business in EDI established security and control standards among themselves.[14] Compliance with these standards is a unique control feature of the Canadian FEDI environment.

9.11 EVALUATED RECEIPT SETTLEMENT AND FINANCIAL EDI: AN APPLICATION AT THE MACRO LEVEL

As organizations reap the benefits of EDI, they begin to realize that, because of the timeliness and quality of the information, they no longer need to wait for that additional piece of documentation called an *invoice* to initiate payments. Once receipt of materials is verified against the advance shipment notice (ASN), payment can be made based on information in the ASN and the receiving organization's purchasing system. This process, called *evaluated receipt settlement* (ERS), eliminates not only the invoice, but also the backend checking and manual processing. ERS is widely implemented in the automotive industry and is gaining popularity in other industries, such as petroleum. (See Figure 9.3.)

ERS implementation does present issues that deserve special control consideration. These issues are described below.

Synchronization and integrity of the pricing data. Maintaining an accurate reflection of the vendor's catalog of products and services, as well as pricing information, is critical to an

---

13.   Cash concentrator and deposit (CCD), corporate trade payment (CTP), and corporate trade exchange (CTX) are NACHA payment formats that can carry limited remittance information.

14.   The Canadian Inter-FI EDI Committee established standards in seven categories: security, standards, legal, audit, settlement and timing, network, and volume. The standards were approved by the participating FIs.

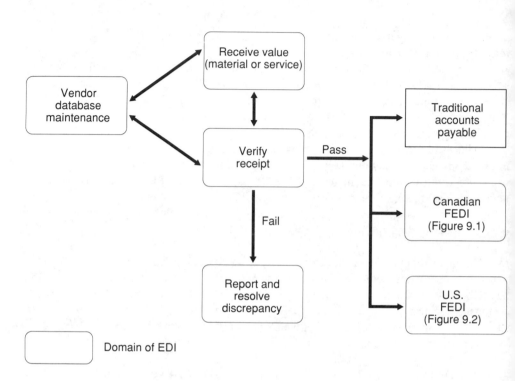

Domain of EDI

Figure 9.3 Evaluated receipt settlement and FEDI.

ERS implementation. The prices and terms must be accurate so that staff remit the exact amounts anticipated by the seller's receivables system. Special pricing algorithms and discount schemes must be available to both trading partners.

Procedures for reporting and resolving discrepancies. In an ERS implementation, discrepancies must be reported immediately. This can be accomplished electronically through EDI. For example, if quantities on the ASN or part numbers on the purchase order transaction set differ from the product received or if damage occurs during shipment, organizations can report the discrepancies using the receiving/discrepancy advice transaction set.

Added application capabilities. In traditional invoicing environments, the accounts payable system validates invoices by matching the invoicing information with the purchasing and receiving data. Once invoices are matched, the system updates the payable balance with the amount specified on the invoice, minus any discounts. Then, on the appropriate date (i.e., the last day discounts are allowed, based on the payment terms specified in the database) the system produces a check. The vendor's application must also be able to update receivable balances based on shipments and adjustments data without creating invoices, or at least without printing them.

Commercially reasonable security procedures and other potential audit impacts of UCC Article 4A. UCC Commercial Code Article 4A addresses several issues that deserve additional consideration from an audit and control perspective. One key issue is a commercially reasonable security procedure for verification (of authorization) and error detection. To determine what is commercially reasonable, organizations can look at common practices of other organizations or FIs that are similar in size and face similar exposures (determined by such factors as frequency and size of payment orders). Even though Article 4A applies only to wholesale EFT transactions, the concept of a commercially reasonable security procedure is gaining attention in the EDI community. (The security aspects of EDI are discussed in Chapter 4.) But Article 4A governs only funds transfer; it does not consider the issues raised by computer-to-computer communication of remittance information. To adequately address EDI requirements for controlled and secured information transfer and, at the same time, place FEDI in its proper context, organizations must review Article 4A alongside the ABA's draft Model Electronic Payments Agreement.

Segregation of duties and system access. Through the use of ERS and FEDI, organizations consolidate previously segregated processing functions within the EDI application. For these functions to operate effectively, the organization must ensure that application support functions remain segregated from processing and communications functions and that adequate balancing and reconciliation procedures exist to detect irregularities. Organizations should also review the segregation of support duties and access to EDI functions, programs, and data files, to ensure that no single individual can make unauthorized changes, additions, or deletions to any EDI data that can affect the entire business cycle [7].

9.12 SUMMARY

There are major differences between EFT and FEDI and, while most EFT security procedures and controls are applicable to FEDI, the FEDI information component must be considered in its own right. What controls FEDI applications require will depend on the extent to which the FEDI information component is utilized. Interest and usage in this area is presently limited, but management should be proactive and cognizant of the potential benefits of moving beyond EFT. A timely quote from Tom Anderson, vice president and director of the Canadian Bankers' Association, addresses the future direction of FEDI [8].

> In future, banks won't be handling just the payments portion of the business world. They'll want to handle all the information associated with a transaction. And money will become a more dynamic medium—it won't just be sitting around in accounts. There will be tighter cooperation between corporations and their banks, and business will have more immediate decision-making control over their accounts via computer.

REFERENCES

[1]   Vezina, Gilles, chair of JTC/EDI Finance Working Group. Personal correspondence, September 25, 1992.

[2]   Bort, Richard, "The ANSI X12 820 Transaction Set," *EDI Forum*, No. 2, 1991, p. 80.

[3]   Deeks, Brian, and Paradine, Carol, "EDI Security: The Feeling's Mutual," *CA Magazine*, November 1991, p. 51.

[4]   *Introduction to Model Electronic Payments Agreement and Commentary,* American Bar Association, p. 8.

[5]   Chan, Sally, et al., *EDI for Managers and Auditors*, Toronto, Canada: EDI Council of Canada Library Publication, 1991, p. 122.

[6]   Jones, Peter, *Essentials of EDI Law*, Toronto, Canada: EDI Council of Canada Library Publication, 1992.

[7]   Institute of Internal Auditors Research Foundation, *Audit, Control, and Security of Paperless Systems: Trends, Guidelines, Practices and Techniques* (from the proceedings of the 1990 Advanced Technology Forum), Florida: O. Jack McGill, 1991, pp. 45–48.

[8]   Anderson, Tom, "EDI or DIE," Globe and Mail, June 11, 1992.

Chapter 10

EDI Audit Considerations

10.1 THE AUDITOR AS CONTROL CONSULTANT

In today's business environment, which is characterized by rapid change and technological innovation, auditors cannot provide effective audit services unless they keep pace with current IT developments. As Ben Wright aptly puts it, "The problems of the information age must be tackled with knowledge [1]." To offer informed opinions and advice to management on the nature, types, and attributes of controls—and to maintain the professionalism and credibility of the auditing profession—auditors must keep abreast of emerging technology. (In the Epilogue, Frank Allen, manager of Advanced Technology at the Institute of Internal Auditors, discusses continuing education and the professional requirements of IT auditors in the 1990s and beyond.)

Over the years, IT auditors moved away from after the fact quality control and policing and became positive contributors to an ongoing quality management process. They recognized that quality must be managed in throughout an organization and that everyone in the organization shares the responsibility for that task. IT auditors are increasingly asked to act as control consultants, and EDI provides excellent opportunities for them to apply advanced audit techniques. Such techniques enable them to inform management up front and then keep it informed about how controls behave throughout the EDI transaction processing cycle.

10.2 GENERAL AUDIT IMPLICATIONS FOR EDI

In fulfilling their mandate to offer independent opinion to stakeholders in an organization, IT auditors face several issues that are specifically related to EDI [2]. Is a substantive approach still adequate in a paperless environment? How can an opinion be arrived at that relates to the adequacy of controls over a lengthy period, rather than simply a point in time? Are embedded audit modules needed to continuously monitor the functioning of controls? Which EDI records are to be retained and in what form? Should trading partners rely solely on mutual trust?

Suffice it to say that for auditors to review exception reports and compare results of manual and computer calculations for sample transactions is not enough. Instead, in the EDI environment, auditors should consider the following points.

EDI control considerations:

- Auditing around the computer is no longer effective.
- Good systems should rely more on effective controls than on substantive testing.
- Control failures can have far-reaching consequences.
- Contingency planning should be top priorities.
- Retention policies and statutory and legal requirements must be revisited.

EDI's impact on controls:

- EDI alters the traditional audit trail.
- Low human intervention requires automated audit programs that allow 100% checking of electronic records.
- System outages can involve all partners in the business cycle.
- The EDI system must have a place on the corporate contingency plan.
- Electronic records, not paper, must be safeguarded.

Because they cannot take into account the online, real-time nature of EDI transaction processing, traditional audit techniques do not yield adequate information about the behavior of automated controls throughout a transaction processing cycle. In online, real-time processing environments, online, real-time testing procedures must be used to preverify automated controls. In other words, auditors can use this type of testing to observe the actual adequacy and functionality of controls in operation.

In EDI, as in other technologies that authorize transactions electronically, auditors should be able to preverify the controls for user IDs, passwords, trading partner access profiles, terminal sources, digital signatures, and message authentication. They should also be particularly focused in their evaluation of timing, recognition, storage, retrieval, and their review of financial documentation. For an EDI system to succeed, auditors and users must fully understand the system EDI is replacing, including the flow of information (in paper, verbal, or electronic form) and the data structure of application programs.

The following are key questions auditors or end users should raise prior to EDI implementation.

- What information will pass between trading partners?
  To answer this question, implementors must review formal documents, such as purchase orders and invoices, and informal documents, such as messages, memos, and records of phone calls checking on transaction status.
- What control and reporting measures will be implemented?
  Will a status report be generated? How about audit trails? If so, what type?

- What information is available from application programs?
  What is the form of output?

Identifying and understanding the current flow of information enables implementors to identify the changes that are necessary for EDI implementation. These changes can include using electronic data entry instead of manual entry, developing a data link between the application program and the translation package, and creating a bridge between applications so multiple departments can use the same information.

Before implementation, auditors should also examine file retention issues to ensure that EDI transaction files and data will be retained for appropriate periods for tax, audit, backup, and management purposes and that data will be stored in an appropriate form (e.g., suspense files). Additional issues include developing policies for initial retention periods, evidence formats, hardware and software compatibility, and system auditability and security.

10.3 THE EXTERNAL AUDITOR'S ROLE

In much the same way that organizations are using EDI to change the way they do business, EDI is changing the way external auditors perform audits.[1] This section considers how EDI impacts external auditors'

- Knowledge of the business;
- Assessment of risk;
- Evaluation of general controls;
- Evaluation of processing controls;
- Testing;
- Use of computer-assisted audit techniques.

In some situations, the impact of EDI is so significant that external auditors must call upon personnel with specialized experience to help plan and execute the work. This experience, which might be provided by internal or external IT auditors, is particularly valuable during the development of new EDI applications.

10.3.1 Knowledge of the Business

External auditors must fully appreciate the total impact EDI will have on an organization's business and the extent to which the technology will be integrated with the organization's other application systems. They should assess the significance of the EDI processing for each EDI application. In many cases, a relatively small number of trading partners will use EDI to process a material portion of the overall transaction volume.

---

1. Section 10.3 was written by Peter Blaiklock and Leigh Morris, partners, Ernst and Young, Toronto.

10.3.2 Assessment of Risk

External auditors must consider the general effects of EDI when they assess the inherent risks of a transaction stream or account balance. EDI changes the nature of the risks associated with the business communication of trading partners.

One piece of good news is that EDI can significantly reduce errors associated with data entry. Because information is transferred electronically, it does not need to be keyed and rekeyed as it moves between trading partners. In fact, the errors generated by the keying in of source documents can be completely eliminated. By minimizing data entry, EDI reduces one of the highest sources of error in information systems.

Listed below are changes to business transaction processing that typically accompany EDI and the risks associated with those changes. In well-designed systems, the weight of these risks can be countered by the benefit of fewer errors, such as data entry errors. Transaction processing changes include:

A higher volume of smaller transactions and increased processing speeds. Integrating EDI into an organization's standard business processes increases the volume and speed of data processing, and, consequently, the need for appropriate and timely error resolution. In addition, connecting multiple parties' systems increases the risk and impact of system failure. Organizations must develop, test, and implement appropriate recovery steps.

Increased system complexity, as controls migrate from being managed by humans to being managed by system and application programs. Many organizations already depend heavily on their automated systems and networks and on the controls those systems provide. As EDI is used more extensively, this dependence will continue to increase.

At the same time that dependence on systems increases, human involvement in the EDI environment will decrease. EDI systems perform many business processes without human intervention. For example, payment of an EDI invoice typically receives minimal scrutiny from a clerk, and the underlying transaction receives no real examination. Users in an EDI environment do not have an opportunity to use their intuition to identify unusual or inconsistent transactions. Increased dependence on technology concentrates control in the hands of fewer individuals, and sometimes, organizations that implement EDI fail to replace manual controls with comparable automated controls.

Reduced balance sheet amounts, as EDI and just-in-time (JIT) processing techniques cause working capital requirements to shrink.

Increased dependence on the internal controls of trading partners and value-added networks (VANs). EDI brings organizations closer to their trading partners. Shorter lead times increase interdependence and exposure to error; therefore, all parties must strive to get it right the first time, on time, every time. Organizations also become vulnerable to trading partners' control failures. A failure in a supplier's computer system can, for example, delay the entire supply chain.

Trading partners also face an increased risk of system tampering. For example, one partner can act upon a seemingly genuine EDI message from another partner, only to discover that the message was sent by a disgruntled employee or an external hacker. Previously, the consequences of poor security were limited to the victim; with the advent of EDI, poor security can also affect a victim's trading partners. The most serious security failures include:

- Unauthorized access, which can result in unauthorized messages and transactions;
- Disclosure of confidential data—more data is maintained in electronic form in EDI systems than in other systems, thus increasing the risk of disclosure;
- Failure of computer hardware and software;
- Loss of computing facilities due to system failure.

Most organizations use one VAN for EDI processing, which concentrates risk and dependence on one organization. This risk increases if the VAN uses a centralized hub. The greatest fear of many EDI users is the temporary loss of their VAN service, which can seriously disrupt operations. System reliability is particularly critical in JIT operations, in which lead times are short.

Uncertainty of the legal status of EDI documents. The absence of laws governing the enforceability of contracts and the treatment of unforeseen liabilities creates a potential for substantial loss. Some organizations use TPAs to formally document the trade terms and conditions of how EDI transactions will be conducted. Legal and EDI organizations in several countries have developed model TPAs.

Lack of hard-copy audit trails. Use of EDI means auditors have fewer hard copy records to rely on. If they are unable to obtain adequate or appropriate hard-copy audit evidence, they might find the tasks of reconstructing, reconciling, or reviewing transactions impossible.

10.3.3 Evaluation of General Controls

Implementation and use of EDI affects external auditors' assessments of the general control environment. They must look for adequate management involvement as a critical factor for the successful implementation and use of EDI.

In reviewing an EDI control environment, external auditors perform these control evaluations:

Hardware and software components. Determine the supplier of the EDI translation software and consider whether the organization uses a VAN for processing EDI transactions. The significance of the VAN will depend on the nature of the processing performed. External auditors should obtain independent confirmation of the effectiveness of any critical control procedures performed by the VAN. Third-party auditors' reports on the adequacy of internal controls at the VAN are available in some countries to meet this need.

Organization. Consider management's (user and information systems) involvement in EDI implementation; senior management and steering committee involvement in EDI; and the new segregation of the duties of recording, authorization, and error resolution.

Logical access. Access control software will be important to prevent access from unauthorized parties, both inside and outside the organization. The absence or inadequate use of access control software should be investigated carefully to assess whether the organization has adequate protection against unauthorized transactions and access.

Physical and logical security. Currently EDI translation processing often resides on a microcomputer. Physical and logical security over telecommunication devices, such as modems and microcomputers, are important.

User involvement in system development. Consider user involvement in the design of EDI application controls. This is particularly critical given EDI's increased speed of processing and reduced human intervention. The auditors must also determine whether trading partner control responsibilities have been clearly communicated during EDI implementation. This will be especially important in the organization's first EDI projects.

Data ownership. Consider the effect of trading partners on the data ownership structure. Normally, data ownership should be assigned to organization staff who have the closest dealings with trading partners.

Contingency planning. Consider the need to assess the contingency plans of VANs and trading partners.

10.3.4 Evaluation of Processing Controls

External auditors must evaluate the processing control requirements that characterize the EDI environment.

10.3.4.1 Understand the Flow of Transactions

In the early phases of implementation, an organization will likely use EDI to automate current processes. For example, instead of receiving paper invoices in the mail from suppliers, an organization might receive EDI "envelopes" directly from suppliers via a VAN, use translation software to interpret the messages, and then read the messages directly into its payment application system. In this example, there is little difference between the actual flow of transactions; instead, there is a change in the medium for receiving the invoice documents. From the organization's perspective, mail, paper handling, and data entry are replaced by translation and communication software and a VAN.

In more advanced phases of implementation, EDI will alter or even eliminate the flow of significant transactions. Building on the above example, the organization might use EDI for all phases of the purchasing process: sending requests for quotes, sending purchase orders, and receiving shipping notices and bills of lading. The organization and its trading partners might agree that payment will be due upon receipt of goods and that, therefore, invoices are unnecessary. This is an important change in the flow of significant transactions. To the extent that significant aspects of the transaction flow are processed at a VAN, the external auditors need to understand the specific aspects of VAN processing.

10.3.4.2 Determine Control Objectives

In EDI applications, the control objectives over the processing of data do not change. Specifically, external auditors still look for controls that are designed to ensure that all transactions that should be recorded are recorded and that each recorded transaction is

- Real;
- Properly valued;
- Reflected in the proper accounting period (timely);
- Correctly classified, summarized, and posted.

Auditors should consider how processing might go wrong, given the additional opportunities for error that the EDI translation and communications software layers introduce. For example, with respect to the control objective of ensuring that all transactions that should be recorded are recorded, the possibility that transactions might be lost between the business application and the translation software or vice versa must be addressed. With respect to the control objective of ensuring that all transactions are real, auditors must address the possibility of duplicate, retransmitted, or fictitious EDI transactions occurring prior to translation and application processing.

The possibilities for error in the non-EDI aspects of transaction processing will likely remain, depending on the nature and extent of changes in significant transaction flows. For example, in instances in which EDI automates paper-based processes, questioning the completeness of billings—such as asking whether products are being shipped without invoices being generated—is still appropriate.

10.3.4.3 Consider Control Procedures

In addition to traditional control procedures, EDI systems have unique control features that are integrated into the standards, included in the translation and communications software (at the organization, its trading partner, and the VAN), and part of the business or accounting applications. Auditors must, therefore, consider control procedures in all these areas.

EDI standards, such as those set by ANSI or EDIFACT, include features that address a number of control objectives. External auditors differentiate between controls that are part of the standards and those that the organization actually uses (i.e., some features might be optional). For example, in assessing billing completeness, auditors look for controls in the organization's billing application to ensure that an invoice record is generated every time goods are shipped. In addition, the translation and communications software should ensure that all invoice records are transmitted to and understood by customers.

Earlier it was noted that the higher speed of EDI transactions increases the importance of timely control mechanisms. As external auditors review organization controls, they should question whether each control is responsive enough, or fast enough, in an EDI environment. And they should continue to look for high-quality detective controls to complement the preventive controls in an EDI system.

Auditors recognize that an organization that uses a VAN is really using a computer service bureau for EDI message traffic. Consequently, they need to understand the effect a VAN has on the organization's routine data processes. Some controls might be located at the VAN rather than at the organization. For example, the VAN might be responsible for control procedures that: ensure the completeness of messages, ensure that messages are only routed to authorized trading partners, and prevent unauthorized changes to messages.

Ordinarily, external auditors should obtain a third-party auditor's report on the effectiveness of control procedures at the VAN. They can use this report, along with information from the organization, to understand and evaluate the EDI flows and controls. If a third-party report is not available, they should either visit the VAN or determine whether the organization has sufficient controls to prevent or detect processing errors by the VAN.

10.3.5 Testing

For external auditors, one of the biggest differences between EDI and other environments is the lack of paper-based evidence of controls and of the transactions themselves. In well-designed EDI applications, there are adequate electronic transaction trails. If the trails are well indexed, auditors should be able to trace electronic transactions through the EDI system more easily than through a paper-based system.

As in other information systems, external auditors must review access and program change controls in the EDI environment. Adequate controls provide a basis for ensuring that programmed EDI controls operate over the period an auditor deems appropriate.

Most EDI organizations rely heavily on access controls because their applications are open not only to their staffs but also to trading partners. In addition, because of their paperless nature and high transaction volumes and speed, EDI applications do not allow for as much supervisory review (detection controls) as other systems.

10.3.6 Use of Computer-Assisted Audit Techniques

Computer-assisted audit techniques (CAATs) are useful for organizations whose systems do not provide paper-based audit trails. For example, an external auditor might develop a CAAT to track all EDI transmissions not yet matched to acknowledgments and flag the transmissions that are older than a specified period. In another example, the external auditor might use a CAAT to track advance shipping notices that have not yet been matched to invoices, and thus identify potential liabilities. Using an ageing and reporting technique to facilitate following up on unmatched transactions could be a powerful tool in system quality control.

In the future, external auditors will develop increasingly powerful CAATs, taking advantage of the standard EDI transaction formats that facilitate porting CAATs from one organization to another. Indeed, auditors might develop their own EDI transaction sets, to confirm interorganizational transactions almost as quickly as they are created.

10.4 THE INTERNAL AUDITOR'S ROLE

In some ways the role of internal auditors in EDI implementation projects is different from that of external auditors. Specifically, internal auditors must

- Be proactive and focus on preventive controls;
- Add value to the business;
- Help eliminate unnecessary controls;
- Shift from fixing blame to endeavoring to make things better;
- Act as agents of change, not criticizers;
- Possess a broad-based perspective on EDI issues;
- Provide timely recommendations;
- Place independence and objectivity above all other concerns;
- Be a team player.

Ultimately, management is responsible for controls. Given that task, business managers rely on internal auditors as control consultants. Managers

- Demand that, as control consultants, internal auditors serve as resident experts in technology and controls—and base their recommendations more on this expertise than on historical findings;
- View the audit function as more than simply a cost of doing business;
- View EDI first as a business strategy and second as a tool for moving data;
- Involve the audit function up front in the EDI development process;
- Provide auditors with an environment in which they can work closely with the organization and, at the same time, independently.

The objective of internal auditors is to provide useful information to business managers. Organizations benefit if internal auditors can advise management about the risks and control issues that new technology brings. The advent of EDI brought to light several new control issues, and internal auditors must address these issues before they can establish the adequacy of internal EDI system controls. IT auditors, who are the dedicated experts in system controls, must regularly update their knowledge of new technologies to evaluate the risks and controls required of new environments.

Many companies in a variety of industries are adopting business strategies that are based on EDI. Recent survey findings show that the most frequently mentioned benefits of EDI are quick response, quick access to information, and improved customer service. Similarly, auditors' quick responses to auditees' business needs will enhance their image.

EDI changes the control and audit environment by introducing new complexities in the initiating, recording, and executing of transactions by the various participants in the EDI network. The means for maintaining adequate control and auditability include data encryption and authentication and the use of continuous process monitoring systems or embedded audit modules. Auditors must employ informed planning skills and predefined audit programs to address control issues.

EDI system planning, implementation, and operations require special emphasis on security, transaction completeness, and data integrity. EDI implementations are generally more cost effective when organizations purchase hardware, software, and e-mail services from outside suppliers or VANs. Using external vendors to process confidential company data, however, places additional risk on the security and integrity of that data.

Internal EDI system auditors must: (a) identify their company's internal control systems and (b) establish relationships between the three main EDI risk factors. These three risk factors are (1) control objectives; (2) errors in transmission, receipt, or processing; and (3) control techniques. The internal audit function must establish an integrated program of assessing risk and monitoring early warning indicators, thus permitting audits to focus on high priority areas. Optimally, auditors should document and assess risks and controls during systems development. They should also be proactively involved during the business requirement and design stages of an EDI project.

The objectives of this book, as previously stated, are to raise auditors' awareness of the risks associated with EDI, to assist them in assessing the adequacy of their organizations' EDI system controls, and to champion the need for auditors to become proactively engaged in auditing this emerging business tool. Corporations on the leading edge of innovation are positioning themselves to be worldwide leaders. And continued growth of and corporate reliance upon innovative information technologies, if properly addressed, will place internal audit departments in a prominent role. Consequently, if auditors fail to address EDI control issues or to become involved on a consistent basis with EDI system operation, they can seriously undermine not only the functioning of the audit department but also the ability of the corporation to remain competitive in the global marketplace.

Accounting and auditing are now completely interwoven and heavily dependent on IT. As society reflects back on the 1990s, it will likely consider the most significant information technology developments to be the impacts of networking, advances in the man/machine interface, and EDI on business practices. As the number of EDI implementations grows and the trend to move from man/machine to machine/machine interfaces continues, tension and conflicts between accountants and auditors will no doubt increase.

Although advances in IT increase end users' involvement with and proximity to data, thus enabling them to perform their activities with greater efficiency, the advances also inevitably create control problems. Technological changes and developments have shifted responsibility for controlling many work tools and methods from staff in the data processing department to end users in the computing environment. In the case of EDI, the key challenge for auditors is to evaluate systems by balancing trust and creativity against control and security.

Growing dependence on IT heightens demand for computer security techniques that safeguard the investments companies have made. EDI strains the effectiveness of traditional security approaches The changing computer environment and businesses' growing reliance on networked computers calls for information security architecture that can deliver such benefits as common identification and authentication processes across computing environments. IT auditors should be familiar with the current trends in this field and its relevance in the EDI context.

Increasingly, the internal auditing profession will be driven by technology that is constantly and dramatically evolving. Internal auditors will be required to deal with rapid growth in the scope and nature of the services they are expected to perform and with a slow but consistent growth in their personal and professional liability. These days, when companies fail, shareholders and the public ask: Where were the external auditors? Very soon, they will start asking: Where were the internal auditors? Internal auditing is a staff function. It does not generate revenue (though internal auditors can help save costs). Therefore, auditors must spend money wisely. Only through continual training, education, and proactive involvement with business and emerging technologies will auditors of the 21st century be able to give back to their companies value equal to or exceeding the cost of their salaries.

REFERENCES

[1]   Wright, Benjamin, "The Taxman Has Spoken: IRS Rule 91-59," A special edition of *EDI Forum, EDI Legal and Audit Issues*, 1992.

[2]   Chan, Sally, et al., *EDI for Managers and Auditors*, Toronto, Canada: EDI Council of Canada Library Publication, 1991, p. 8.

Chapter 11

Final Thoughts on the Auditor's Changing Role

The future direction of EDI is evolving and changing daily. As the number of implementations of EDI systems increase, so do concerns for maintaining adequate financial and security controls within companies. For this reason, internal audit groups should become part of the EDI development process. George Grilley, EDI systems coordinator at Deeretech Services comments, "I'd make sure the audit control department works with MIS to ensure that proper controls are in place as the EDI system is being installed. EDI's elimination of order processing steps, for example, automatically changes internal auditing procedures." Traditional internal controls might not be adequate within an EDI system, and the participation of auditors in EDI development can help ensure well-controlled and properly designed systems.

Supporting this philosophy, Arjan Sadhwani explains that "the auditor must play a significant role during the design and development of EDI systems and must assure management that secure, auditable, and properly controlled systems are developed and that adequately designed programmed procedures are effectively implemented [1]."

Lack of involvement of internal auditors could create a risk factor that, if not addressed, could undermine internal controls throughout a corporation. Left unchecked or uncontrolled, all systems interactively linked to the EDI system would be suspect.

Coopers & Lybrand conducted a survey of its top 100 clients to identify the most important EDI control issues management faces today. All those issures are covered in this book. The survey concluded that management must perform the following control functions [2]:

- Ensure that data transmissions are accurate and complete, so business operations and financial accounting are not affected;
- Maintain an audit trail of transactions, so there is a record of visible evidence leading to a financial operation;
- Set in place procedures to correct errors identified by the system;
- Limit access to the system, as a security measure;

- Use control codes to verify the authenticity of transmissions (otherwise users cannot identify the originators of transmissions).

It might be that the expanding global implementation of EDI is not a total EDI revolution—at least, not yet. But the revolution has begun. The use of EDI for competitive advantage is a wave gaining momentum. It will have an impact on those not prepared to integrate this technological tool into long-range strategic plans for day-to-day operations. Reactive or proactive? The decision to implement EDI might be made for some companies by their business partners, leaving no room for discussion or customization of the EDI implementation.

The potential ramifications both of implementing EDI and of deciding not to implement EDI could have serious impact on a firm's future financial success. The practice of implementing processes that enable business to be conducted electronically has raised and will continue to raise questions about internal controls, access to and control of data, privacy of transactions, and the security, reliability, and accountability of applications, systems, and networks.

Auditors must prepare now. They must begin to examine EDI, and not so much as a technology but as a business strategy and process—a process that changes how business is conducted and provides significant benefits in the form of reduced costs, improved productivity, and more reliable access to information.

EDI will change how controls are viewed, what controls are required, and how controls are verified. It will also change how auditors view transaction processing, audit trails, and traditional policies and procedures for establishing internal controls over transactions. The evolution of EDI technologies will force auditors to renew their level of control awareness and challenge existing controls as they are applied to EDI. (Appendices A through F offer internal control questions and audit checklists and programs that auditors can use to begin to assess EDI's impact on an organization and ensure that internal controls exist within EDI environments.)

EDI significantly increases an organization's reliance on automated systems to conduct business with customers, suppliers, distributors, and subsidiary units. In fact, it becomes unrealistic for organizations that use EDI to think they can "audit around the computer." Internal controls, the nature of the audit trail, the amount and form of evidentiary material, risk assessment procedures, the entire audit process itself—all these components are changing in ways that are both unavoidable and unstoppable.

The auditor's role in the design and development of EDI systems is crucial; they must provide reasonable assurance to management that the system being developed possesses proper controls and is auditable. This responsibility requires that auditors conduct preimplementation reviews to verify the adequacy of controls. In EDI systems that use third-party networks, auditors will also be required to review any new application features (at the third-party network level) that use network facilities and can impact internal processing at the company.

Companies in a variety of industries are expressing interest in faster forms of EDI, notably event-driven or real-time EDI. Auditors and organizations should be aware that the next step in electronic communications between trading partners will probably move toward some type of interenterprise system, most likely in the form of shared databases. A move in this direction creates new risks and control exposures (e.g., opening up the firm's databases to suppliers) that auditors must be prepared to incorporate into thorough EDI audit plans.

REFERENCES

[1]   Sadhwani, Arjan, et al., "EDI's Effect on Internal Controls," *EDPACS*, July, 1989, p. 2.

[2]   "Coopers & Lybrand Study: IS Reveals Hefty Increase in Volume of Transactions Occurring Electronically," *EDI News*, Vol. 3, No. 11, April 1989, p. 6.

Epilogue

EDI is only the tip of the iceberg in a sea of emerging and enabling technologies. It relies on technological advances in the communications area, which, themselves, will eventually support a business community that is truly worldwide. This community will be independent of time and geographic location, as well as the hardware and software platforms on which applications run. It will require a rethinking of the audit process because that process will have to serve a global market in which the "store" is always open for business somewhere and for which systems must be up and running 24 hours a day, 7 days a week, worldwide.

Many auditors are already concerned with paperless systems in their own organizations. They will be more concerned when these systems are connected with other systems in other organizations a world away. The systems will communicate via electronic mail. The traditional paper trail used by generations of auditors will begin to disappear at an even more rapid rate.

Without the paper trail, auditors will find it more and more difficult to evaluate systems of internal control without a fairly high level of technical IT knowledge. The Institute of Internal Auditors' Advanced Technology Committee recently published a document titled *Model Curriculum for Information Systems Auditing—A Knowledge/Skill Set for Information Systems Auditing in the 90s*. This document lists 13 areas of knowledge and skill that information systems auditors need. Each of the areas is broken down into three levels of expertise, a summary of which is given below.

Level 1. At this level of expertise, auditors must possess a conceptual knowledge of some aspects of IT auditing for all types of PC-based end user computing systems, as well as for midrange and mainframe systems. Approximately two years of training is required for an auditor to become fully conversant in the practical application of this knowledge. It is expected that, in future years, internal audit candidates will receive much of this knowledge in colleges and universities.

The level 1 auditor will be able to execute any information systems audit program, recognize control weaknesses, and assess the materiality of control weaknesses back to the scope and objectives of the audit.

Level 2. At this level of expertise, auditors must be fully conversant in the conceptual knowledge of all aspects of IT auditing. They must possess the knowledge and practical experience to set the scope and objectives of individual audits, prepare audit programs, lead audits, and approve the overall results.

The level 2 auditor will be able to relate symptoms back to causes and determine if the scope of an audit needs to be expanded to encompass those causes. This level includes any requirements for level 1 auditors. An auditor who is proficient at level 2 will have at least two years of practical audit experience.

Level 3. At this level of expertise, auditors must be fully conversant in specific vendor hardware and software products. Level 3 auditors must be able to formulate audit programs that incorporate appropriate testing mechanisms, execute audit programs, recognize control weaknesses, assess the materiality of these weaknesses, and relate them back to the scope and objectives of the audit.

Ideally, level 3 auditors will be fully qualified at level 2. However, this might not always be the case. For example, in terms of overall audit knowledge and experience, a level 3 auditor might be operating primarily at level 1, relying instead on a depth of technical knowledge provided by a systems background. That auditor will be seriously challenged to perform with level 2 proficiency many of the tasks related to technical audit (noncomputer) responsibility.

When work started on the model curriculum, the Advanced Technology Committee believed that a fully qualified IT auditor should possess the expertise defined at each of the three levels. Later, in the writing and review process, it dawned on the group that level 1 was not solely the domain of the IT auditor—*all* auditors need to be proficient to at least that level! Much of this proficiency can be gained only by books such as this one.

The 13 major elements in the model curriculum show the depth and breadth of knowledge that aspiring IT auditors must be conversant in. These elements are

1. Information systems organization and administration
2. Information systems security
3. System development
4. System maintenance and change control
5. Information systems problem management
6. Information systems contingency planning
7. Information processing operations
8. Application systems
9. Systems software and environmental control programs
10. Data management

11. Database management and data dictionaries
12. Telecommunications networks
13. Artificial intelligence, expert systems, and image processing

EDI is an excellent example of a system that integrates most of an organization's applications. These applications can include purchasing, ordering, shipping, receiving, warehousing, receivables, payables, and cash. And the applications and departmental systems are not only integrated within the organization, but, through EDI, they interface with counterpart systems in other organizations as well. This integration is, in retrospect, a natural outgrowth of technological advances over the last few years that have led to the integration of communications, processing, analysis, and design components within individual systems. These changes and their ready availability have made such innovations as EDI not only possible but mandatory.

The Institute's landmark *Systems Auditability and Control* (SAC) study is another work that drives home the need for a better knowledge base for auditors. It states [1]:

> The responsibility of the internal auditor is to identify controls over information and process integrity and to test such controls for evidence of ongoing compliance and effectiveness. When appropriate, the auditor should make recommendations for cost-effective improvements to controls.
>
> In order to fulfill these responsibilities in the information systems environment of the 1990s, all internal auditors should understand information technology and be technically proficient in certain areas. It is and will continue to be virtually impossible to perform an audit of any activity without encountering some degree of automation. Technical skills, therefore, are necessary in order to review information systems, to explore control issues, and to formulate meaningful recommendations.

ACKNOWLEDGMENT

The authors acknowledge the generous contribution of Frank Allen, manager of Advanced Technology at the Institute of Internal Auditors, for providing this Epilogue.

REFERENCES

[1]   *Systems Auditability and Control*, The Institute of Internal Auditors, 1991, Module 1, p. 1-15.

Appendix A

General Considerations for an EDI Audit

This appendix contains the auditor's view of EDI at a macro level. Auditors should be familiar with the new potential risks that EDI can bring and with general management concerns, which are described in Chapter 1.

A.1 MANAGEMENT CONTROL CONCERNS

A.1.1 Loss of the Paper Audit Trail

Auditors must address the issue of the reliability of electronic audit trails. The issue is not whether an audit trail is electronic or paper, but whether it can be certified (i.e., by audit evidence, a compliance program, or control procedures) as a true copy of the records kept.

A.1.2 Business Continuity

The domino effect of system outages cannot be overlooked. Organizations must incorporate workable recovery plans not only in their systems and technology plans but also in their business resumption plans. In addition, auditors must verify that the priority processing assigned to EDI systems, among all other applications, is reasonable and agreed upon by the users. They must also verify that service level agreements spell out the systems' and performance requirements for EDI.

A.1.3 Exposure of Data to Third Parties

Organizations that use third-party networks or service bureaus must ensure that the contracts cover liability and risk apportionment. Any third party's access to an organization's data should be restricted.

Auditors should have a good understanding of the service provider's control environment. They should obtain a copy of the external auditor's report for review and relay any concerns to the service provider. (These concerns are, in turn, addressed by the service provider's external auditor.) If a service provider has not been audited, the auditor must determine whether a request for controls review is warranted.

A.1.4 Potential Legal Liability

The role of auditors is to advise management on controls that can minimize risk. They should also assist users in identifying and evaluating the control and audit features that are desirable for EDI trading to be considered in TPA negotiations. These control procedures can also be used to prequalify trading partners.

A.1.5 Records Retention and Retrievability

The focus of auditors should be risk-based. Information is an asset. The value attached to that asset, the potential threats to the asset, and any statutory considerations will dictate risk assessment, control, and security requirements. (See Chapter 8 for details.)

A.1.6 Segregation of Duties

The age-old concept of segregation of duties must be applied, whether it is EDI or another information system, and auditors should assess that segregation. They must evaluate EDI controls, and they should also observe closely how controls not specifically designed for EDI operation function in this new environment. An example of a generic control is the dual custody and split knowledge of encryption keys, which is no different from similar safeguarding procedures for opening a safe or vault.

A.2 MANAGING INTERENTERPRISE RELATIONSHIPS

It is in the nature of EDI that trading partners cannot act alone. Initially, auditors must see to it that EDI systems development team members interface with trading partner counterparts to aim at win/win solutions. After the system is implemented, auditors should periodically obtain evidence that trading partner relationships are well maintained. For example, are parties sharing the *float neutrality* promised in new FEDI payment terms?

A.3 IMPLICATIONS FOR INFORMATION SYSTEMS AUDITORS

The advent of EDI does impose new demands on the knowledge and skills that auditors possess. New challenges include:

- Increased need for information technology training and education. To assess the controls that exist in the expanded telecommunications environment of EDI—whether domestic or international—auditors will have to reengineer existing skill sets.

- Advanced audit techniques. There is no value in auditing around the computer. To audit online, real-time systems like EDI, auditors must be familiar with advanced audit techniques, such as embedded audit modules and continuous audit monitoring.
- To effectively evaluate EDI system controls, auditors will have to be aware that controls can exist at locations other than their organization.
- Auditors will have to strike a balance between remaining objective and independent and participating as a proactive team player in the organization they are auditing. This balance requires that 21st-century auditors clearly and continually communicate their role and responsibilities to the auditees. (See Chapter 10 for more details.)

Appendix B

An EDI Implementation Audit Program

B.1 AUDIT OBJECTIVE

The objective of an EDI implementation audit checklist is to ensure that the EDI development project is properly managed from startup to finish, so that a quality system that meets customer (user) expectations is delivered on time and within budget.

B.2 IMPLEMENTATION AUDIT PROGRAM

The organization of this program follows, to a degree, the 10 key control considerations described in Chapter 7. It focuses on EDI project controls; the scope does not include management controls that should be exercised in the overall EDI environment.

1. Education

   - Assess the development team's project and product knowledge. Confirm that knowledge deficiencies are repaired through timely training and education. This task requires auditors to stay current in EDI developments!

2. Management and organization

   - Review EDI management documents to determine that both a long-term business plan for EDI and executive support are evident.
   - Review the project organization chart to determine the adequacy of management and user representation in all areas affected by the development.
   - Obtain evidence of proactive planning and cooperative systems development among trading partners.
   - Obtain evidence that the project manager is constantly managing the expectation gap between the developer (service provider) and the client (user). For example, is project status routinely communicated? Are assumptions and con-

straints routinely tested? Do all parties understand the high risks associated with certain functions?

- Determine whether the organization is participating to an adequate degree in appropriate industry and standards groups.
- Obtain evidence that adequate communication takes place between the project manager and the trading partner's counterpart.
- Ensure that legal counsel has been consulted in the contractual arrangements, specifically, the TPA and third-party network and software agreements.

3. Quality project plan

- Review and comment on the project plan and look for evidence of the three dimensions in a quality plan (i.e., quality as a function of cost, time, and the fulfillment of client expectations).
- Check that an auditor and a lawyer are included in the project plan as control and legal consultants and that their time is factored into the plan.
- Ensure that the project plan is treated as a living document and updated during the life of the project, as required; verify that key players and their roles and responsibilities are well defined and understood.
- Obtain evidence that the plan was approved by clients and senior management and that quality can be attained in the prescribed cost and time structure.

4. Internal systems and business procedures review

- Based on the results of a risk assessment, evaluate system controls to verify that system designers have built appropriate controls (application and environmental), as specified by the users.
- Assess the viability of the control assessment (CSA) program as a means for identifying and evaluating controls. If the project team uses the CSA technique, assess the effectiveness of the CSA techniques and worksheets.
- Communicate control deficiencies to the project team on a timely basis.

5. EDI surveys

- Ensure that EDI surveys (trading partner, communications, and hardware) are properly conducted and use checklists established for those purposes.
- Review with the project manager any newly designed checklists and evaluate them for missing control issues.

6. Standards and document review

- Learn about the standard and the transaction sets. Identify the control data elements that will be tested by the project team and verified by the auditor.

- Tell project management what documents will be audited. Provide timely controls evaluation.
- Ensure that any deviations from standards, including system bypasses and overrides, have been approved and fully documented. Compensating controls, if required, must be in place.

7. Translation software and VAN selection review

- Verify that the vendor selection process follows established corporate policy and procedures.
- Ensure that legal counsel is consulted in matters relating to apportionment of risk, liability, etc.
- Assess the financial stability and long-term viability of the vendor.
- Make sure a sound business case supports the selection of a vendor.
- Assess the software capabilities and control features offered by the vendor in relation to user needs and the current systems environment.
- With regard to the VAN, ascertain that such issues as third-party control reviews and restriction of the VAN's access to sensitive and competitive information are resolved with the assistance of legal counsel.
- With regard to the translation software, assess the vendor's ability to support multiple standards and versions of the same standard concurrently.

8. Implementation and postimplementation review
(This area of review is similar to any development audit review. It should focus on finding evidence of open communication with trading partner counterparts.)

- Review the master test plan and selected test cases and verify a sampling of test results to confirm that both the organization and the trading partners have performed adequate and sufficient testing.
- Assure that training is properly conducted and that job aids (e.g., user documentation, hot line, help desk) are available.
- Verify that sufficient data are collected for a postimplementation review.
- Review and comment on the postimplementation report. Whether it is a lesson to be learned or a true success story, the postimplementation evaluation report should accurately reflect the major events in the EDI project life cycle.

Appendix C

A Financial EDI Audit Program

C.1 OVERVIEW

FEDI, like EFT, is unique in application, primarily because of the nature of the assets the data represents and the fact that transfer of ownership or custodial responsibility of these assets occurs through electronic channels. (Refer to the risks and exposures identified and the internal control structure described in Chapter 9.)

Internal controls are most effective in a funds transfer system when

- The controls are developed throughout the systems development effort rather than retrofitted.
- No one control is relied upon to independently satisfy a control objective.
- The controls are integrated with the functions of the system, whether manual or automated.

Auditors should approach an FEDI audit with a thorough understanding of the major differences between EFT and FEDI, so that existing EFT audit procedures can be fully utilized and customized to suit FEDI audit needs.

With regard to *control* objectives, auditors must ensure that FEDI internal controls enhance the integrity and confidentiality of payment messages and provide appropriate levels of security, reliability, and availability.

With regard to the *audit* objective, auditors must seek to obtain, through independent verification, testing, and confirmation, assurance that control objectives are being met and that the controls built into the system are working as promised.

C.2 AUDIT PROCEDURES FOR GENERIC FUNDS TRANSFER

These procedures for generic funds transfer apply to both EFT and FEDI transactions [1].

The nature of funds transfer demands that attention to controls focus on establishing and attesting to the existence of preventive controls (i.e., controls that prevent errors). In the use of detective controls (i.e., controls that detect errors), timely feedback becomes critical. In addition, sophisticated and advanced feedback mechanisms, such as expert systems, continuous process monitoring systems, context-sensitive help, or embedded audit modules, must be in place to adequately protect the funds transfer system.

To ensure effective operation, auditors should test the sets of controls listed below.

C.2.1 Management and Administrative Controls

To test management and administrative controls, auditors follow these steps:

1. Review established policies that define usage and penalties for misuse.
2. Examine insurance coverage for protection against unauthorized or inaccurate transmissions.
3. Assess management controls to ensure their operability and adherence. In particular, assess
   □ The control atmosphere of the organization, which is reflected in data security policies and procedures; the level of management support; and the formal identification of system risks.
   □ The adequacy of segregation in such duties as dual authorization for transaction processing.
   □ Audit trail requirements.
4. Ensure that management gives due consideration to the applicability of UCC Article 4A, Funds Transfer. Although the Article governs U.S. wholesale funds transfer, U.S. courts might apply it to U.S. funds transfers involving non-U.S. participants. Both U.S. and non-U.S. financial institutions should be aware of this Article and take steps to minimize their potential liability.[1]
5. Consult with the legal counsel on critical legal issues surrounding international electronic trade. These issues can provide insight into the controls that are necessary for international commerce, particularly financial transfers. A study by the United Nations Commission on International Trade Law (UNCITRAL) covered such areas as evidentiary requirements, writing requirements, authentication, and risk of loss or liability, which are also relevant to auditors in their definition of the scope of an EFT or FEDI audit.

C.2.2 System Controls

The controls listed below are typical of funds transfer applications. They are designed to fulfill the control objectives of integrity and confidentiality at the transaction level and security, reliability, and availability at the system environment level.

---

1. Robert Ballen and Natalie Diana's article "Walking a High Wire," *Banking Technology*, July/August, 1991, discusses the potential impact of Article 4A on U.S. and non-U.S. financial institutions. Also see recommended readings on UCC Article 4A in Appendix G.6.

Auditors should devise tests to verify effective functioning of these system controls:

- System access
- Message validation and authentication
- Terminal validation and authorization
- Encryption
- Completeness verification, e.g., of batch or hash totals
- Transaction sequencing
- Dual storage
- Smartcards
- Data recovery and retrieval capabilities
- Message status feedback and error recognition
- Message intercept capability
- Message time logging
- Message statistics reporting
- Automatic redundancy checks

Auditors can use audit software, query language, or expert systems to perform the following tests:

- Detect suspicious funds transfer profiles;
- Analyze large and unusual transactions;
- Select transactions for confirmation and preparation of confirmation letters;
- Produce reports of payments to verify against source and summary accounts.

C.2.3 User (Operational) Controls

These controls are exercised by users who are responsible for the security and control of their portions of the system. The controls might be exercised by internal or external users. The primary user controls that auditors should test are

- Access control, which includes both physical and logical access and administration of the authorization process (e.g., the physical location of stored passwords);
- Message authentication, which includes controlling the use of headers in messages and managing key assignment for electronic user signatures to protect built-in message controls from compromise and manipulation;
- Encryption, which protects the confidentiality of payment data, if warranted;
- Monitoring of overdraft limits and adjustments;
- Message reconciliation, which includes reconciling message traffic at all end points and queues and notifying users of undelivered messages on a timely basis;
- Troubleshooting controls, which include timely investigation of reported problems and provisions for emergency or alternate delivery methods of payment.

C.3 FINANCIAL EDI-SPECIFIC AUDIT PROCEDURES

To ensure effective operation, auditors should test the sets of controls listed below.

C.3.1 Management Controls

Auditors should be familiar with FEDI payment agreements and guidelines and verify that management has given sufficient consideration to recommendations in these documents:

1. Model Electronic Payments Agreement and Commentary (for Domestic Credit Transfers), from the American Bar Association [2]. This document details issues trading partners should consider when exchanging payment orders or remittance information via EDI. Auditors should confirm that FEDI controls accommodate the receipt, acknowledgment, and verification procedures the document provides.
2. The Inter-FI EDI Control and Audit Standards, authored by the Audit Task Force of the Canadian Inter-FI EDI Committee under the auspices of the Canadian Bankers Association (CBA). This task force has established control and audit standards for the exchange of FEDI. When FEDI is fully operational among Canadian FIs, compliance with these standards should be part of the scope of the auditor's review of EDI-capable Canadian FIs.
3. CPA Standard 023—Standards and Guidelines Applicable to EDI Transactions, Canadian Payments Association, November 199.
4. Corporate to FEDI Control Guidelines, distributed by the CBA and EDI Council of Canada.[2] Corporate auditors should be familiar with these guidelines and able to assess their applicability to a given audit environment.

In addition to following the guidance provided by these documents, trading partners' corporate staff and their FI auditors should discuss control concerns, to ensure that links between trading partners along the value chain are reliable. This step is in line with the cooperative spirit fostered by EDI.[3] Finally, auditors should obtain evidence that liability transfer is well defined and reflected in the TPA or electronic payments agreement.

C.3.2 Application Controls

Auditors should perform these tests to verify the functioning of application controls:

- Ascertain that the suggested verification procedures in Section 6.3 (D) of the Model Electronic Payments Agreement and Commentary have been adequately considered.

---

2. The Corporate to Financial EDI Control Guidelines can be obtained free of charge from the CBA or EDI Council of Canada.

3. The biggest obstacle in auditing interenterprise relationships seems to be differing corporate policies and philosophies about risk, controls, and specific industry practices. As an example, the security procedures that FIs follow and the procedures their low-end clients follow can be difficult to reconcile.

- Verify that settlement and timing requirements are clearly stated in agreements.
- Ascertain that the criteria for application-level acknowledgment are functioning as intended. The common criteria are based on the results of authenticating such data as transfer limits, account numbers, FI codes, and partner profiles.
- Review and confirm the operation of customized edit features.
- Because FEDI can eliminate the payor or purchaser's *float advantage,* examine this aspect to ensure that the payor's loss of float advantage is compensated by other terms, such as an adjustment of the electronic payment due date to conform with the perceived amount of check float. The objective is to ensure that neither party gains or loses availability of funds as a result of the payment method changing from paper to electronic form [3].
- In FEDI systems in which the FI or third-party network vendor provides the warehousing of payments, examine this service in light of such factors as the timeliness of payment deliveries, advance notices of payments coming due, and cancellation notices and the protection of the confidentiality of the stored information.
- If remittance information is bundled with payment, determine that the information is utilized in a cost-effective manner. Also, determine if this bundling of information requires that changes be made to accounts receivable or payable functions.
- Verify that FIs exchange end-of-day reconciliation and settlement reports.
- Verify that such documents as status and exception (e.g., missing accounts) reports, credit returns, invoice and payment receipt reports, and remittance advice are available to the payor or payee regularly or upon request.

C.3.3 Environmental Controls

Auditors should evaluate these aspects of environmental controls:

- Verify that mutually agreed upon commercially reasonable security procedures exist between or have been independently implemented by the payor and the FI and the payee and the FI.
- Determine that message authentication codes (MACs) are effectively employed to ensure message integrity. Review security breaches or MAC failures and obtain evidence that such incidents are immediately investigated and acted upon. (In applications in which Canadian Inter-FI EDI control and audit standards apply, compliance with those should be reviewed.)
- Ascertain that adequate consideration is given to encrypting the payment message or database to ensure confidentiality. (It is the widely held view of the Canadian FEDI community that integrity of payment messages is mandatory, whereas confidentiality is left to the discretion of individual organizations.)
- Review contingency provisions for emergency or alternate deliveries. The objective is to minimize the domino effect on downstream partners and avert liability, penalties (e.g., interest charges), and other damages.

- Assess the suitability of employing advanced audit techniques, such as expert systems, embedded audit modules, and continuous process monitoring tools, to automate the review of high risk areas. Many of these techniques allow 100% sampling and enable auditors to report on controls for entire periods rather than just discrete points in time.

REFERENCES

[1]   Canaglia, Don, EDP audit manager, American Automobile Association, personal correspondence, September, 1991. (Edited, with permission, by the authors.)

[2]   *Model Electronic Payments Agreement and Commentary (for Domestic Credit Transfers)*, draft prepared by the EDI and Information Technology Division, Section of Science and Technology, American Bar Association, August 1992.

[3]   *Introduction to Model Electronic Payments Agreement and Commentary*, American Bar Association, p. 2.

Appendix D

Audit Considerations for Trading Partner Agreements

Auditors should be familiar with the major clauses and the terms and conditions in the TPA. While lawyers are concerned with the reliability of the actual EDI records, auditors seek to assure that sufficient controls exist in the EDI environment so that reliability can be ascertained. As Joseph Rosenbaum put it, "the legal and audit concerns seem almost married in the EDI world."[1]

Auditors should view the TPA as an excellent opportunity for control agreements to be reached between trading partners. Auditors can add value to agreements by advising lawyers about what controls should be included in the TPA and how they should be implemented throughout the life of the agreement.

D.1 REVIEW MODEL TRADING PARTNER AGREEMENTS

To understand the legal environment in which EDI operates, auditors should familiarize themselves with the available model TPAs and the legal guidelines for electronic commerce. These documents are

- Model Electronic Data Interchange Agreement and Commentary (American Bar Association)
- Model Form of Electronic Data Interchange Trading Partner Agreement and Commentary (EDI Council of Canada)
- Uniform Rules of Conduct for the Interchange of Trade Data by Teletransmission (UNCID) (International Chamber of Commerce)

---

1. See Joseph Rosenbaum's section on the legal aspects of EDI in Chapter 5.

D.2 EVALUATE CONTROLS TO BE INCLUDED IN THE TRADING PARTNER AGREEMENT

From the audit perspective, the TPA is a control agreement bilaterally agreed upon by trading partners. The agreed upon controls included in the TPA define the mutual obligations partners must fulfill. (Refer to Chapters 6, 7, and 8 for more controls considerations.) Auditors must ensure that the TPA includes the following controls:

- *Application controls.* These are EDI-specific controls, such as trading partner validation, syntax checking, application editing, and levels of acknowledgment.
- *Environmental controls.* These controls include:
  - □ Backup and recovery provisions, contingency planning, standards maintenance, error reporting and investigation procedures.
  - □ Confidentiality and integrity requirements. Auditors should assess the appropriateness of security techniques.
  - □ Record retention and evidence of authenticity. Auditors should be aware that write once optical devices do not automatically qualify as nonalterable devices. In assessing retention periods, they must consider the short life span of today's media and technology.
- *Testing.* Auditors must assess the nature and extent of testing of EDI software by trading partners, especially in the areas of transaction authorization, data validation, security, authentication, and transmission. They should also recommend that the contingency plan be tested on an interorganizational level. In particular, timing and interval must be specified.

D.3 EVALUATE INTERORGANIZATIONAL CONTROL ASSURANCES

In addition to the standard contract items vetted by lawyers, auditors should recommend that trading partners exchange audit reports (internal or external) on a regular basis and that trading partners' auditors exchange mutual control assurances (these are less formal than audit reports).

Appendix E

Audit Considerations for Third-Party Network Agreements

While this appendix focuses on the terms and wording requirements that legal counsel should ensure are met in third-party network agreements, the requirements are also useful for auditors reviewing such agreements. Using the requirements as steps in the audit process would be especially useful for auditors who are asked by trading partners to provide independent assurance of a network provider's control environment.

A number of the requirements, or audit steps, described below are not strictly related to the agreement itself, but are included as reminders of additional considerations for third-party network audits. Daggers (†) identify these additional steps.

E.1 COMPLETE STATEMENT OF TERMS

- Ensure that the agreement states the complete obligations of the network provider, including such responsibilities as user support and data transmission, translation, storage, and delivery.
- Determine if the third-party vendor has clearly defined all technical terms.
- To establish the legality of transaction processing, ensure that the agreement clearly states the determination of where a message has to be (i.e., destination, such as the wholesaler's EDI mailbox) and when it has to get there (e.g., by 4:00 pm EST) to have legal effect.
- Determine that the agreement specifically identifies the methodology for confirming messages sent and received by trading partners (e.g., functional acknowledgments).
- Verify that the agreement details the company's obligations, if any, to acquire equipment and services from the third-party network provider, and its liability to the third-party vendor or trading partners if it fails to implement a working EDI system.
- Examine the agreement for appropriate wording (which, in a non-EDI operating environment, is usually found on the reverse side of purchase orders and invoices) of such concerns as warranties, return policies, product liabilities, and credit terms.

- Examine the agreement for such clauses as
  - (a) "Vendor does not warrant that the software or network will support the customers processing requirements."
  - (b) "Should vendor breach the terms of this contract as set herein, the vendors liability will not exceed (a percentage) of the fee paid by the company for the EDI service."

  Statement (a) limits the grounds on which the vendor *can even be considered* to be in breach of its contract. Statement (b) also favors the vendor by assuming that the company is in a better position than the vendor to secure its transmissions.
- Particularly if the agreement contains one or both of the clauses listed above, protect the company from vendor processing failures by ensuring that both the EDI software and EDI system users perform daily backups of critical and changed data, transmissions, functional acknowledgments, and any critical documentation.†
- Ascertain that issues relating to records retention at external locations are adequately addressed. While records retention decisions—such as retention periods for individual message and data element types—are typically covered in TPAs, they should also be discussed with third-party network providers and service bureau representatives, at whose external locations transactions are affected.
- If the company's EDI transactions will cross international trade borders, verify that the agreement specifically states under which laws it will be interpreted and considered binding. The agreement must also identify any previously agreed upon terms that will be waived for international transactions.

E.2 DATA OWNERSHIP

- Just as an unpaid mechanic can assert a lien for servicing an automobile, a network provider can retain data if a customer fails to pay network charges. To preclude the possibility of a business disruption resulting from a billing dispute, verify that the agreement confirms the customer's (company's) absolute right to data.
- Ensure that the agreement establishes a methodology for sequencing transactions that require processing (e.g., requests for quote and responses, purchase orders, vendor responses or acknowledgments, shipping notifications). Such controls let partners base obligations to perform services on when EDI messages are exchanged.
- Determine that the agreement prohibits the third-party vendor from having access to or being able to statistically analyze the company's transmissions. Statistical information collected without the company's knowledge could be used to place the company in a competitively disadvantaged position.

E.3 CONFIDENTIALITY

- Determine that the service contract establishes precise obligations to protect company data confidentiality.

- Determine that the third-party provider uses proper and complete data and network access security measures. Although laws inhibit a network provider from voluntarily disclosing data, they do not require that security measures be used on networks.†
- Verify that the vendor performs a periodic purging of backup files, according to the schedule supplied.†
- Confirm that EDI transaction and pricing data (which could prove quite a tempting target for a corporate spy or antitrust plaintiff's lawyer) is secured by the third-party vendor and unavailable to unauthorized access.†
- Obtain evidence to confirm that the third-party vendor has established a secure operating and processing environment.†

E.4 INVESTIGATIONS AND AUDITS

- A tax authority or investigative agency can order a network provider to release a client's information. Verify that the contract contains a clause requiring the third-party provider to notify the company before releasing any information, so that the company can monitor or contest such attempts.
- Ensure that the agreement contains a right to audit clause, enabling the company to conduct an independent, internal audit of the third-party vendor's operations. If this is not feasible, request a copy of the vendor's external auditor's report and obtain assurances from the external auditors that the control environment is adequate.

E.5 LIABILITY FOR ERRORS

Insist that the third party provider be held liable, up to a defined point, for mistakes. After all, the provider is often in the best position to prevent errors. Verify that the agreement divides the responsibility (equally or in some appropriate manner) for risk, including data loss, delay, misdirection, and total cessation of data traffic.

E.6 AMENDMENTS

- Since services provided by the vendor inevitably change over time, determine that the agreement is subject to amendment by the company.
- Verify that the agreement provides the company with an advanced warning (not less than 90 days) of any adverse changes (such as altered protocols) the vendor intends to make that could impact the functionability, security, and operation of the network.
- Analyze the agreement to determine if it authorizes *only the third-party vendor* to make modifications or enhancements to the software. Such a restriction can bind the company into accepting the vendor's philosophy on processing scope and direction. This restriction can also expose the company to dependence on a sole source vendor,

which can present a control exposure if the company and vendor disagree and one party wishes to terminate the relationship or if the vendor ceases to exist.

- Verify that the agreement restricts the vendor from increasing its maintenance fees on an annual basis.

E.7 TERMINATION

Determine that the agreement provides the company with sufficient warning (not less than 90 days) of the contract's termination by the third-party vendor (for whatever reason) and, if feasible, with the option to extend services beyond the effective expiration date.

Appendix F

Environmental Audit Considerations: Contingency Planning and Disaster Recovery

Internal auditors play many roles in organizations. One of their functions is to keep management informed of business threats. In today's computerized business environment, a threat to availability of computer services can impact the future of an entire organization.

Online, real-time applications have become commonplace in today's business environment. In fact, since computer systems and business goals are often interdependent, computer applications are essential to a business's success. As such, creating a disaster contingency plan (DCP) has become a concern for senior management. The proliferation of business-critical, real-time transaction processing applications makes availability a key information processing issue. However, the very nature of interactive online systems significantly complicates recovery strategy. Despite hardware redundancies and fault-tolerant operating systems, fires, floods, and numerous other disasters pose risks that a comprehensive contingency plan *should* address. The auditor's role is to assist management by providing timely, complete, and accurate reviews of the organization's DCP.

F.1 TELECOMMUNICATIONS SERVICES AND SUPPORT

Comprehensive and functional DCPs are necessary because today's automated information services critically affect the very life of an organization. Within moments of a disruption in system availability, a business can experience inefficiencies and inconveniences. As a direct result of the prevalence of critical real-time systems, computer disasters are now viewed as potential corporate disasters [1].

According to a survey by *Disaster Recovery Journal*, one in eight companies has no network recovery plan. Designing functional and secure telecommunications networks and associated systems is critical to the long-term success of any EDI environment. The EDI process is so dependent on an effective, stable, and protected network that the auditor's review of network survivability is an essential part of a well-conducted IT audit. A well-designed and functionally efficient EDI system is worthless to a company if the system is unusable. This critical corporate resource must be protected by structured contingency planning, disaster recovery and prevention activities, and periodic review via system and network performance audits.

By definition, a *network audit* is an examination of the processes associated with a network's overall operations. The objective for conducting a network audit is to highlight the importance of analyzing assets, operations, and management controls of the organization's EDI system, which depend so heavily on corporate-wide telecommunications. In contrast, a *technical systems audit* is a review of essentially the same activities but it concentrates on the hardware and software elements that comprise the network infrastructure. The entire systems audit process is detailed and goes well beyond a simple, periodic inventorying of network assets. A well-planned and implemented technical systems audit provides management with a concise summary of the firm's network assets as well as of the nature of the controls associated with network operations. In the end, the technical systems audit identifies for management any suspected or actual network risk points.

Embedded in the broad term *telecom network asset* are a wide range of telecommunications control concerns that auditors must review when they examine the controls related to the disaster contingency plan (DCP) and disaster recovery plan (DRP). Areas of concern include: transmission facilities, cables and connectors, switching systems, modems and multiplexers, connectivity devices (e.g., routers and bridges), specialized software (especially software that establishes and maintains the EDI link with the firm's VAN or direct-connect trading partners), terminals, testing and diagnostic equipment, and of course, telecommunications personnel.

Together, these assets (in strategic combination within or surrounding the organization's EDI environment) support the firm's telecommunications network infrastructure and, consequently, the EDI process. Unfortunately, each asset also represents a potential point of exposure and network deficiency.

When they audit DCP and DRP strategies for network operations in EDI environments, auditors should perform these tasks:

- Identify the EDI applications that must be supported by the network or networks and that have processing priority among the organization's applications;
- Quantify the existing network assets;
- Verify that the existing network hardware and software infrastructure can support the firm's EDI objectives, both now and over a longer term;
- Verify that the network's design and topology meet the EDI strategy;
- Determine that network operations are meeting or exceeding overall corporate EDI performance objectives;
- Identify any EDI system, VAN, or trading partner link or performance problems that require corrective action;
- Identify EDI and network risk points in relation to the system's ability to
  □ Use the existing telecom environment to recover EDI operations in the event of a local disaster;

□ Switch to an alternate VAN on an alternate telecom network if the primary link is destroyed or out of service for an extended period;

□ Establish access and utilization controls to the EDI environment from temporary or emergency telecom links across unsecured networks;

□ Establish secured telecom links to complete FEDI/EFT transaction processing.

Before beginning detailed audit field work, auditors should learn the major parts of the firm's general disaster recovery plan. For example, a typical contingency plan might contain the following sections:

    I. Assumptions and Definitions
    II. Activation of Plan
    III. Management and Control
    IV. Damage Assessment
    V. Personnel
    VI. Offsite Storage Facilities
    VII. Ongoing Plan Maintenance

Auditors reviewing contingency plans for network operations (in general as well as in relation to EDI requirements) should determine the existence, within the plan, of major recovery components, such as

- Redundant lines (voice and data) from alternate carriers;
- Fall-back data processing sites;
- Automatic backup of local data;
- Basic inventory of equipment, circuits, and personnel;
- Testing plans for infrequently used offsite recovery equipment;
- Procedures for implementing voice network recovery.

In addition, auditors should look for evidence that the DCP and DRP address such items as regional telephone company failures, local telecom failures, local power black-outs, site power failures, local weather conditions, equipment failures, and, of course, natural disasters.

F.2 ADDITIONAL AUDIT CONSIDERATIONS

The preceding discussion concentrated primarily on how auditors must assess a firm's disaster recovery preparedness in the area of telecommunications services and support. But there are other system characteristics auditors must evaluate to obtain a complete picture of a firm's disaster recovery preparedness. These range from functions that support overall data processing operations to characteristics that directly effect EDI, such as the ability of the VAN to survive or recover from a disruption in its operation, identification of critical

EDI application software required at a recovery site, or procedures required for processing FEDI payments through a common carrier across unsecured phone lines.

Management should be cognizant of the domino effect of EDI systems outages, which are more probable and frequent than a total disaster, and should make every effort to minimize impact on operations. Companies can employ these key control techniques to ensure timeliness and recoverability in the event of an EDI systems outage[1]:

- The TPA should detail the requirements and periodic testing of a recovery plan (which can be an outage recovery plan or a disaster recovery plan). Evidence of such testing should be retained for an agreed upon period and available for audit review.
- The roles and responsibilities for recovery should be well defined and communicated between trading partners and service providers.
- Operating procedures for restart and recovery procedures should be in place to enable orderly execution of the recovery plan.
- Recovery should be followed by either manual or system verification that all transactions are accounted for. It might be necessary to issue a statement of compliance to a counter party that such procedures were followed.

This text does not claim to be a definitive resource on DCPs and DRPs for EDI environments. Readers interested in additional information on this topic can see Appendix G, Section 10.

REFERENCES

[1]   Marcella, Albert, et al., *Automated Contingency Planning and Disaster Recovery System,* Altamonte Springs, Florida: Institute of Internal Auditors, October 1992, p. 3.

---

1. Adapted from *EDI for Managers and Auditors,* by Sally Chan, et al., EDI Council of Canada Library Publication, 1991, pp. 60–61.

Appendix G

Recommended Readings

For easier reference, the selected texts, journals, periodicals, papers, articles, and association addresses are grouped into eleven categories. The categories are

G.1 General readings
G.2 Management topics
G.3 Standards
G.4 Audit and control issues
G.5 Security issues
G.6 Legal issues
G.7 Network and telecommunication issues
G.8 Software and third-party network vendors
G.9 Productivity enhancements
G.10 Contingency planning and disaster recovery
G.11 Association addresses

G.1 GENERAL READINGS

Bolles, Gary A., "Gearing Up for EDI: A Primer on Electronic Data Interchange," *Network Computing*, September 1991, p. 88.

Booker, Ellis and FitzGerald, Michael, "Retailers Try EDI Hard Sell," *ComputerWorld*, July 9, 1990, p. 1.

Brooks, Jack, "Electronic Data Exchange: Where Do We Stand Today?" *Canadian Datasystems*, June 1989.

Burch, John, "The Case of the Reluctant EDIer," *Journal of Systems Management*, March 1989.

Cafiero, William, and Dearing, Brian, "Electronic Data Interchange: A Tutorial," *EDI Forum*, 1989, p.10.

Carroll, Paul B., "Computers Bringing Changes to Business Documents," *The Wall Street Journal*, March 6, 1987, p. 33.

Cerf, G. Vinton, "Prospects For Electronic Data Interchange," *Telecommunications*, January 1991.

Cheene, Dominique, "The World of EDI," *PC Today*, April 1991.

Chester, Jeffery, "Electronic Data Interchange," *InfoSystems*, Vol. 33, June 1986, p. 48.

Daly, James, "EDI Comes to the Mac," *ComputerWorld*, January 28, 1991.

Edelson, L.W., "Electronic Data Interchange," paper presented at the Los Angeles EDPAA chapter meeting on March 14, 1989.

EDI Executive Publications, Inc., 1685 Barn Swallow Place, Marietta, Georgia 30062-2860, (404) 578-4980.

"EDI Forum," *The Journal of Electronic Data Interchange*, EDI Publications, Inc., 1989.

EDI, Spread the Word!, P.O. Box 811366, Dallas, Texas 75381-1399, (214) 243-3456.

Flanagan, P., "A Cascade of Fiery Woes," *Computer Decision*, September 1988.

Gregory, T., and Palmer, C., "Paperless Payments," *Business Credit*, December 1988.

Hall, D., "Electronic Payments Ready to Take Off," *American Bankers Association Banking Journal*, May 1989.

Harris, Catherine, et al., "An Electronic Pipeline That's Changing The Way America Does Business," *Business Week*, August 3, 1987, p. 80.

Hinge, Kathleen Conlon, *Electronic Data Interchange from Understanding to Implementation*, New York, NY: American Management Association, 1988.

Horwitt, Elizabeth, "Global Players Winning With EDI Technology," *ComputerWorld*, November 12, 1990.

Jackson, Kelly, "EDI Is Opening Up," *Communications Week*, December 10, 1990.

Jackson, Kelly, "Auto Group Unveils EDI Guide," *Communications Week*, May 6, 1991.

Layne, Richard, "How Will Banks Plug Into EDI?" *Computers in Banking*, September 1989.

Leech, Tim, "Control Self-Assessment: The Dawning of a New Era in Control Governance," unpublished paper, Leech & Associates, 1990.

Lee, Yvonne, "GE Adds Task Automation, Windows Interface To EDI PC Software," *Network World*, September 16, 1991, p. 46.

Linden C., Susan, "EDI: Brief Cases," *3X/400 Information Management*, January 1991.

McCusker, Tom, "GE Spreads EDI Gospel," *Datamation*, April 15, 1991, p. 55.

Meier, Jeffrey J., "EDI: A Practical Approach," *CMA Magazine*, September 1992.

Molloy, Maureen, "Global EDI Group To Focus On Implementation Issues," *Network World*, September 23, 1991.

Moses, James, "Getting By With Just The Basics," *ComputerWorld*, March 26, 1990, pp. 90–91.

Naegele, Tobias, "Automating Paperwork: A Matter of Survival," *Electronics*, February 1989, pp. 126–27.

Nash, Foster, "When Push Comes To Shove," *ComputerWorld*, March 5, 1990.

Nash, Jim, "EDI Growth May Be Leveling Off," *ComputerWorld*, January 21, 1991.

The 1992 EDI Directory, Philips Publishing, Inc.

The 1992 EDI Source Book, Philips Publishing, Inc.

Norris, Richard C., "Electronic Data Interchange," *Data Communications Management*, Boston, MA: Auerbach Publishers, Inc., Vol. 1, 1987.

"Paperless Purchasing—Is It Finally Here?" *Purchasing*, July 1988.

Payne, Robert A., "EDI Implementation: A Case Study," *Journal of Systems Management*, March 1989.

————, "Keys to EDI Success," *Transportation and Distribution*, April 1989, p. 40.

Rush, Tom, "Gauging The Corporate Impact of EDI," *Network World*, March 1988.

Silber, Sigmund, "A Case for Electronic Document Interchange," *InfoSystems*, January 1987, p. 58.

Stone, Bernell, K., "One To Get Ready: How to Prepare Your Company for EDI," Philadelphia, PA: The Corestates Banks, 1988.

Taylor, David, "A Step Beyond EDI," *ComputerWorld*, October 9, 1989, SR/27.

Tutt, Nigel, "The EDI Trials," *Banking Technology*, September 1991, p. 22.

Vedock, Frank, and Wheeless, Bob, "EDI Revolutionizes The Auto Insurance Industry," *ASM Journal of Systems Management*, October 1990.

————, "Coopers & Lybrand Study: IS Reveals Hefty Increase in Volume of Transactions Occurring Electronically," *EDI News*, Vol. 3, No. 11, April 31, 1989, pp. 5–6.

————, "EDIA Chief Discusses Hurdles Facing EDI," *Network World*, July 1991, p. 23.

————, "Keys to EDI Success," *Transportation and Development*, April 1989.

————, "Kids' Chain Tests EDI/OR," *Stores*, March 1989.

G.2 MANAGEMENT TOPICS

Barr, Robert, "Are EDI and EFT In Your Tax Filing Future?" *Journal of Systems Management*, April 1991, p. 32.

Booth, Grayce M., "Designing Integrated Information Systems," *Handbook of Communications Systems Management*, James W. Conrad, Boston, MA: Auerbach Publishers, Inc., 1988. pp. 101–12.

Bruce, David G., "The Future of EDI," *The EDP Auditor Journal*, Vol. 1, 1990, pp. 11–13.

Carter, Joseph, et al., "Education and Training for Successful EDI Implementation," *Journal of Purchasing and Materials Management*, Vol. 23, 1987, p. 13.

Eckerson, Wayne, "Firms Look to Boost Interenterprise Nets," *Network World*, March 11, 1991.

————, "Maritime Group Navigating Through EDI Net Pilot Test," *Network World*, May 13, 1991.

————, "EDI's Future In The Automotive Industry," *Network World*, May 20, 1991.

————, "Ford Profits By Letting Suppliers Tap Into System," *Network World*, July 1, 1991, p. 1.

Emmelhainz, Margaret A., *Electronic Data Interchange: A Total Management Guide*, NY: Van Nostrand Reinhold, 1990.

Emmett, Arielle, "Breaking Barriers to EDI," *Datamation*, April 1, 1991.

Evans-Correia, K., "EDI: The Future Frontier?" *Purchasing*, February 1989.

FitzGerald, Michael, "Sears Puts Foot Down, Insists on EDI Ability," *ComputerWorld*, July 16, 1990, p. 132.

Gelford, Susan M., and Davis, Joe Ellen, "Now the 'Paperless' Expense Account," *Business Week*, September 7, 1987, p. 106.

Ghrist, John, "The EDI Game Plan at Nintendo," *3X/400 Information Management*, April 1991.

Guisbond, Lisa, "Retailers Dress Up EDI Systems," *ComputerWorld*, March 26, 1990.

Harrington, L., "EDI Gains Ground in US Companies," *Traffic Management*, September 1988.

Harris, K., and Hall, T., "How to Start an Electronic Data Interchange Program," *Electrical World*, February 1989.

Iida, Jeanne, "Wesco Plans to Drop Suppliers Not Using EDI," *Metalworking News*, May 1, 1989, p. 38.

Jackson, Kelly, "Doing Business By EDI," *Communications Week*, January 14, 1991.

Kiely, Tom, "The Two Faces of EDI," *CIO*, October 1990.

Kolodziej, Stan, "EDI: Use It or Lose It," *ComputerWorld Focus on Integration*, August 7, 1998, pp. 36–41.

Korzeniowski, Paul, "EDI Popularity Grows Sharply," *Communications Week*, September 23, 1991.

LaPlante, Alice, "EDI Booms As Global Outlook Blooms," *ComputerWorld*, February 18, 1991.

McCormick, Patricia, "Electronic Business Pitfalls Avoided," *Journal of Commerce and Commercial*, Vol. 377, July 21, 1988, pp. 1A–10A.

McDonald, Hal, "EDI Implementation Considerations," *The EDP Auditor Journal*, Vol. 1, 1990, pp. 43–46.

Molloy, Maureen, "Firm Consolidates But Keeps Customers Happy With EDI," *Network World*, April 29, 1991.

Monczka, R., and Carter, J., "Implementing Electronic Data Interchange," *Journal of Purchasing and Materials Management*, 1967.

Norris, Richard, "Corporate Strategies for Making EDI Standards Work," *EDI Forum*, 1990, pp. 96, 99.

Robins, G., "EDI and the Buyer: Less Grunt Work," *Stores*, May 1988.

Ryan, Alan, "Smaller Firms Drawn to EDI Fire," *ComputerWorld*, December 1989, p. 6.

Salamone, Salvatore, "EDI: Bottomline Booster or Budget Breaker?" *Network World*, April 1, 1991.

Sehr, Barbara, "Levi Strauss Strengthens Customer Ties With Electronic Data Interchange," *ComputerWorld*, January 30, 1989, p. S12.

Shapiro, Gabriel, "EDI Finally Accepted By Auto Industry As the Norm," *ComputerWorld*, September 10, 1990.

Sokol, Phyllis K., *EDI: The Competitive Edge*, McGraw Hill, 1989.

"The Strategic Value of EDI," *I/S Analyzer*, August 1989.

Tsay, Bor-Yi, "Electronic Data Interchange—Current Developments and Prospects," *Journal of Systems Management*, September 1988, pp. 20–23.

"25 Key Issues in EDI: Challenges for Users and Vendors," Alexandria, VA: The Electronic Data Interchange Association and the Gartner Group, Inc., 1988.

Wexler, M. Joanie, "EDI Matches Strike User Interest," *ComputerWorld*, April 9, 1990.

Wheatman, Victor, "It's Time For EDI Project Managers To Stand And Deliver," *Network World*, May 13, 1991.

———, "Electronic Data Interchange (EDI)—Ushering in a New Decade of Corporate Information Exchange," *Electronic Cash Management*, Vol. 4, No. 3, 1989, p. 2.

———, "ATM Scam: Anatomy of a Failed Computer Fraud," *EDPACS*, Vol. XIX, No. 3, September 1991.

———, "From EDI to Inter-Enterprise Systems: A Scenario for the 1990s," *EDI Forum*, No. 1, 1991, p. 22.

———, "Closing the EDI Loop," *Banking Technology*, May 1992, pp. 29–30.

G.3 STANDARDS

"ASC X12 Status Report: Standards Development and Maintenance Activities," Alexandria, VA: Data Interchange Standards Association, Inc., February 1992, pp. 61–84.

Berge, John, *The EDIFACT Standards*, NCC Blackwell, Ltd., 1991.

Booker, Ellis, "Automotive Group Thwarts EDIFACT Protocol Proposal," *Computer-World*, June 17, 1991.

Bushaus, Dawn, "EDI Billing Standard," *Communications Week*, May 13, 1991.

Carley, Joseph G., "The EDI Standards Debate," *EDI Forum*, 1989.

Eckerson, Wayne, "Car Industry Mulls Move To EDIFACT," *Network World*, May 27, 1991.

———, "Users Applaud Passage of EDI-Over-X.400 Standard," *Network World*, July 1, 1991, p. 4.

———, "New EDI Message Standard Criticized By Users, Vendors," *Network World*, August 26, 1991, p. 2.

Emmett, Arielle, "Breaking Barriers to EDI," *Datamation*, April 1, 1991.

Frye, Collean, "EDI Beginning to Stretch National Business Bounds," *Software Magazine*, May 1992.

Horwitt, Elizabeth, "Standard Developed To Unite EDI With X.400," *ComputerWorld*, November 19, 1990.

Messmer, Ellen, "Customs Moves Ahead Despite EDIFACT Delays," *Network World*, August 19, 1991, p. 6.

Wheatman, Victor, "Is X.435 The EDI Interconnection Solution?" *Network World*, July 1, 1991, p. 24.

"X12.58 Security Structure," Alexandria, VA: Data Interchange Standards Association, Inc. 1990.

Zita, Ken, "The Progress of EDI—Standards in the Pacific Rim," *Global Networks*, Vol. 1, No. 1, 1991.

———, "Implementing the EDI Standard: Mapping the Data to the Corporate Database," *EDI News*, Vol. 3, No. 7, April 1989, pp. 6–7.

———, "Introduction to UN/EDIFACT," United Nations Economic Commission for Europe (UN/ECE), April 1991.

———, "Voluntary Interindustry Communication Standards," *Retail Industry Conventions and Implementation Guidelines for Electronic Data Interchange*, VICS Publication, 1990.

G.4 AUDIT AND CONTROL ISSUES

Ahwish, Philip A., "Who Pays for Risk in Worldwide EFT Networks?" *Information Technology: The Executive's Journal*, Spring 1991.

"The Effects of Computer Processing on the Examination of Financial Statements," New York, NY: American Institute of Certified Public Accountants, Inc., AICPA SAS 48, 1988.

"Consideration of the Internal Control Structure in a Financial Statement Audit," New York, NY: American Institute of Certified Public Accountants, Inc., AICPA SAS 55, 1988.

Carlin, Anna, "Audit Concerns in Electronic Data Interchange," *EDPACS*, Vol. 17, No. 7, January 1990.

Chalmers, Leslie, "New Technology Introduces New Risks," *Journal of Accounting and EDP*, Winter 1990.

Chan, Sally, et al., *EDI for Managers and Auditors*, EDI Council of Canada Library Publication, Toronto, Canada, 1991.

———, "Managing and Auditing EDI Systems Development," *CMA Magazine*, Vol. 65, No. 9, November 1991.

———, "Establishing Reliability in an EDI Environment," *EDP Auditor Journal*, Vol. 2, 1992.

Dove, G., and Kandel, S., "EDI Implications for the EDP Auditor," paper presented at the Los Angeles EDPAA chapter meeting on June 13, 1989.

"Control Objectives, Controls in a Computer Environment: Objectives, Guidelines, and Audit Procedures," EDP Auditors Association, April 1990.

Control Objectives: Controls in an Information Systems Environment: Objectives, Guidelines, and Audit Procedures, EDP Auditors Foundation, April 1992 (P.O. Box 106, Carol Stream, Illinois 60188-0180).

EDI Control Guide, EDI Council of Australia and EDP Auditors Association, Sydney, Australia, 1990.

Fitzgerald, Jerry, "Security and Control in Data Communications Systems," *Data Security Management* (Volume 1), Boston, MA: Auerbach Publishers, Inc., 1987.

Fullerton, Kenneth H., "EDI and Auditing: Opportunity or Threat?" *EDI Forum*, Vol. 2, 1989.

Gibbons, Kathy, *Control Considerations in the Microcomputer Environment*, Southern California Edison, 1989.

Gundi, Jeffrey, "Auditing Beyond the Balance Sheet," *Financial Post*, May 28, 1992.

Harker, Samuel, "Audit Trails: Today's High-Tech/High-Touch Audit Challenge," *EDPACS*. January 1989, pp. 1–13.

Lecker, David L., "Record Retention—A Critical Internal Control," *EDP Auditor Journal*, Vol. 1, 1991.

McGill, Jack, Institute of Internal Auditors Research Foundation, "Audit, Control, and Security of Paperless Systems: Trends, Guidelines, Practices, and Technologies," Proceedings of the 1990 Advanced Technology Forum, pp. 45–48.

Mar, Steve, Burns, David, and Sorkin, Horton Lee, *Understanding and Auditing EDI and Open Network Controls*, Institute of Internal Auditors Research Foundation and the Bank Administration Institute, Rolling Meadows, IL, 1991.

Marcella, Albert, Sampias, William, and Kincaid, James, "Audit and Control Issues Surrounding Electronic Data Interchange," *EDI Forum*, No. 1, 1992, pp.48–52.

Mathias, Paul, "Auditing In Crisis," (a five-part series), *Financial Post*, March 19th through 23rd, 1990.

Moo, Paul, "Auditing and EDI: A Practical Guide for Management," *EDI Forum*, September 1992.

Norris, Daniel, and Waples, Elaine, "Control of Electronic Data Interchange Systems," *Journal of Systems Management*, Vol. 22, March 1989, pp. 21–25.

Powers, William J., "EDI Control and Audit Issues," Monographs of TDCC, Alexandria, VA: The Electronic Data Interchange Association, 1989.

———, "EDI Control and Audit Issues," *EDI Forum*, No. 1, 1991, p. 124.

———, "EDI Control and Audit Issues: For Managers, Users, and Auditors," Coopers & Lybrand, and the Electronic Data Interchange Association, Alexandria, Virginia.

Sadhwani, A.T., and Kim, I., "Audit Implications of Electronic Data Interchange in Just-In-Time Systems," *EDI Forum*, Vol. 1, 1988.

Sadhwani, A. T., Kim, I., and Helmerci, J., "EDI's Effect on Internal Controls," *EDPACS*, Vol. 17, No. 1, July 1989.

Skupsky, Donald S., "Recordkeeping Requirements," Information Clearinghouse, 1989.

Weber, Ron, "Controls in Electronic Funds Transfer Systems: A Survey and Syntheses," *Computers and Security*, Elsenier Science Publishers, Ltd., Vol. 8, No. 2, 1989.

Wright, Benjamin, "Auditors Should Be Aware of EDI's Legal Issues," *The EDP Auditor Journal*, Vol. 1, 1990, pp. 53–58.

———, "Data Communications System Controls for Auditing," *The Faulkner Report on Data Communications*, Faulkner Technical Reports, Inc., Vol. 1, December 1987.

———, "Growing Interest in Electronic Document Interchange Could Create EDP Auditing Problems," *EDPACS,* September 1988, p. 16.

G.5 SECURITY ISSUES

Carroll, John M., *Computer Security,* (2nd ed.) Stoneham, MA: Butterworth, 1987.

Deeks, Brian,and Paradine, Carol, "EDI Security: The Feeling Is Mutual," *CMA Magazine*, October 1991.

Gallegos, Frederick, and Wright, David M., "Evaluating Data Security: The Initial Review," *Data Security Management*, Boston, MA: Auerbach Publishers, Inc., 1986.

Garon, Gilles, and Outerbridge, Richard, "DES Watch: An Examination of the Sufficiency of the Data Encryption Standard for Financial Institution Security in the '90s," *Cryptologia*, November 1990, p. 3.

Hellman, Martin E., "The Mathematics of Public-Key Cryptography," *Trends in Computing*, August 1979.

Isaacson, Gerald I., "Security and Reliability: Design and Operational Concepts," *Data Communications Management*, Boston, MA: Auerbach Publishers, Inc., Vol. 1, 1989.

Lewis, Barry, "Electronic Authorization—The Next Wave In Automation," *Journal of Systems Management*, Vol. 40, No. 3, March 1989, pp. 21–25.

Schwartz, Michael, "Data Authentication," *Data Communications Management*, Boston, MA: Auerbach Publishers, Inc., Vol. 1, 1987, pp. 1–12.

G.6 LEGAL ISSUES

Ballen, Robert, and Natalie Diana, "Walking a High Wire," *Banking Technology*, July/ August 1991, p. 38.

Baum, Michael S., "EDI and the Law," *EDI Forum*, 1989 pp. 80–82.

Baum, Michael S., and Henry Perritt, *Electronic Contracting, Publishing, and EDI Law*, NY: Wiley Law Publications, 1991.

Betts, Mitch, "Lawyers Fret Over Risks of EDI Growth," *ComputerWorld*, January 16, 1989, p. 17.

Booker, Ellis, "I'll See You in Court," *ComputerWorld*, March 19, 1990, p. 58.

Carruba, Paul A., *A Practical Guide to U.C.C. Article 4A Funds Transfer*, Bank Administration Institute, 1992.

The Commercial Use of Electronic Data Interchange—A Report, Chicago, IL: American Bar Association, publication no. PC5070258, (312) 988-5555.

Electronic Data Interchange Agreement, EDI Association, 1991.

Greco, Thomas J. (Editor), *UCC Article 4A: A Practical Guide for Bankers and Bank Consul*, American Bankers Association, 1992.

Homrighausen, Paul, et al., *Uniform Commercial Code Article 4A and the Automatic Clearing House System*, NACHA, 1992.

Horwitt, Elizabeth, "Errand EDI Sparks Vendor Action," *ComputerWorld*, August 12, 1991, p. 1.

Jones, Peter, *Essentials of EDI Law*, EDI Council of Canada Library Publication, Toronto, Canada, 1992.

Kerr, Susan, "Legal Laissez-Faire," *Datamation*, Vol. 35, No. 8, April 15, 1989, pp. 54–56.

Kutten, L.J., and Reams, Bernard D., *Electronic Contracting Law: EDI and Business Transactions*, New York, NY: Clark Boardman, 1991.

Model Electronic Payments Agreement and Commentary (for Domestic Credit Transfers), Chicago, IL: American Bar Association, publication no. PC5070233 B-10, (312) 988-5555.

Model Form of Electronic Data Interchange Trading Partner Agreement and Commentary, Toronto, Canada: EDI Council of Canada, 1990.

Pinsky, Donne, "Bidding By EDI," *Communications Week*, June 10, 1991, p. 1.

"Safe Paying the Goal of the Newly Created Model Electronic Payments Agreement," *EDI News*, May 18, 1992.

Salamone, Salvatore, "Legal Groups Working On Rules For International EDI," *Network World International Networks*, March 12, 1990, p. 26.

Wright, Benjamin, "Authenticating EDI: The Location of a Trusted Recordkeeper," *Software Law Journal*, Vol. 4, 1991.

————, "EDI Legal Issues: Important but Not Alarming," *EDI Forum* (Special Edition), 1990, p. 126.

————, *The Law of Electronic Commerce EDI, Fax, and E-Mail: Technology, Proof, and Liability*, Boston, MA: Little Brown and Company, 1991.

————, "Legal, Audit,and Control: Second Generation Issues," *EDI News*, Vol. 3, No. 11, May 31, 1989, pp. 1–2.

————, *Legal Issues Impacting EDI*, Alexandria, VA: The Electronic Data Interchange Association, 1988.

————, "The Taxman Has Spoken: IRS Rule 91-59," *EDI Forum* (Recordkeeping Issue, Special Edition), June 1992, pp. 71–75.

Wright, Benjamin, and Takach, George, "Legal Issues in EDI Implementation: The Canadian and American Perspectives," *EDI for Managers and Auditors*, Toronto, Canada: EDI Council of Canada Library Publication, Toronto, Canada, 1991, p. 106.

G.7 NETWORK AND TELECOMMUNICATIONS ISSUES

Bacon, Michael, "Assessing Public Network Security," *Telecommunications*, December 1989, pp. 19–20.

Brown, Bob, "AT&T Embraces New Standard For EDI Billing," *Network World*, September 23, 1991.

————, "Carriers Travel Tough Road In EDI Market," *Network World*, December 24, 1990.

————, "Vendors Respond To Move To Faster EDI Networking," *Network World*, May 20, 1991.

Brown, Jim, "PacBell to Test EDI-Based Service For Billing Users," *Network World*, May 6, 1991.

Crockett, Barton, "AT&T EasyLink Establishes International EDI Services," *Network World*, September 16, 1991, p. 25.

Diamond, Sam, "EDI Applications Take Off," *Telecommunications*, December 1990.

Eckerson, Wayne, "Companies Strive to Consolidate EDI Nets," *Network World*, April 1, 1991.

————, "Sprint International Service Allows EDI Document Exchange Over X.400," *Network World*, June 24, 1991, p. 6.

Gross, Steve, "Sears Preps Net For EDI," *Communications Week*, June 17, 1991, p. 18.

Isaacson, Gerald I., "Data Communications Security: Design and Operational Concepts," *Data Security Management*, Boston, MA: Auerbach Publishers, Inc., Vol. 1, 1987.

Smith, Tom, "EDI Package Features Applications Gateway," *Network World*, March 19, 1990.

————, "Electronic Data Interchange (EDI)," *The Faulkner Report on Data Communications*, Faulkner Technical Reports, Inc., Vol. 1, October 1989.

————, *Telecommunications Dictionary and Fact Book*, Ramsey Center for Communications Management, Inc., 1984.

G.8 SOFTWARE AND THIRD-PARTY NETWORK VENDORS

Bruce, David, "EDI Trading Partners," *3X/400 Information Management*, May 1991.

Cashin, Jerry, "Business Transactions Take Electronic Route," *Software Magazine*, December 1991.

Dalton, Gary, "The Relationship between EDI and E-Mail," *EDI Forum*, 1991, p. 28.

Diamond, Gerry, and Howe, Edward, "Understanding and Choosing a Value-Added Network," *External Affairs and International Trade*, Canada Transportation Services Division, Federal Government of Canada, 1992.

Desmond, Paul, "IBM EDI Software to Run In Near Real-Time Mode," *Network World*, April 15, 1991.

Eckerson, Wayne, "EDI Trading Pacts A Blessing and A Curse," *Network World*, March 5, 1990.

————, "EDI Forces Companies To Hammer Out Trading Terms," *Network World*, March 5, 1990.

The EDI Group, Ltd., "An Analysis of the U.S. EDI Software Market for Users and Vendors," Phillips Publishing, Inc., December 1991.

————, "Extol Translation Software for EDI on AS/400s Debuts," *Network World*, March 25, 1991.

————, "Integrating EDI Into Application Systems at Crompton & Knowles," *EDI News*, Vol. 3, No. 6, March 22, 1989, pp. 4–6.

Gerson, Gordon M., "Data Mapping: The Integration of EDI into the Corporate Information Structure," *The EDP Auditor Journal*, Vol. 1, 1990, pp. 59–70.

Micro Translation Software Comparison Chart," *EDI News* (Special Report), March 23, 1992.

Molloy, Maureen, "EDI Users Tell VAN Reps: Here's How You Can Help," *Network World*, December 10, 1990.

————, "User Enlists Help of AT&T In Readying EDI Partners," *Network World*, April 8, 1991.

————, "TI Irons Out Wrinkles In Its Worldwide EDI System," *Network World*, April 8, 1991.

Stahl, Bob, "The Ins and Outs of Software Testing," *ComputerWorld*, October 24, 1988, pp. 87–92.

G.9 PRODUCTIVITY ENHANCEMENTS

Annis, Ted, "JIT Via EDI," *Manufacturing Systems*, Vol. 4, November 1986, p. 62.

Anthens, Gary, "EDI May Save Time, Money for Defense Department," *ComputerWorld*, August 26, 1991, p. 32.

Eckerson, Wayne, "Pioneering Users Moving to Faster Methods of EDI," *Network World*, May 6, 1991.

————, "Health Care Recognizes Value of EDI," *Network World,* September 1991, p. 23.

Heidkamp, Martha M., "Reaping the Benefits of Financial EDI," *Management Accounting*, May 1991.

Klein, Lawrence, "'Pillow Talk' For Productivity: Bar Coding and EDI," *Management Accounting*, February 1991, p.47.

Mandell, Mel, "EDI Speeds Caterpillar's Global March," *ComputerWorld*, August 12, 1991, p. 58.

Miller, Hannah, "Just-In-Time: Some Textile Industries Call It 'Linkage,'" *Purchasing*, April 9, 1987, p. 58.

Rizzo, Terry, "EDI For Efficiency's Sake," *Network Computing*, September 1991, p. 78.

Sadhwani, Arjan, and Sarhan, M. H., "Electronic Systems Enhance JIT Operations," *Management Accounting*, Vol. LXIX, No. 6.

————, "Cost-Justifying EDI: When To Do It and Why," *EDI News*, Vol. 3, No. 7, April 5, 1989 pp. 2–3.

G.10 CONTINGENCY PLANNING AND DISASTER RECOVERY

Andrews, William C., "Contingency Planning for Physical Disasters," *Journal of Systems Management*, July 1990, Vol. 41, No. 7, p. 28.

Axt, Jeff, "Keep Your Business Systems Going When Your Computer Is Not," *3/X400 Information Management*, October 1991, p. 67.

Betts, Mitch, "Ignore Archive Issues At Your Peril," *ComputerWorld,* March 2, 1992, pp. 71–74.

Bolles, Gary A., "Whipping Up An Emergency Response Plan," *Network Computing*, February 1992, pp. 81–89.

Briere, Daniel, "The Best Way To Prevent A Disaster: Plan for One," *Network World*, November 27, 1989, p. 1.

Crockett, Barton, "Users Seek Damages From Illinois Bell," *Network World*, May 23, 1988, pp. 11–13.

———, "CO Fire Shows Need For Recovery Plans," *Network World*, May 1988, p. 21.

———, "Sea-Land Rethinks Recovery Plan After Comdisco Outage," *Network World*, November 11, 1991, p. 15.

Desmond, Paul, "Software Provides Disaster Relief On Transaction Nets," *Network World*, February 4, 1992, pp. 13–15.

Hamilton, Rosemary, "Picking Up The Bytes and Pieces After A Wind Storm," *Computer-World*, February 19, 1990, p. 6.

Handbook of Effective Disaster Recovery Planning, Dialog Management, Inc. (1945 Bryon Road, Merrick, NY 11566).

Harris, Alison, "Planning Your Recovery," *Service News*, May 1989, pp. 22–35.

Henkel, Tom, and Bartolid, Peter, "A Special Report: Protecting the Corporate Data Resource," *ComputerWorld*, November 18, 1983, p. 25.

Hirsch, Steven A., "Disaster: Could Your Company Recover?" *Management Accounting*, March 1990, p. 50.

Jenkins, Avery, "Firms Need Data-Protection Policies," *PC Week*, March 1984, p. 38–41.

LeGallee, Julie, "Power Protection Now, Not After A Disaster," *The Office*, February 1992, pp. 40–1.

Llana, Andres, "Drill For Disaster," *Connect,* Spring 1989, pp. 20–21.

Magid, Robin F., "Recovering The Business: A Daily Journal," *Tech Exec*, February 1990, pp. 19–26.

Marcella, Albert, et al., "Automated Contingency Planning and Disaster Recovery System," *Institute of Internal Auditors*, October 1992, p. 3.

Pastore, Richard, "Disasters Shine Light On Micro Recovery System," *ComputerWorld*, November 27, 1989, p. 37.

Radding, Allan, "Disaster Planners: Prices Are More Flexible Than Products," *ComputerWorld*, January 6, 1992, p. 81.

Roberts, Mary Lou, "Choose Your Disaster Protection," *3X/400 Information Management*, October 1991, pp. 45–48.

Roberts, Mary Lou, "Planning For Business Continuity," *3X/400 Information Management*, January 1991, pp. 64–70.

Saunders, Laura, "Disaster Without Relief," *Forbes*, November 27, 1989, pp. 124–28.

Semilof, Margie, "Work-Area Disaster Services Catch On," *The Office*, February 1992, p. 27.

Wallace, Bob, "Disaster Recovery Group Expects More Members As Outages Mount," *Network World*, January 13, 1992, p. 14.

Weixel, Suzanne, "Disaster Prevention and Recovery," *ComputerWorld*, March 13, 1989, pp. 75–84.

Whaley, Richard L., "Blueprint For Survival," *3X/400 Information Management*, October 1991, pp. 36–43.

White, David, "After The Fire," *Industrial Fire World*, October 1988, pp. 17–20.

Zane, Richard B., "Real-World Disaster Recovery Planning," *Chief Information Officer*, Spring 1989, Vol. 1, No. 4, p. 36.

Order the books listed below from DIANE Publishing Company, (600 Upland Avenue, Upland, Pennsylvania 19015).

Guide for Selecting Automated Risk Analysis Tools, 1989

Recovery-Site Strategies: How to Select an EDP Recovery Site, 1988

Contingency Planning: Preventing, Surviving and Recovering From Disaster, 1990

Effective Disaster Recovery Planning: How to Prevent and Recover from Major Catastrophes, 1990

Disaster Recovery Planning Manual for Financial Institutions, 1990

Disaster Recovery for Banks: A Comprehensive Program for Today's Regulatory Climate, 1988

Disaster Recovery and Restoration for Telecommunications Facilities and Networks, 1990

G.11 Association Addresses

American Bar Association, Order Fulfillment
750 North Lake Shore Drive
Chicago, IL 60611
(312)988-5555

Association of Records Managers and Administrators (ARMA)
4200 Somerset Drive, Suite 215
Prairie Village, Kansas 66208-5287
(913) 341-3808

The Canadian Information and Image Management Society (CIIMS)
86 Wilson Street
Oakville, Ontario L6K 3G5
(416) 842-6067

Canadian Payment Association
50 O'Connor Street, Suite 1212
Ottawa, Ontario K1P 6L2

Data Interchange Standards Association, Inc.
1800 Diagonal Road, Suite 355
Alexandria, Virginia 22314-2852

EDI Council of Canada
5401 Eglinton Avenue West, Suite 203
Etobicoke, Ontario M9C 5K6

The EDP Auditors Association
3701 Algonquin Road, Suite 1010
Rolling Meadows, IL 60008
(708)253-1545

Institute of Internal Auditors (ITA)
249 Maitland Avenue
Altamonte Springs, Florida 32701-4201
Systems Auditability and Control Report, February 1991

National Archives and Record Administration (NARA)
NE Office of Public Programs, Room G-8
National Archives
8th at Pennsylvania NW
Washington, DC 20408

Glossary

ABM Automated banking machine. Also known as an automated teller machine (ATM), an ABM is a 24-hour, stand-alone minibank, located outside branch bank offices or in public places like shopping malls. Through ABMs, clients can access deposits, withdrawals, account inquiries, and transfers. Typically, the ABM network is comprised of two spheres: a proprietary sphere, in which the bank manages the transactions of its clients, and the public or shared domain, in which a client of one financial institution can use another's ABMs. The shared networks are regulated by national standards (ANSI X9 series). ABM networks in North America make extensive use of cryptography.

ACH Automated Clearinghouse. A nationwide electronic payments system, which more than 15,000 financial institutions use, on behalf of 100,000 corporations and millions of consumers in the United States. The funds transfer system of choice among businesses that make electronic payments to vendors, it is economical and can carry remittance information in standardized, computer processable data formats. (See NACHA.)

ADMA Administration management domain. Used by X.400.

ADMD Administrative management domain, as defined by the X.400 standard.

AIAG Automotive Industry Action Group. Develops EDI standards for the automotive industry.

ALFA An automated clearance system for German customs and the Frankfurt Airport.

agorithm A clearly specified mathematical process for computation; a set of rules which, if followed, give a prescribed result.

ANA Article Numbering Association. Originally formed to establish and coordinate bar coding activities in the retail and wholesale markets in the United Kingdom.

ANSI American National Standards Institute. The parent organization of the X12 standard and the recognized clearinghouse for information on U.S. national standards.

ANSI standard A published transaction set approved by ANSI. The standards are reviewed every six months.

application acknowledgment X12 transaction 824, which responds when a transaction set is received for processing by an application program.

application advice [824]   X12 transaction 824, which identifies any errors beyond the normal syntax checks of a transaction set and accepts or rejects the transaction set.

application interface   The component of EDI software that passes electronic transactions to and from the appropriate application system.

application link software   A software program that links an application program and an industry data or fixed field format.

application message type   A basic message type adapted to suit an application area.

application program   A computer program designed to process a particular function, e.g., accounts receivable, order processing.

application-to-application   The direct interchange of data between computers, without rekeying.

archive   To store backup files and associated journals for a given period of time for security, backup, or auditing.

ASAP   Analytic Systems Automated Purchasing. An electronic order entry system for hospitals.

ASCII   American Standard Code for Information Interchange. The standard code for information exchange among data processing systems. Uses a coded character set consisting of 7-bit coded characters (8 bits including parity check).

ASC X12   Accredited Standards Committee X12. ANSI committee that develops and maintains U.S. EDI standards.

ASN   Advanced shipping notice. A transaction that indicates that shipment was made by a supplier.

assumed receipt   The principle of assuming that the contents of a shipping or delivery note are correct. Shipping and receiving personnel do not check the delivery quantity. Used in conjunction with bar codes and an EDI-delivered ASN to eliminate invoices.

asynchronous transmission   Transmissions in which, while the start of the transmission of a character or block of characters is arbitrary, each subsequent signal, representing a bit within the character or block, has the same relationship in a fixed time frame.

AT&T   American Telephone and Telegraph, now also owners of Istel, a British EDI service provider.

auditability   A characteristic of modern information systems, gauged by the ease with which data can be substantiated by tracing it to source documents and the extent to which auditors can rely on preverified and monitored control processes.

audit trail   Manual or computerized tracing of the transactions affecting the contents or origin of a record.

authentication   (1) The process of verifying the eligibility of a device, originator, or individual to access specific categories of information or to enter specific areas of a facility. This process involves matching machine-readable code with a predetermined list of authorized end users. (2) A practice of establishing the validity of a transmission, message, device, or originator, which was designed to provide protection against fraudulent transmissions.

authentication key   A short string of characters used to authenticate transactions between trading partners.

auto dial   A function of some modems that automatically dials up and accesses a network on a given command, at a given time, or on recognizing a given condition in a program.

batch control totals   The result of grouping transactions at the input stage and establishing control totals over them to ensure proper processing. These control totals can be based on document counts, record counts, quantity totals, dollar totals, or hash (mixed data, such as customer AR numbers) totals.

batch processing   The processing of computer information after it has been accumulated in one group, or batch.

baud   A rate of transmission over a channel or circuit. The baud rate is equal to the number of pulses that can be transmitted in one second, often the same as the number of bits per second. Common rates are now 1200, 2400, 4800, 9600 bits and 19.2 and 56 kilobytes.

binary   A system of numerical notation that assumes only two possible states or values, zero (0) and one (1).

bisynchronous   A communication protocol whereby messages are sent as blocks of characters. The blocks of data are checked for completeness and accuracy by the receiving computer.

bit   The basic unit of information in a binary numbering system (BInary digiT).

BT   British Telecom.

BT-Tymnet   The merged McDonnell Douglas-EDINet/BT company, which is an EDI service provider.

byte   A string of 7 or 8 bits, or binary digits. The length of the string determines the amount of data that can be represented. The 8-bit byte can represent numerous special characters, 26 uppercase and lowercase alphabetic characters, and 10 numeric digits, totalling 256 possible combinations.

CAAT   Computer-assisted audit technique. The use of computers in the audit process.

CARGO-IMP   An IATA standard for airline cargo messages.

CARGONAUT   An internal clearinghouse system at Schipol Airport in Amsterdam.

CCC   Customs Cooperation Council, based in Brussels.

CCD   Cash Concentration and Disbursement. Developed by NACHA for the electronic transfer of funds between companies and trading partners. Allows 60 characters of information in addition to the dollar amount.

CCD+   Cash Concentration and Disbursement Plus. An ACH format for electronic payments. Expansion of CCD. Allows additional remittance information. Addendum can be executed in X12 format. The "plus" refers to the 705 addenda.

CCDX   Cash Concentration and Disbursement with Addendum.

CCITT   Consultative Committee on International Telegraph and Telephone. A committee within the ITU. Among other tasks, it creates conventions and set standards that enable incompatible networks and computer systems to exchange data.

CDC   Control Data Corporation. Operates REDINET, a third-party service operation for EDI.

CEBIS   Commission EDIFACT Board Information System.

CEC　Commission of the European Communities. The governing body of the European Economic Community.

CEFIC　Federation of European Chemical Industries. Provides EDI for the chemical industry in the United Kingdom and in Western Europe. One of the first transactional projects in Europe; the pilot was launched in September 1987.

CEN　Commission of the European Communities.

CGSB　Canadian Government Standards Board

challenge and response　A method of user authentication. The user enters an ID and password and, in return, is issued a challenge by the system. The system compares the user's response to the challenge to a computed response. If the responses match, the user is allowed access to the system. The system issues a different challenge each time. In effect, it requires a new password for each logon.

CHAPS　Clearinghouse Automated Payments System. Great Britain.

CHIEF　Customs Handling of Import and Export Freight. A U.K. customs project that succeeded DEPS.

CHIPS　Clearinghouse Interbank Payments System. A computerized clearinghouse system used by banks to settle interbank foreign exchange obligations.

CIDX　Chemical Industry Data Exchange. The U.S. chemical industry's EDI guidelines, which are based on X12 standards. Also the term for the industry association that develops CIDX standards and guidelines.

cipher or ciphertext　Encrypted, or enciphered, data, which can be stored and transmitted in a nonreadable format. An encryption key is required to convert the data back into readable form.

clearinghouse　A conventional or limited purpose entity generally restricted to providing specialized services, such as clearing funds or settling accounts.

codifying　The process of detailing a new standard.

common carrier　In the United States and Canada, a public data transmission service, such as a telephone or telegraph company, that provides the general public with transmission service facilities.

communications controller　A hardware and software unit that monitors and controls telecommunications traffic, or data, within a computer network. It optimizes line usage, allocates priorities, and talks to the outside world.

communications envelope　An enveloping function of EDI management software that identifies such components as communications protocols and line speeds for an interchange envelope.

communications interface　The component of EDI software that transmits and receives EDI documents electronically.

completeness controls　Controls that ensure that all transactions are accepted and recorded by a system only once. The conrols should also report all rejected or duplicated transactions.

compliance checking　The function of EDI processing software that ensures that all transmissions contain the mandatory information demanded by the EDI standard. Compares information sent by an EDI user against EDI standards and reports exceptions.

Does not ensure that documents are complete and fully accurate, but does reject transmissions with missing data elements or syntax errors.

compliance program A method by which two or more EDI trading partners periodically report conformity to agreed upon standards of control and audit. Management produces statements of compliance, which briefly note any exceptions, as well as corrective action planned or taken, in accordance with operating rules. Auditors produce an independent and objective statement of opinion on management statements.

confirmation A formal notice (by message or code) from a electronic mailbox system or EDI server indicating that a message sent to a trading partner has reached its intended mailbox or been retrieved by the addressee. (See also functional acknowledgment.)

contingency planning Planning for events and occurrences that *might* happen.

control Maintaining the quality of the organization and incorporated systems.

control envelope Used to validate the receipt of correct and complete data.

control number Identifies a standard data element (data element identifier) or a standard segment (segment identifier). Also called a reference number.

control objectives Techniques and procedures for conducting audits of various activities across a wide spectrum of technical and organizational settings, resulting in a normative model of how activities should be performed. Information control objectives are accuracy and completeness, security (including authorization), auditability, timeliness, and recoverability.

control segment A segment, structured like a data segment, that transfers control information for the grouping of data segments.

control structure The beginning (header) and ending (trailer) segments that identify transactions in EDI.

control validation Confirmation that information in the control segments is correct.

corrective controls Controls that correct errors.

COSAC The Hong Kong air terminal's system for import and export clearance.

CPA Canadian Payments Association. Federally regulated organization that plans, develops, and administrates the Canadian payments system, which includes the national clearing and settlement system, both paper-based and electronic.

CPA 005 Canadian Payment Association Standard 005. Standard for exchanging check transactions using magnetic tape.

CPA 023 Canadian Payment Associaltion Standard 023. Standard for exchanging EDI transactions among Canadian financial institutions.

cryptographic equipment Hardware that performs cryptographic functions, e.g., encryption, authentication, key generation.

cryptographic key A parameter that determines the transformation of plaintext to ciphertext or vice versa.

CSA Canadian Standards Association.

CSM Cryptographic service message. A message that transports the keys or related information that controls a keying generation.

CTP Corporate trade payment. An electronic message system that allows one dollar amount to cover several invoices.

CTX   Corporate trade exchange. Also, an electronic funds transfer format, compatible with X12, that both carries information about a payment and transfers values.

CUSDEC   EDIFACT standard for European customs declaration format.

CUSRES   Customs response, an EDIFACT coded message.

Customs   Excise, duty, and tariffing agency that handles national customs processing.

data dictionary   Lists the elements for which standards exist. The Joint Electronic Document Interchange (JEDI) committee developed a data dictionary that is employed by many EDI users.

data element   The smallest named item in a transaction set. Together with a segment ID, data elements form data segments.

data element directory   Lists identified, named, and described data element attributes, along with specifications for representing the data element values.

data key   A working key used to encrypt and decrypt or to authenticate data.

data mapping   The relationship between a user's data and the X12 message syntax.

data segment   The intermediate unit of information in a message, or transaction set, enclosed by a segment identifier, which identifies each segment, and a segment terminator. (In EDIFACT, a segment identifier code is composed of three uppercase alphabetic characters; in X12, it is two or three uppercase characters or digits.) A data segment consists of a predefined set of functionally related data elements, which are identified by their sequential positions in the message. When data segments are combined to form a message, their relationship is specified by a data segment designator and a data segment sequence. An EDI data segment is analogous to a logical record.

data transfer   Transmission of data signals from any data source to a data sink, or receiving device.

DCE   Data circuit (terminating) equipment (e.g., the packet switch).

DEA   Data encryption algorithm. The algorithm, specified by ANSI X3.92, combines a binary number with a 64-bit cryptographic key that allows more than 72 quadrillion combinations to scramble the transmission of a message. Detailed in the Federal Information Processing Standard Publication 46, January 15, 1977. (See also DES and encryption algorithm.)

decryption   Transforming ciphertext into plaintext.

delimiters   Two levels of separators and a terminator that are integrals part of a transferred data stream. Delimiters are specified in the interchange header. From highest to lowest level, the separators and terminator are segment terminator, data element separator, and component element separator (used only in EDIFACT).

DEPS   Departmental entry processing system. Used in the U.K. customs control system.

DES   Data Encryption Standard. The standard, created by ANSI X3.92 specifies a data encryption algorithm for enciphering and deciphering data. (See also DEA and encryption algorithm).

detective control   Controls that detect errors.

dial up   Access a network by dialing a phone number or initiating a computer to dial the number. The dial-up line connects to the network access point via a node or a PAD.

digital signature Electronically generated, digitized (as opposed to graphically created) authorization that is uniquely linkable and traceable to an empowered officer.

direct transmission A transmission whereby data is exchanged directly between sender and receiver computers, without an intervening third-party service. Also called a point-to-point transmission.

DISA Data Interchange Standards Organization. The secretariat for the ANSI ASC X12 committee, which manages X12 activities.

disaster recovery planning Contingency planning specifically related to recovering hardware and software (e.g. data centers, application software, operations, personnel, telecommunications) in information system outages.

document In EDI, a form, such as an invoice or a purchase order, that trading partners have agreed to exchange and that the EDI software handles within its compliance-checking logic.

double length keys Keys whose bit length is doubled to make their codes harder to break. Keys are numbers that are combined with confidential data to conceal the data. The longer the key, (i.e., the more characters it contains), the larger the number of values it can assume, hence, the more difficult it is to infer. For example, a binary key of 4 characters has 2^4 or 16 possible values. Extended to 8 characters, the key can assume 2^8 or 256 values. Previously, keys were 64 bits long. Currently, important keys, such as master file keys, are 128 bits long. (Typically, 8 bits are needed for parity.)

DSD Direct store delivery. Delivering products directly to retail stores and notifying stores of deliveries electronically rather than by paper.

DTI Direct trader input. Allows direct traders or their forwarding agents to input shipment details into U.K. customs computers.

dual control Using two or more separate entities (usually people) operating in concert to protect sensitive functions or information. Both entities are equally and separately responsible for protecting vulnerable transaction materials from access or use.

EAN International Article Numbering Association

EB EDIFACT Board. Advisory and support team for the UN/EDIFACT Rapporteurs of North and South America, Western Europe, Eastern Europe, Australia and New Zealand, and Japan and Singapore.

EC (1) European Community, consisting of the 12 members of the European Economic Community. (2) Electronic commerce. Conducting business between computers through digital exchange (U.S. Department of Defense EC/EDI/PLUS program).

ECE Economic Commission for Europe. One of five regional commissions of the United Nations. Includes North America, Western Europe, and Eastern Europe.

EDI Electronic data interchange. Intercompany, computer-to-computer transmission of business information in a standard format. For EDI purists, "computer-to-computer" means direct transmission from the originating application program to the receiving, or processing, application program, and an EDI transmission consists only of business data, not any accompanying verbiage or free-form messages. Purists might also contend that a standard format is one that is approved by a national or international standards organization, as opposed to formats developed by industry groups or companies.

EDIA   Electronic Data Interchange Association. A national body that propagates and controls the use of EDI in a given country. All EDIAs are nonprofit organizations dedicated to encouraging EDI growth. EDI associations include:

EDIA	EDI Association in the United States
EDICC	EDI Council of Canada
EDICA	EDI Council of Australia
EDIA	EDI Association in the United Kingdom
EDIANZ	EDI Association of New Zealand

The EDIA in the United States was formerly TDCC and administered the development of standards in transportation and other industries. The EDIA in the United Kingdom is very active, as is the EDIA in New Zealand.

EDI clearinghouse   In contrast to a conventional clearinghouse, which performs a specialized service, such as clearing funds or settling accounts, an EDI clearinghouse is an administrative, legal, and technical infrastructure that provides telecommunications and computerbased commercial trading services to facilitate electronic trade, reduce legal uncertainty, and bolster the reliability and enforceability of electronic transaction records.

EDIFACT   EDI for Administration, Commerce, and Transport. EDI standards established for these business functions by the United Nations Economic Commission for Europe.

EDIFICE   Electronic data interchange forum for companies interested in computing and electronics. EDI for the electronics industry in the European Community.

EDIFRANCE   The organization that administrates EDI in France.

EDI interface phase   The phase of EDI processing in which the EDI translator and the application interface perform functions for inbound and outbound transactions.

EDI standards   Criteria that define the data content and format requirements for specific business transactions (e.g., purchase orders). Using standard formats allows companies to exchange transactions with multiple trading partners easily.

EDI translation   Converting application data to and from a standard format.

EDI translator   The component of EDI software that performs authorization checking against the trading partner master file, transaction syntax checking against the appropriate EDI standard, and translation of the transaction into application format. Translates outbound transactions from the application format to the appropriate EDI standard format. Also generates FAs, which are transmitted to sending partners, and builds FA control records to match against trading partner FAs upon return receipt.

EDI transmission   A functional group of one or more EDI transactions that are sent to the same location, in the same transmission, and are identified by a functional group header and trailer.

EDP   Electronic data processing.

EDP audit   Electronic data processing audit. Auditors give an impartial, independent judgement of the quality of the automated information processing system under review. Also referred to, in the 1990s, as an IS or IT audit.

EDX Electronic data interchange for the electrical industry. Stands for both the standards organization and the published industry guidelines.

EFT Electronic funds transfer. Sending payment instructions across a computer network, or the company-to-company, company-to-bank, or bank-to-bank electronic exchange of value. (See FEDI.)

EFTA European Free Trade Association. Composed of the non-EEC countries—Austria, Finland, Iceland, Norway, Sweden, and Switzerland.

EIDX Electronics Industry Data Exchange. Industry group that makes recommendations to X12.

electronic mail Also called e-mail. The computer-to-computer exchange of messages. E-mail is usually unstructured (free-form) rather than in a structured format. X.400 has become the standard for e-mail exchange.

electronic mailbox A designated holding location for electronic mail. It can be located on the receiver's computer or, more commonly, on a third-party network. Trading partners log onto their VAN mailbox systems to retrieve EDI transactions. Also the software used by a VAN to store EDI documents in its computer system.

element The smallest item of information in an electronic data message, or transaction set. Analogous to a field.

element delimiter A single character that follows the segment identifier and each data element in an electronic data message except the last.

embedded audit module Programming added to system software that permits auditors to monitor and test controls and audit procedures. As an automatic monitoring device, the module might monitor and report on integrity controls for authorization, accuracy, security, authentication, and encryption.

encryption Transforming confidential plaintext into ciphertext to protect it. Also called encipherment. An encryption algorithm combines plaintext with other values called keys, or ciphers, so the data becomes unintelligible. Once encrypted, data can be stored or transmitted over unsecured lines. Reversing the process, or decrypting data, strips the keys of their encrypted values and makes the plaintext available for further processing. (See encryption algorithm.)

encryption algorithm The algorithm that performs data encryption. (See encryption.) Often programmed into a specialized computer called a hardware security module. Combines plaintext with keys, or ciphers, to obscure the data. An algorithm has to be reversible to be useful, but reversibility, or *symmetry*, is an exposure. If the keys of a reversible algorithm are stolen or deciphered by computers, the encrypted values can easily be returned to plaintext. For this reason, cryptographers are developing *asymmetrical* algorithms.

The most prominent symmetrical algorithm is the data encryption standard (DES), which has been in the public domain for many years and is available in any large public library. The DES combining process is called *exclusive or* (XOR). It is also called *modulus 10 without carry*, which refers to the fact that when DES adds 7 and 6, the result is 3, not 13. This concealment method carefully merges keys and plaintext. As a result, even if fraudsters know the text and the encrypted value—and even if they have a copy of the algorithm—they cannot infer the keys.

The Rivest, Shamir and Adelman (RSA) algorithm, which is asymmetrical, reduces the risk of reversibility. It uses two keys, a public key and a private key. The public key encrypts the sender's data and the private key decrypts the recipient's data. The keys are generated at the same time and stand in a complex mathematical relationship. RSA calculations are very processor intensive. In the future DES and RSA might be used together—DES to perform routine concealment and RSA to encrypt electronic signatures, so true nonrepudiation is achieved.

enveloping   An EDI management software function that groups all documents of the same type, or functional group, and bound for the same destination into an electronic envelope.

ERS   Evaluated receipt settlement. When, to take advantage of the timeliness and accuracy of EDI, organizations do not wait for a paper invoice to pay vendors. Once they verify receipt of materials against the ASN and their purchasing system, organizations can initiate payment.

event-driven EDI   When EDI processing is triggered by predetermined criteria, such as receipt of a purchase order from a specific trading partner. It can also be extended and expanded to include triggers at the transaction set level, such as when, in FEDI, application acknowledgment is triggered by a limit check on quantity or amount. Embedded audit modules are also examples of event-driven EDI.

EXIT   An Australian system for automated EDI export clearances.

FA   Functional acknowledgment. Sent to a trading partner to indicate that a document was received and successfully entered into the EDI interface phase.

FCP 80   A U.K. computerized port cargo handling system.

FEDI   Financial electronic data interchange. Also known as electronic funds transfer EDI (EFT/EDI). In FEDI, payments and remittance data are passed between financial institutions and companies. FEDI allows remittance information to be collected, analyzed, and reported to the payor, thus compressing the reconciliation cycle and obviating some accounts payable functions. FEDI documents include payment orders, balance inquiries, bank statements, deposit notices, and remittance advice.

FedWire   The funds transfer system owned and operated by the Federal Reserve Banks. Allows banks to use their reserve or clearing accounts with Federal Reserve banks to transfer funds. Typically used for transactions that require immediate settlement and finality. A FedWire transaction can carry only limited administrative or remittance information, and FedWire fees are high compared to ACH and other payment mechanisms. Since remittance information must often accompany commercial electronic payments and same-day settlement is often not required for routine payments between trading partners, most corporate trading partners do not use FedWire.

FIATA   International Federation of Freight Forwarders Associations.

flat file   Any file having fixed-record length or, in EDI, the file produced by EDI translation software to serve as input to the interface. Usually has the same fields as the original file, but each field is expanded to its maximum length. Does not have delimiters.

front end   The computer that performs EDI preprocessing. Usually performs communications functions, translates EDI documents, and is connected to a host computer, which performs final processing. Can perform line control, message handling, and code conversion and control special purpose terminals.

functional group   A group of related transaction sets. For example, a purchase order functional group could contain purchase orders and purchase order acknowledgments. Organizing similar transactions into distinct functional groups (e.g., differentiating invoices from purchase orders) allows multiple transaction sets to be sent in the same package.

gateway   The connection that permits messages to flow freely between two networks.

GATT   General Agreement on Tariffs and Trade.

GE.1   Committe of members of the UN/ECE WP.4 (on Facilitation of International Trade Procedures) who are experts on data elements and automatic data interchange. (See WP.4.)

GE.2   Committee of members of the UN/ECE WP.4 who are experts on procedures and documentation. (See WP.4.)

GTDI   The UN/ECE guidelines for trade data interchange.

hardware security module   A self-contained, physically secured computer that performs securityrelated processes and stores security parameters and sensitive data.

header record   Precedes a group of related data records (e.g., transaction sets or a functional group of transaction sets) and contains control information, such as batch control totals and sequential control numbers.

HIBCC   Health Industry Business Communications Council. Develops EDI guidelines for the health industry.

HMC&E   Her Majesty's Customs and Excise (United Kingdom).

HOTLINE   A VAN in the port of Hong Kong.

hub   Also called a sponsor. Any large company that uses EDI and encourages its paper-based business partners to use EDI; the responding partners are, in turn, called spokes.

IAPH   International Association of Ports and Harbors.

IATA   International Air Transport Association.

ICAA   International Civil Airports Association.

ICAO   International Civil Aviation Organization.

ICC   International Chamber of Commerce.

ICS   International Chamber of Shipping.

IDEA   International Data Exchange Association, based in Brussels. Promotes global expansion of EDI.

integrity controls   Manual or programmed controls that ensure that the objectives of maintaining the accuracy, completeness, and confidentiality of data during input, processing, output, and storage are met.

interchange   In EDI, the exchange of electronic information between companies. Also, the group of transaction sets transmitted from one sender to one receiver at one time. Delineated by interchange control segments.

interchange envelope   An EDI management software function that groups multiple electronic envelops.

interconnect   Connecting two VANs so that documents can be exchanged between subscribers who do not use the same VAN.

interface   A shared boundary; a recognized and definable crossover point between two systems. (See gateway.)

INTIS   An EDI project in the port of Rotterdam, in the Netherlands.

IRC   International record carrier. Transnational communication and carrier companies, e.g., ITT, RCA.

IS   Information system.

ISDN   Integrated services digital network. The networks and equipment for integrated broadband transmission of data, voice, and image, from rates of 144 Kbps to 2 Mbps. Allows integration of data, voice, and video over the same digital links.

ISO   International Standards Organization. An organization within the United Nations to which all national and other standard setting bodies (should) defer. Develops and monitors international standards, including OSI, EDIFACT, and X.400.

ISO 7372   The United Nations trade data element directory, adopted by the ISO.

ISO 9735   The UN/EDIFACT syntax standards adopted by the ISO.

IT   Information technology.

ITU   International Telecommunications Unit.

JEDI   Joint Electronic Document Interchange. A United Nations committee established by WP.4 to develop syntax, messages, and related procedures for EDI. Brought together standards for X12, GTDI, TDCC, UCS, WINS, etc. The work is now being performed by EDIFACT.

JIT   Just in time. A manufacturing and inventory philosophy according to which materials are scheduled to be delivered to a production line only as needed.

JTC/EDI   Joint Technical Committee on Electronic Data Interchange. Composed of the Canadian groups CGSB and CSA.

KEK   Key exchange key. Used to protect either other key encryption keys or data keys during an exchange between two trading partners.

key custodians   The persons, assigned by the security administrators of trading partners, that send or receive a component of either the master key or exchange key used to encrypt data encryption keys. This control technique involves dual control, with split knowledge that requires two key custodians.

key exchange   The exchange of keys between partners, so messages can be validated before and after transmission.

key management   Generating and storing keys, or ciphers, for encrypting, or concealing, confidential data. Also, organization and change procedures for cryptographic algorithms.

key material   The data required for establishing and maintaining cryptographic keying relationships.

key relationship   When trading partners or financial institutions share at least one cryptographic key.

knapsack algorithm One of the first methods for constructing a public key cryptosystem, it used puzzles of a known complexity. The *trapdoor knapsack cipher* employs as its puzzle the knapsack problem, which is known to be very difficult to solve. The problem involves a set of eight assorted weights that must be balanced with a "knapsack" containing an unknown selection of the same weights. The puzzle specifies a *knapsack vector*, which is the set of integer weights, and a *knapsack total*, which is the weight that must be matched. The solution is the subset of weights that adds up to the total. Like any public key system, the trapdoor knapsack cipher comprises a method of forming the secret and public keys, a method of encipherment, and a method of decipherment.

KOMPASS A system for data exchange used in the port of Bremen, West Germany.

KPE Key encryption key. Also known as the data key or working key. Used exclusively to encrypt and decrypt keys.

label The code at the front of a file of documents that enables the EDI server to recognize the batch.

LAN Local-area network. Connects computer terminals or PCs together, generally within a range of less than 2000 feet.

MAC Message authentication code. Generated as a result of an authentication algorithm (e.g., DES) processing a data string and a secret key. Verifies that the data has not been altered.

mapping Diagraming data that is to be exchanged electronically, including how it is to be used and what business management systems need it. Preliminary step for developing an applications link. Performed by the functional manager responsible for a business management system.

master key The encryption key used to encrypt key encryption keys and data keys for file storage.

matching check Comparing input data with information stored in master or suspense (holding) files. Unmatched items are usually reported for manual investigation.

message The EDIFACT term for a transaction set. A message is the collection of data, organized in segments, exchanged by trading partners engaged in EDI. Typically, a message is an electronic version of a document associated with a common business transaction, such as a purchase order or shipping notice. A message begins with a message header segment, which identifies the start of the message (e.g., the series of characters representing one purchase order). The message header segment also carries the message type code, which identifies the business transaction type. EDIFACT's message header segment is called UNH; in ANSI X12 protocol, the message header is called ST. A message ends with a message trailer segment, which signals the end of the message (e.g., the end of one purchase order). EDIFACT's message trailer is labelled UNT; the ANSI X12 message trailer is referred to as SE.

MHS Message handling service. Generic term for the X.400 services, capabilities, and message handling entities under development (and already implemented in some countries).

modem Modulator/demodulator. Enables digital signals (i.e., from a computer) to be transmitted over analog transmission facilities (i.e, telephone lines).

MTA Message Transfer Agent. A network through which X.400 messages pass.

multiplexer A device that allows one communication line to be shared by several terminal devices and vice versa.

NACHA National Automated Clearinghouse Association. A confederation of regional clearinghouse associations that establishes rules and regulations and provides education, training, and marketing services for the ACH network. Established in 1974 as a regulatory body. (See ACH.)

NACS National Airfreight Clearance System. An automated system run by the Japanese Ministry of Finance, airlines, and forwarding agents.

NAWGA North American Wholesale Grocers Association. Led the successful introduction of microcomputers into EDI and facilitated integration of small users into the EDI community.

NIST National Institute for Standards of Technology. A U.S. organization. Formerly the National Bureau of Standards.

nonrepudiable A message is said to be nonrepudiable if trading partners are absolutely certain of the message source and thus can accept the message for contractual purposes. Currently, message authentication coding is used widely to verify the origins of messages. This book advances the position that because machine authentication coding is intended to protect data, not to verify the origin of data, it can only establish a sender's identity inferentially. To be certain of a message's origin, organizations might have to use complex, nonreversible cryptography, which is not widely used today.

NSA National Security Administration. A U.S. group that sets and enforces data encryption standards. ANSI committee X9.9 is taking over the responsibility for encryption standards for public systems while NSA concentrates on military systems. DES was originally overseen by the U.S. National Bureau of Standards. (See DES.)

ODETTE Organization for Data Exchange by Teletransmission in Europe. An EDI group in the automotive industry. Similar to AIAG in the United States.

open network A network with which outside parties can communicate.

O/R name Originator/recipient name. The addressing scheme used in the P1 message transfer protocol.

OSI Open system interconnect. A 7-layer architectural model for standardizing interaction that enables networks and computers to communicate freely.

P1 envelope The "envelope" that holds electronic messages. Envelopes are identified by a naming convention called the P1 message transfer protocol. A P1 message carries the contents of an EDI message through a message transfer agent (MTA) to its intended destination, where the envelope is discarded.

P1 message transfer protocol See P1 envelope.

P2 Protocol that defines the header information in the X.400 message handling standard.

P7 Protocol for accessing stored messages in the X.400 message handling standard.

packet switching Dividing a transmission into packets of up to 256 characters for efficient transmission of messages via radio or phone circuit paths.

PAD Packet assembler/disassembler. An interface device that buffers data sent to and from character mode devices and assembles and disassembles the packets needed for X.25 operation; an extension of CCITT X.25.

password A unique, generally 6-digit word that, along with a user ID, identifies a user to a computer system. Systems must perform user and system validation and authentication before they will send or receive messages. Messages are subject to compliance checking.

payment data The payment portion of an FEDI transaction. Includes such items as identity of creditor and debtor, transaction value, value date, and message origination date.

Pedi The committee developing EDI specifications for the X.400 standards family. Also known as X.435.

PIDX Petroleum Industry Data Exchange. A petroleum industry group that defines industry guidelines for X12 and promotes EDI. Secretariat is the American Petroleum Institute.

plaintext Data before it has been encrypted or after it has been decrypted, e.g., an ASCII text file. (See encryption.)

POS Point-of-sale. Also, a national network of merchant terminals, at which customers can use client cards and personal security codes to make purchases. Transactions are directed against client deposit accounts. POS terminals are sophisticated cryptographic devices, with complex key management processes. POS standards draw on ABM network experiences and possess extremely stringent security requirements.

preventive controls Controls that prevent errors.

preverification of controls Online, real-time testing of data processing environment controls, such as user identification codes, user authorization profiles, terminal source, message authenticity, and encryption.

private formats Unique formats developed by trading partners who choose not to adopt standard industry or public formats.

private key A unique key assigned to only one entity in a data encryption system.

proprietary standard A data format developed by an industry or a company for the data exchanged by its trading partners. Proprietary formats do not comply with the ASC X12 series of standards.

protocol Communication standards that determine message content and format, enabling uniformity of transmissions.

PSD A cryptography device that has a built-in safeguard that prevents users from revealing all or part of the cryptography. To be successful, such a device must respond to tampering by erasing or rendering unusable any cryptographic keys. In addition, tampering should produce noticeable damage, and successful penetration must require skills, equipment, and facilities that are not generally available.

PTT Post Telephone and Telegraph Administration. Nationalized organizations that oversee public use of communications facilities in such areas as Europe, South America, and the Pacific Rim.

public key Within a public key encryption scheme, an encryption code that is associated with a specific individual and is known to all parties within a communications circle.

QR Quick response. An inventory philosophy, borrowed from the apparel industry, that holds that businesses must respond quickly to customer orders and should rely on EDI to do so. Analogous to the just-in-time philosophy in manufacturing.

QRS Quick response system. Systems that combine EDI with other time-saving devices, such as databases, bar codes, container and goods codes, and universal product codes. Used in fast-moving industries, such as retail and apparel.

QRT Quick response trading. A trading methodology that combines universal product codes (UPCs) and EDI. Retailers and distributors endeavor to order smaller quantities more frequently from associate suppliers and manufacturers, thereby allowing members of the distribution chain to respond more quickly to customer demand, maintain lower stock levels on a wider selection of products, and reduce the quantity of unsalable or slow-moving inventory items. Participants use UPC codes to track inventory as it is sold and use EDI to transmit orders.

rapporteur A person nominated by a government and appointed by UN/ECE WP.4 to initiate and coordinate UN/EDIFACT development work in a geographical area of jurisdiction.

real-time EDI EDI in which transaction sets are sent and received on line and entire transactions can be completed in a single session. Presently, most EDI transactions are still in the store-and-retrieve or store-and-forward mode.

reasonableness check Using software to test whether the contents of a transaction fall within predefined limits (e.g., a range of values) or satisfy predefined criteria (e.g., a relationship to previous input).

recoverability In EDI, the control objective of ensuring that recovery from a failed transaction or system occurs within an acceptable time frame. Requires adequate backup, retention, and contingency plans.

redundancy bits A communications control technique for detecting distorted data during transmission.

remittance Any data, or supporting documentation, that accompanies payment data in FEDI transactions. Includes purchase orders, invoice stubs, and invoice numbers.

RINET Reinsurance and insurance network. A European EDI insurance and reinsurance network.

RSA An asynchronous public key scheme, named after its inventors Rivest, Shamir, and Adelman. (See encryption algorithm).

SAGITTA A national Dutch customs clearance system.

SAS Statement of Auditing Standards issued by the AICPA.

SCC JTC/EDI Standards Council of Canada Joint Technical Committee on Electronic Data Interchange.

SEAGHA System for electronic and adopted interchange in the port of Antwerp, Belgium.

security The desired level of integrity, exclusiveness, availability, and effectiveness to protect data from loss, corruption, destruction, and unauthorized use.

security incidents Incidents related to the security of FEDI. Can include MAC verification failure, cryptographic service message counter out of sequence, known or suspected compromise during the manual key distribution process, known or suspected penetration of a physically secure device, known or suspected compromise of a key.

segment A line of data in a standard EDI transaction set format. Analogous to a record in a computer data file. EDI messages are made up of segments and the segments are made up of elements.

segment code A unique code that identifies a segment specified in a segment directory. An EDIFACT term.

segment diagram A schematic of the format and composition of a segment.

segment directory A publication that defines the format of all segments for which standards exist.

segment name One or more words that identify a data segment type. An EDIFACT term.

SISTEMI TELEMATICA A VAN for the port of Genoa, Italy.

SITPRO Simpler International Trade Procedures. A government agency formed to respond to DIT. Developed Interbridge sofware. Takes a leading role in developing standards in Great Britain.

SMMT The Society of Motor Manufacturers and Traders. A U.K. organization that represents British auto manufacturers. Commissioned the first auto-specific EDI scheme, in close coordination with ODETTE.

split knowledge When two or more parties each possess key components that individually convey no knowledge of the cryptographic key that results from their combination.

store and forward The term commonly applied to messaging systems (i.e., electronic mail systems) that store messages in electronic mailboxes before delivering them to recipients, i.e., systems that perform direct delivery. A second messaging method is store and retrieve, whereby systems store messages and recipients retrieve them. Actually, most mailbox systems both perform direct delivery and allow retrieval, provided they incorporate time delays. Both methods are considered acceptable by most telecommunications regimes.

store and retrieve The term commonly applied to messaging systems (i.e., electronic mail systems) that store messages in electronic mailboxes, where they reside until either addressees retrieve them or, if they lie dormant for a predefined period, they are purged to an archive file. Purging routines vary. A second messaging method is store and forward, whereby systems store messages before delivering them to recipients, i.e., direct delivery. Actually, most mailbox systems both perform direct delivery and allow retrieval, provided they incorporate time delays. Both methods are considered acceptable by most telecommunications regimes.

S.W.I.F.T. Society for Worldwide Interbank Financial Telecommunications. An international financial communications system. Although not technically an EFT system, it facilitates transfers with a fast, secure, reliable and economical international communications network. Formed as a Belgian company in May 1973, S.W.I.F.T. began to offer a standardized interbank system for continuous automated international message processing and transmission on October 29, 1976. Live service actually began on May 9, 1977. Around-the-clock services include international payments between banks, foreign exchange, and trade finance transactions. Currently, it has over 2,300 users representing 1,500 banks in over 70 countries.

syntax check   Comparing an input transaction to the appropriate EDI standard format.

table-driven   When a programming process is driven by data that is maintained in a table, or matrix.

table-driven program   A program for which such components as factors, variables, and data reside in a table, or matrix. The program "looks up" these elements and holds them in a file or in memory.

TC154   Technical Committee 154. A UN committee affiliated with UNECE WP.4 that establishes agreement on EDIFACT documentation standards through the ISO.

TCIF   Telecommunication Industry Forum. An industry group that develops telecommunications industry guidelines for X12.

TDCC   Transportation Data Coordinating Committee. An industry trade group that originally promoted the development of standards for EDI messaging and a communications structure based on transaction sets for the transportation industry.

TDI   Trade Data Interchange. EDI standards developed in Great Britain and currently used throughout Europe. Used in the development of EDIFACT.

technical systems audit   (1) A formal examination and evaluation of the effectiveness of telecommunications systems controls. (2) Performing compliance and substantive tests on systems as an integrated unit.

TEDIS   Trade Electronic Data Interchange System. Set up to promote awareness of EDI in Europe. Extends the concept of the standardized approach of EDI to all users in business, industry, and government.

third party   A party involved in the trading relationship that exists between two or more trading partners but with whom neither of the trading partners trades. (See third-party network.)

third-party network   A service provider that functions as a clearinghouse for EDI messages. Third-party networks usually provide mailbox services as well as value-added services, such as data translation from one format to another.

TPA   Trading partner agreement. The written contract that spells out agreed upon terms between EDI trading partners.

tracing request   A request by trading partners to a third-party network for information on the location or routing of an EDI transaction. Made to resolve a conflict.

Tradacoms   Developed by ANA, this message standard is used for data interchange between major U.K. retailers and their suppliers.

trading partners   Companies that do business with each other via EDI (e.g., send and receive business documents, such as purchase orders).

trading partner master file   Also called a trading partner directory. Computer file that contains information about all authorized trading partners.

trailer records   Records that designate the end of a group of related data records (e.g., a transaction set or a functional group of transaction sets) and contain control information, such as batch control totals.

transaction   A single completed transmission, e.g., transmission of an invoice over an EDI network. Analogous to usage of the term in data processing, in which a transaction can be an inquiry or a range of updates and trading transactions. The definition is important for EDI service operators, who must interpret invoices and other documents.

transaction reference number   The unique number in an EDI transaction that identifies the transaction.

transaction set   One electronic document (e.g., a purchase order). The data included in a transaction set conveys the same information as a conventional printed document.

translation   When documents received in one format are translated into another format (e.g., a document can be translated from a format that is standard for an industry to EDIFACT).

translation software   The EDI software that translates an incoming document, or flat file, into the format that a receiving party specifies. The format can be a specific industry standard, ANSI, or EDIFACT.

translator   The application system that links flat files from an internal application system and the EDI X12 transaction set. Essentially, the link performs data conversion to make bidirectional EDI communication possible.

transmission acknowledgment   Acknowledgment that a total transmission was received with no errors detected.

UCC   Uniform Code Council. A U.S. association that administrates UCS, WINS, and VICS and provides UCS identification codes and UPCs. Also, a model set of legal rules governing commercial transmissions, such as sales, contracts, bank deposits and collections, commercial paper, and letters of credit. Individual states give legal power to the UCC by adopting its articles as laws.

UCC Article 4A   A comprehensive set of rules that define the rights and obligations of parties to wholesale wire transfers, including transfers executed over electronic transfer systems, such as FedWire and CHIPS.

UCS   Uniform Communications Standard. An EDI document standard for the grocery industry in the United States. (See also VICS.)

UNCID   Uniform Rules of Conduct for Interchange of Trade Data by Teletransmission. Rules developed by the International Chamber of Commerce (ICC).

UNCITRAL   United Nations Commission on International Trade Law.

UNCTAD   United Nations Conference on Trade and Development.

UN/ECE   See ECE.

UN/GTDI   United Nations Guidelines for Trade Data Interchange.

UNICORN   An EDI project for ferry sailings in Europe.

UNIDO   United Nations Industrial Development Organization.

UN/JEDI   United Nations Joint Electronic Data Interchange Committee. Established by the WP.4 to develop syntax, messages, and related procedures for EDI.

UNSM   United Nations Standard Message. A standard EDIFACT message used by business partners that is registered with the UN/ECE WP.4.

UNTDED   United Nations Trade Data Elements Directory. Defines standard data elements and codes. Jointly maintained by UNECE and ISO. Contains ISO 7372.

UPC   Uniform Product Code. A standard bar code system used by the retail industry. Identifies manufacturer, item, style, color, etc.

user agent   A computer process that links the originating end user's computer and the X.400 standard used to carry electronic messages. (See MTA and P1 message transfer protocol.)

validation   Check whether a document is the correct type for a particular EDI system, as agreed upon by the trading partners, and determine whether the document is going to or coming from an authorized EDI user.

value chains   Links to suppliers who furnish goods and services that add value to a company's product or service. Includes all goods and services, from raw material to the furnished product. Can be extended to include the services provided by third-party network suppliers and paying agencies.

VAN   Value-added network. Also called a third-party network or public network. An independent, third-party service that provides communication links, storage, message forwarding, and other services to facilitate electronic messaging between EDI trading partners. Many companies use VANs to exchange EDI documents because of the accessibility and convenience of the electronic mailbox setup.

variable-length file   A file whose segments contain data elements that can vary between minimum and maximum requirements but have no fixed length. A data element delimiter marks the end of each element and a segment delimiter marks the end of each segment.

vendor agreement   A contract between third-party network service providers or EDI software suppliers and EDI trading partners. Typically maximizes the vendor's rights and minimizes the vendor's exposure.

VICS   Voluntary Interindustry Communications Standards. The EDI document standards for the retailing and supermarket industries. (See also UCS and QRS.)

WINS   Warehouse Information Network Standard. An EDI standard for the warehousing industry developed by the International Association of Refrigerated Warehouses and the American Warehouseman's Association.

WP.4   Working Party 4 (on Facilitation of International Trade Procedures). A UN/ECE committee for the development of trade. Comprised of experts on procedures and documentation, appointed by governments or organizations recognized by the UN/ECE. Thirty member states regularly participate. Members include the United States, the United Kingdom, France, Canada, Bulgaria, Italy, and Turkey. Other members of the United Nations can participate as observers.

X12   The ANSI standard for interindustry electronic interchange of business transactions.

X12.5   Interchange Control Structure. This standard provides the interchange envelope of a header and trailer for electronic interchange through data transmission and a structure for acknowledging receipt and processing of the envelope. X12.22 and X12.3 do not contain separate segments and data elements.

X12.6   Application Control Structure. This standard describes the control segments used to envelop loops of data segments, transaction sets, and groups of related transaction sets.

X12 Finance The ANSI ASC X12 subcommittee that develops and maintains EDI standards and guidelines for EDI documents associated with financial functions.

X12 Mailbag The most recent development in the X12 standard, completed in 1991 for VAN-to-VAN interconnection. The standard provides a means for controlling the exchange of EDI messages between VANs. Both basic and advanced audit and control concepts of X400 are contained in this operating standard. X12 Mailbag is simpler to use and less expensive to implement than X400. It is anticipated that X12 Mailbag will be the "hottest" method of interconnection in North America by the end of 1992.

X.25 International standard for packet switching.

X.400 An international standard for connecting electronic message (e-mail) networks. Generally, X.400 is a CCITT and ISO standard for communications protocol, a message handling facility. Because of the cost, complexity, and overall lag in development of the standard, X.400 has been used to connect few trading partners with the same (or even differing) VANs. X.400 is actually a series of recommendations for message handling systems, such as e-mail; for example, it allows e-mail users to interchange mail between any mailbox on any X.400-compatible network.

X.435 International standard for sending EDI over X.400. (Scheduled to be completed by the end of 1992).

X.500 Equivalent to an ordinary telephone book in electronic database format. Typically employed by users of X.400 electronic messaging services.

X Series A somewhat misleading label, X applies to either a committee setting a standard or the standard itself. ANSI has several independent committees, e.g., X9.9 for data encryption standards and X12 for EDI. The CCITT's X.25 provides recommendations for communication standards and X.400 provides recommendations for messaging standards. The X followed by a period refers to CCITT recommendations, the X is not followed by a period in ANSI ASC committee prefixes. (ISO established its own series of alternate numbers for CCITT recommendations.)

SOURCES

American Bar Association, *The Commercial Use of Electronic Data Interchange—A Report,* Chicago, IL: American Bar Association, 1990.

Chan, Sally, et al., *EDI for Managers and Auditors,* Toronto, Canada: EDI Council of Canada Library Publication, 1991.

Data Interchange Standards Association, Inc., *ASC X12 Status Report: Standards Development and Maintenance Activities,* Spring 1992.

Davis, D. W., and Price, W. L., *Security for Computer Networks: An Introduction to Data Security in Teleprocessing and Electronic Funds Transfer,* New York, NY: John Wiley & Sons, 1984.

EDI Council of Australia, EDP Auditors Association, *EDI Control Guide*, Australia: EDI Council of Australia Publishers, 1990.

Emmelhainz, Margaret A., *Electronic Data Interchange: A Total Management Guide*, New York, NY: Van Nostrand Reinhold, 1990.

Jenkins, Gordon, and Ray Lancashire, *The Canadian EDI Handbook: A Quick Read on EDI*, Toronto, Canada: EDI Council of Canada Library Publication, 1990.

Institute of Internal Auditors, *Audit, Control, and Security of Paperless Systems: Trends, Guidelines, Practices and Techniques*, Orlando, FLA: Institute of Internal Auditors, September 1990.

Kimberley, Paul, *Electronic Data Interchange*, New York, NY: McGraw-Hill, 1991.

Pfaffenberger, Bryan, *Que's Computer User's Dictionary*, Carmel, IN: Que Corporation, 1992.

Wright, Benjamin, *The Law of Electronic Commerce EDI, FAX, and E-Mail: Technology, Proof, and Liability*, Boston, MA: Little Brown and Company, 1991.

Sokol, Phyllis, *EDI: The Competitive Edge*, New York, NY: McGraw-Hill, 1988.

———, *Introduction to UN/EDIFACT*, Rapporteurs' Teams, April 1991.

About the Authors

Albert J. Marcella, Jr., COAP, CQA, CSP, CDP, CISA, is the president of Business Automation Consultants, a data processing management consulting firm that specializes in designing and implementing EDP audits, disaster contingency planning, system development life cycle reviews, EDI, and systems programming. Prior to forming his own firm, Mr. Marcella was employed by the Dun & Bradstreet Corporation, where he established and formalized the EDP audit function.

Mr. Marcella's professional experience also includes providing internal systems consulting services to Hartford Insurance Group and designing and executing operational, financial, and data processing audits for the Uniroyal Corporation, both in the United States and abroad. He has contributed numerous articles to audit-related publications and has authored and coauthored several audit-related text books, including *Auditing IBM's Customer Information Control System*, *End-User and Departmental Computing*, and *Auditing Disaster Contingency Planning*.

Mr. Marcella holds a Bachelor of Science degree in Business Administration, with a dual major in Management Information Systems and Management from Bryant College in Rhode Island and a Masters of Business Administration in Finance from the University of New Haven in Connecticut. He is currently completing his doctoral studies in Management at Walden University. He has been designated a certified systems professional (CSP) by the Association for Systems Management, a certified quality assurance analyst (CQA) by the Quality Assurance Institute, a certified office automation professional (COAP) by the Office Automation Society International, a certified information systems auditor (CISA) by the EDP Auditors Association and holds a certificate in data processing (CDP) from the Data Processing Management Association. He has also been recognized as a distinguished adjunct faculty member by the Institute of Internal Auditors.

Sally Chan, MA, CMA, is the audit manager of Treasury and Investment Banking Systems at Royal Bank, Canada's largest bank. Before assuming her present position, Ms. Chan was the audit manager of Corporate Banking Systems, responsible for auditing and reviewing all Royal Bank's EDI systems, which included both purchasing and payments functions.

Ms. Chan was chairperson of the EDI study group that wrote *EDI for Managers and Auditors*, published by the EDI Council of Canada in November 1991. She is a leading member of the Canadian Inter-FEDI Audit Task Force, which established the control and audit standards for the Canadian financial institutions engaging in EDI. This task force also prepared *Corporate to Financial Institutions EDI Control Guidelines*, which is free to the EDI community through the Canadian Bankers Association and the EDI Council of Canada. Ms. Chan is also a contributing member of the Legal and Audit Committee of the EDI Council of Canada.

Ms. Chan's previous experience includes systems analysis and consulting in design and project management for the manufacturing, insurance, educational, and banking sectors. She was a part-time community college instructor in systems design, accounting information systems, and project management for five years.

Ms. Chan, who is a certified management accountant, holds a Bachelor of Arts from the University of Hong Kong and an Masters from the University of British Columbia, Canada.

Index

The Artech House Telecommunications Library

Vinton G. Cerf, Series Editor

Numerical Analysis of Linear Networks and Systems, Hermann Kremer *et al.*

Optimization of Digital Transmission Systems, K. Trondle and Gunter Soder

The PP and QUIPU Implementation of X.400 and X.500, Stephen Kille

Packet Switching Evolution from Narrowband to Broadband ISDN, M. Smouts

Principles of Secure Communication Systems, Second Edition, Don J. Torrieri

Principles of Signals and Systems: Deterministic Signals, B. Picinbono

Private Telecommunication Networks, Bruce Elbert

Radiodetermination Satellite Services and Standards, Martin Rothblatt

Residential Fiber Optic Networks: An Engineering and Economic Analysis, David Reed

Setting Global Telecommunication Standards: The Stakes, The Players, and The Process, Gerd Wallenstein

Signal Processing with Lapped Transforms, Henrique S. Malvar

The Telecommunications Deregulation Sourcebook, Stuart N. Brotman, editor

Television Technology: Fundamentals and Future Prospects, A. Michael Noll

Telecommunications Technology Handbook, Daniel Minoli

Telephone Company and Cable Television Competition, Stuart N. Brotman

Terrestrial Digital Microwave Communciations, Ferdo Ivanek, editor

Transmission Networking: SONET and the SDH, Mike Sexton and Andy Reid

Transmission Performance of Evolving Telecommunications Networks, John Gruber and Godfrey Williams

Troposcatter Radio Links, G. Roda

Virtual Networks: A Buyer's Guide, Daniel D. Briere

Voice Processing, Second Edition, Walt Tetschner

Voice Teletraffic System Engineering, James R. Boucher

Wireless Access and the Local Telephone Network, George Calhoun

For further information on these and other Artech House titles, contact:

Artech House
685 Canton Street
Norwood, MA 01602
(617) 769-9750
Fax:(617) 762-9230
Telex: 951-659

Artech House
6 Buckingham Gate
London SW1E6JP England
+44(0)71 630-0166
+44(0)71 630-0166
Telex-951-659